THE POLITICS OF EMPIRE

THE POLITICS OF EMPIRE

THE US, ISRAEL AND THE MIDDLE EAST

JAMES PETRAS

CLARITY PRESS, INC.

© 2014 James Petras
ISBN: 978-0-9860731-0-6
Ebook: 978-0-9860731-1-3

In-house editor: Diana G. Collier
Cover: R. Jordan P. Santos

THE COVER IMAGE: Middle Eastern military forces disembark a U.S. Navy landing craft air cushioned during a live-fire rehearsal of the final exercise with the 26th Marine Expeditionary Unit during "'Red Reef 2008'" in the Middle East. Source: Wikimedia Commons

Library of Congress Cataloging-in-Publication Data

Petras, James F., 1937-
 The politics of empire : the US, Israel and the Middle East / by James Petras.
    pages cm
 ISBN 978-0-9860731-0-6
 1. United States--Foreign relations--Israel. 2. Israel--Foreign relations--United States. 3. United States--Foreign relations--Middle East. 4. Middle East--Foreign relations--United States. 5. United States--Foreign relations--2009- 6. Zionism--United States. I. Title.

 E183.8.I7P479 2014
 327.7305694--dc23

                    2014002494

Clarity Press, Inc.
Ste. 469, 3277 Roswell Rd. NE
Atlanta, GA. 30305 , USA
http://www.claritypress.com

TABLE OF CONTENTS

For Robin

PART I

OVERVIEW:
THE STATE OF THE
EMPIRE

THE CHANGING CONTOURS OF US IMPERIAL INTERVENTION IN WORLD CONFLICTS

Introduction

Following the Vietnam War, US imperial intervention passed through several phases: In the immediate aftermath, the US government faced a humiliating military defeat at the hands of the Vietnamese liberation forces and was under pressure from an American public sick and tired of war. Imperial military interventions, domestic espionage against opponents and the usual practice of fomenting coups d'état (regime change) declined.

Slowly, under President Gerald Ford and, especially President 'Jimmy' Carter, an imperial revival emerged in the form of clandestine support for armed surrogates in Southern Africa—Angola, Mozambique, Guinea Bissau—and neoliberal military dictatorships in Latin America. The first large-scale imperial intervention was launched during the second half of the Carter Presidency. It involved massive support for the Islamist uprising against the secular government of Afghanistan and a mercenary jihadist invasion sponsored by Saudi Arabia, Pakistan and the US (1979). This was followed by direct US invasions in Grenada (1983) under President Reagan; Panama (1989) and Iraq (1991) under President Bush Sr. and Yugoslavia (1995 and 1999) under President Clinton.

In the beginning, the imperial revival involved low cost wars of brief duration with few casualties. As a result there were very few voices of dissent, far diminished from the massive anti-war, anti-imperial movements of the early 1970s. The restoration of direct US imperial interventions, unhindered by Congressional and popular opposition, was gradual in the period 1973-1990. It started to accelerate in the 1990s and then really took off after September 11, 2001.

The imperial military and ideological apparatus for direct intervention was firmly in place by 2000. It led to a prolonged series of wars in multiple geographical locations, involving long-term, large-scale commitments of economic resources, and military personnel and was completely unhampered by congressional or large-scale public opposition—at least in the beginning. The 'objectives' of these serial wars were defined by their principal Zionist and militarist architects as the following: (1) destroying regimes and states (as well as their military, police and civil governing bureaucracies) which had opposed Israel's annexation of Palestine; (2) deposing regimes which promoted independent nationalist policies, opposing or threatening the Gulf puppet monarchist regimes and supporting anti-imperialist, secular or nationalist-Islamic movements around the world.

Blinded by their imperial hubris (or naked racism) neither the Zionists nor the civilian militarists within the US Administrations anticipated prolonged national resistance from the targeted countries, the regrouping of armed opposition and the spread of violent attacks (including terrorism) to the imperial countries. Having utterly destroyed the Afghan and Iraqi state structures, as well as the regimes in power, and having devastated the economy as well as any central military or police capacity, the imperial state was faced with endless armed civilian ethno-religious and tribal resistance (including suicide bombings), mounting US troop casualties and spiraling costs to the domestic economy without any "exit strategy". The imperial powers were unable to set up a stable and loyal client regime, backed by a unified state apparatus with a monopoly of force and violence, after having deliberately shredded these structures (police, bureaucracy, civil service, etc) during the invasion and early occupation.

The creation of this "political vacuum" was never a problem for the Zionists embedded in the US Administrations since their ultimate goal was to devastate Israel's enemies. As a result of the US invasions, the regional power of Israel was greatly enhanced without the loss of a single Israeli soldier or shekel. The Zionists within the Bush Administration successfully blamed the ensuing problems of the occupation, especially the growing armed resistance, on their 'militarist' colleagues and the Pentagon 'Brass'. 'Mission Accomplished', the Bush Administration Zionists left the government, moving on to lucrative careers in the private financial sector.

Under President Obama, a new 'cast' of embedded Zionists has emerged to target Iran and prepare the US for a new war on Israel's behalf. However, by the end of the first decade of the 21st century, when Barak Obama was elected president, the political, economic and military situation had changed. The contrast in circumstances between the early Bush (Jr.) years and the current administration is striking.

The 20-year period (1980-2000) before the launching of the 'serial war' agenda was characterized by short, inexpensive, low-casualty wars in Grenada, Panama and Yugoslavia, and a proxy war in Afghanistan; Israeli invasions and attacks against Lebanon, the occupied West Bank and Syria;

and one major US war of short duration and limited casualties (the First Gulf War against Iraq). The First Gulf War succeeded in weakening the government of Saddam Hussein, fragmenting the country via 'no fly zones', establishing a Kurdish client 'state' in the north while 'policing' was left to the remnants of the Iraqi state—all without the US having to occupy the country.

Meanwhile, the US economy was relatively stable and trade deficits were manageable. The real economic crisis was still to come. Military expenditures appeared under control. US public opinion, initially hostile to the First Gulf War, was "pacified" by its short duration and the withdrawal of US troops. Iraq remained under aerial surveillance with frequent US bombing and missile strikes whenever the government attempted to regain control of the north. During this period, Israel was forced to fight its own wars and maintain an expensive occupation of southern Lebanon—losing its own soldiers.

By the second decade of the 21st century everything had changed. The US was bogged down in a prolonged thirteen year war and occupation in Afghanistan with little hope for a stable client regime in Kabul. The seven-year war against Iraq (Second Gulf War) with the massive occupation, armed civilian insurgency and the resurgence of ethno-religious conflict resulted in casualties and a crippling growth in US military expenditures. Budget and trade deficits expanded exponentially while the US share of the world market declined. China displaced the US as the principal trading partner in Latin America, Asia and Africa. A series of new 'low intensity' wars were launched in Somalia, Yemen and Pakistan which show no prospect of ending the drain on the military and the US Treasury.

The vast majority of the US public has experienced a decline in living standards and now believes the cost of overseas wars are a significant factor contributing to their relative impoverishment and insecurity. The multi-trillion-dollar bailout of the Wall Street banks during the economic crash of 2008-09 has eroded public support for the financial elite as well as the militarist-Zionist elite, which continue to push for more imperial wars.

The capacity of the US imperial elite to launch new wars on Israel's behalf has been greatly undermined since the economic crash of 2008-09. The gap between the rulers and ruled has widened. Domestic economic issues, not the threat of external terrorists, have become the central concern. The public now sees the Middle East as a region of unending costly wars—with no benefit to the domestic economy. Asia has become the center of trade, growth, investment and a major source of US jobs. While Washington continues to ignore the citizens' views, accumulated grievances are beginning to have an impact.

A Pew Research report, released in late 2013, confirms the wide gap between elite and public opinion. The Pew Foundation is an establishment polling operation, which presents its questions in a way that avoids the larger political questions. Nevertheless, the responses presented in the report are significant: By a vast margin (52% to 38%) the public agree that the US "should mind its own business internationally and let other countries get along the best they can on their own". This represents a major increase in public opposition to armed US imperialist intervention; the 52% response in 2013 contrasts sharply with 30% polled 2002. A companion poll of elite policy advisors, members of the Council on Foreign Relations (CFR), highlights the gap between the US public and the ruling class. The elite are described by the Pew Report as having a 'decidedly internationalist (imperialist-interventionist) outlook'. The American public clearly distinguishes between 'trade' and 'globalization' (imperialism.): 81% of the public favor 'trade' as a source of job creation while 73% oppose 'globalization' which they see as US companies relocating jobs overseas to low wage regions. The US public rejects imperial economic expansion and wars for the harm done to the domestic economy, middle and working class income and job security. The members of the Council on Foreign Relations, in contrast, are overwhelmingly in favor of 'globalization' (and imperial interventions). While 81% of the public believe the principal goal of US foreign policy should be the protection of American jobs, only 29% of the CFR rate US jobs as a priority.

The elite is conscious of the growing gap in interests, values and priorities between the public and the imperial state; they know that endless costly wars have led to a mass rejection of new imperial wars and a growing demand for domestic job programs.

This gap between the imperial policy elite and the majority of the public is one of the leading factors now influencing US foreign policy. Together with the general discredit of the Congress (only 9% have a favorable view of it), the public's rejection of President Obama's militarist foreign policy has seriously weakened the empire's capacity to begin new large-scale ground wars at multiple sites.

Meanwhile, Israel (Washington's foreign patron), the Gulf State clients and European and Japanese allies have been pushing the US to intervene and confront 'their adversaries'. To this end, Israel and the Zionist Power Configuration within the US government have been undermining peace negotiations between the US and Iran. Saudi Arabia and the other Gulf monarchies, as well as Turkey are urging the US to attack Syria. The French had successfully pushed the US into a war against the Gaddafi government in Libya and have their sights on their former colony in Syria. The US has given only limited backing to the French military intervention in Mali and the Central African Republic.

The US public is aware that none of Washington's 'militarist' patrons, clients and allies has paid such a high price in terms of blood and treasure as the US in the recent wars. The Saudi, Israeli and French "publics" have not experienced the socio-economic dislocations confronting the US public. For these 'allied' regimes, the cheapest way to resolve their own regional conflicts and promote their own ambitions is to convince, coerce or pressure the US to "exercise its global leadership".

Washington's imperial policymakers, by background, history, ideology and past experience, are sensitive to these appeals—especially those from the Israelis. But they also recognize the growing "intervention fatigue" within the American public, the CFR's euphemism for rising anti-imperialist feelings among the American majority, which is saying 'no' to further imperial military interventions.

Faced with choice of acting as an unfettered imperial power with global interests and facing rising domestic discontent, Washington has been forced to revise its foreign policy and strategies. It is adopting a more nuanced approach, one less vulnerable to external pressures and manipulations.

Imperial Foreign Policy in a Time of Domestic Constraints and External Pressures

US empire builders, with increasingly limited military options and declining domestic support, have begun to (1) prioritize their choice of places of engagement, (2) diversify their diplomatic, political and economic instruments of coercion and (3) limit large-scale, long-term military intervention to regions where US strategic interests are involved. Washington is not shedding its militarist polices by any means, but it is looking for ways to avoid costly long-term wars which further undermine the domestic economy and intensify domestic political opposition. In place of large scale ground troops in a limited number of countries, Washington's empire-builders have turned to a massive increase and proliferation of special forces—in 2013, SOCOM forces were deployed in 134 countries around the globe, a 123% increase during the Obama years[1]—to police the world via assassinations, sabotage, destabilization, etc.

In order to decipher US imperial policy in this new context, it is useful to first 1) identify the regions of conflict; 2) estimate the significance of these countries and conflicts to the empire; and 3) analyze the particular interventions and their impact on US empire building. Our purpose is to show how the interplay between domestic and external countervailing pressures affects imperial policy.

Conflicts which Engage US Empire Builders

There are at least eleven major or minor conflicts today engaging US empire builders to a greater or lesser extent. A major premise of our approach is that US empire builders are more selective in their aggression, more conscious of the economic consequences, less reckless in their commitments and have a greater concern for domestic political impact. Current conflicts of interest to Washington include those taking place in the Ukraine, Thailand, Honduras, China-Japan-South Korea, Iran-Gulf States/Israel, Syria, Venezuela, Palestine-Israel, Libya, Afghanistan and Egypt.

These conflicts can be classified according to whether they involve major or minor US interests and whether they involve major or minor allies or adversaries. Among the conflicts where the US has strategic interests and which involve major actors, one would have to include the territorial and maritime dispute between Japan, South Korea and China. On the surface the dispute appears to be over an economically insignificant pile of rocks claimed by the Japanese as the Senkaku Islands and by the Chinese as the Diaoyu Islands. In essence, the conflict involves the US plan to militarily encircle China by provoking its Japanese and Korean allies to confront the Chinese over the islands. Washington's treaties with Japan will be used to come to the 'aid' of its most important ally in the region. The US support of Japan's expansionist claims is part of a strategic shift in US policy from military commitments in the Middle East to military and economic pacts in Asia, which exclude and provoke China.

The Obama regime has announced its 'Pivot to Asia' in an attempt to deal with its largest economic competitor. China, the second biggest economy in the world, has displaced the US as the principal trading partner in Latin America and Asia. It is advancing rapidly as the principal investor in developing Africa's natural resources. In response, the US has 1) openly backed Japan's claims; 2) defied China's strategic interests in the East China Sea by flying B52 bombers within China's Air Defense Identification Zone; and 3) encouraged South Korea to expand its 'air defense' zones to overlap with those of the Chinese. History teaches us that inflexible assertions of dominance by established imperial powers against rising dynamic economies will lead to conflicts, and even disastrous wars.

Imperial advisers believe that US naval and air superiority and Chinese dependence on foreign trade give the US a strategic advantage in any armed confrontation. Obama's "Pivot to Asia" is clearly designed to encircle and degrade China's capacity to outcompete and displace the US from world markets. Washington's militarists, however, fail to take account of China's strategic levers—especially the over two trillion dollars of US Treasury notes (debt) held by China, which, if dumped on the market, would lead to a major devaluation of the US currency, panic on Wall Street and a deeper economic depression. China could respond to US military threats by 1) seizing the assets of the 500 biggest US MNCs located in the country which would crash the stock market and 2) cutting off the source for major supply chains, further disrupting the US and world economy.

Imperialist ambitions and resentment over the loss of markets, status, and supremacy is pushing Washington to raise the stakes and confront China. Opposing the militarists, Washington's economic realists believe the US is too exposed and too dependent on credit, overseas earnings and financial revenues to engage in new military interventions in Asia, especially after the disastrous consequences of wars in the Middle East. Current US policy reflects an ongoing struggle between the militarist imperialists and the defenders of imperial economic interests. For the market-oriented policy advisers, it makes no sense to confront China, when mutual gains from rising trade and economic inter-dependence have proved far superior to any marginal territorial gains offshore. These conflicting outlooks find expression in the alternating bellicose and conciliatory rhetoric of Vice President Biden during his December 2013 visit to Japan, China and South Korea.

The second area involving major actors and interests is the Persian Gulf, especially Israel-Iran-Saudi Arabia and the US. Having gone through costly and disastrous wars in Iraq and Afghanistan and fully aware that US intelligence agencies have found no evidence of an Iranian nuclear weapons program, the Obama Administration is eager to reach an agreement with Iran. Nevertheless, US strategists are pursuing an agreement that would 1) weaken Iran's defense capability; 2) undermine Iranian support for popular revolts among Shiite populations living in the Gulf Monarchies; 3) isolate President Bashar al-Assad in Syria; and 4) facilitate a long-term US presence in Afghanistan by destroying Al Qaeda operations throughout the region. In addition a US-Iran agreement would lift the harsh economic sanctions and 1) allow US oil companies to exploit Iran's richest oil fields; 2) lower the cost of energy; and 3) reduce US trade deficits.

The well-entrenched Zionist strategists and advisers among policymakers, especially in the Executive Branch, including such Department heads and Secretaries as Treasury Undersecretary (for 'Terrorism') David Cohen, Treasury Secretary Jack Lew, US Trade Representative Michael Froman, 'Special Adviser for the Persian Gulf' Dennis Ross, among others, pose a major stumbling block to any US-Iran agreement. An even greater obstacle to the agreement comes from the Zionist-controlled US Congress, which acts more on behalf of Israel's regional ambitions than for US interests. Israel's megalomaniacal rulers seek military, political and economic supremacy throughout the Middle East (from Sinai to the Gulf) and have so far successfully used the US military to destroy and weaken its adversaries at no cost to Israeli soldiers or its economy.

Israel has taken a direct hand in setting the terms, which the US will demand from Iran. According to the *Financial Times*, "A team of senior Israeli officials led by Yossi Cohen, national security adviser, is due to visit

Washington … to begin detailed discussions with the Obama Administration to use its influence in shaping the negotiating agenda."[2]

Secretary of State John Kerry has already caved in to Israeli pressure stating, "We will be stepping up on enforcement (of existing sanctions) through the Treasury Department".[3] Israel and its top Zionist agent within the Obama Administration, Dennis Ross, are pushing for a joint Israeli-US "working group" to discuss tightening sanctions on Iran and punishing any government or business which tries to do business with Iran during the "interim agreement", a position pursued by David Cohen and Treasury Secretary Jack Lew.[4] Israel is behind the US demand that Iran convert its Arak Facilities from a heavy water into a light-water reactor and reduce its centrifuges by 95% from 19,000 to 1,000.

In other words, Israel dictates terms to the US negotiators that will effectively sabotage any possible agreement and put the US on a course toward another war for Israel. Surprisingly, Israel's hardliners and its agents within the US Administration have an important and unlikely ally—Iran's Foreign Minister Mohammed Javid Zarif, the chief negotiator in Geneva, who has downplayed Iran's military capabilities, exaggerated US military capabilities and seems quite willing to dismantle Iran's peaceful nuclear program. In justifying his far-reaching concessions and meager returns, Foreign Minister Zarif publicly declared that 'the US could destroy the country's (Iran's) defense system with one bomb!"[5] Zarif, in effect, is preparing to sell out Iran's nuclear industry, in advance, without any objective consideration of Iran's military power or recognition of US strategic weaknesses.

Saudi Arabia's rulers influence US policy through their contracts with the military-industrial complex, amounting to over $20 billion dollars in arms purchases in 2013. In addition, the Saudi monarch has allowed the construction of US military bases on its territory and maintains close ties with Wall Street investment houses. Saudi opposition to any US–Iran rapprochement arises from Riyadh's fear of Iranian influence over its oppressed Shia minority and Tehran's critique of the absolutist monarchy.

The positive gains, in terms of US strategic military and economic interests, from an agreement with the liberal Iranian regime, are offset by the negative pressures from Saudi and Israeli-Zionist interests. As a result, Washington's policy oscillates between peaceful, diplomatic overtures to Iran and bellicose threats to appease Israel and Saudi Arabia. Washington is desperate to avoid being dragged into another "war for Israel", in order to secure its hegemony in the Persian Gulf region and to avoid a major domestic political and economic crisis. The Obama Administration has yet to exhibit the high degree of statesmanship necessary to restrain and neutralize the deeply embedded Zionist Power Configuration within its ranks and in the Congress, which places Israeli interests over those of the US.

Regional Conflicts: Minor Interests and Major Actors

The Ukraine–European Union (EU)–Russian conflict involves minor US economic interests but potentially major military interests. The US supports the EU's policy of incorporating the Ukraine into its economic and trade system. The EU will be the major beneficiary in the plunder of Ukraine's economy, penetrating its market and reaping mega financial returns. The US is content to watch the EU play the major role in stoking Ukrainian civil unrest. If and when Ukraine joins the EU, it will become another client regime subject to the dictates of the bankers and bureaucrats in Brussels, just like Spain, Greece, Portugal and Italy. The US is mainly interested in bringing the Ukraine into NATO as part of its policy of surrounding Russia.

Syria, like Libya, Mali, Central African Republic and Egypt, is of secondary interest for the US. Washington has let the European Union, especially France, England and their allies, lead and direct military operations directly and through proxies. The Obama Administration already faced intense "intervention fatigue"—widespread popular opposition to war—when it joined the EU in bombing Tripoli to rubble, but it refused to commit ground forces and left Libya a broken country without a viable economy, stable society or functioning state! So much for 'humanitarian intervention'! Intervention in Syria has faced even greater domestic opposition from Congress and the US public—except for the Israeli and Saudi lobbies. Obama was clearly not willing to act as 'Al Qaeda's Air Force' by bombing Damascus and facilitating a jihadist takeover. The US chose a diplomatic solution and accepted the Russian proposal to dismantle Syria's chemical weapons. It appears to support a Geneva-based negotiated solution. Another war, this time with Syria, would inflame US domestic discontent and further erode the economy, with no positive gain for US imperialism. In fact, US military victory over Damascus would expand the territory of operation for Al Qaeda in Iraq and the Levant. US public opinion overcame the massive pro-Israel media barrage and pressure from the 52 Presidents of the Major American Jewish Organizations that had been actively pushing the Obama Administration into a 'Syrian Quagmire'!

French President Francois Hollande is the new face of imperial militarism and interventionism in Africa with its massive bombing in Libya and invasion and occupation in Mali and the Central African Republic. The US is content to play a 'supporting role' to France. There are few large scale ground troop engagements in Africa, yet Washington has established a centralized command structure (AFRICOM) to direct special operations and drone attacks and its proxy wars in Somalia and South Sudan.

With public opinion strongly against any more major direct military intervention Washington has turned to military proxies for conflicts in 'strategic' and marginal countries and regions. Even where significant imperial interests may be involved, Washington increasingly relies on local elites to act on its behalf in conflicts in countries as diverse as in Yemen, Thailand, Honduras, Venezuela, Pakistan, Afghanistan and Egypt. Sending drones and dispatching teams of Special Forces in clandestine operations have been the US Administration's intervention of choice in Yemen, Somalia and Pakistan. In Afghanistan, Special Forces combine with the US military, NATO troops and local client military proxies, as well as drones.

In Honduras, the US-backed military coup, which unleashed death squads with the killing of over 200 dissident activists in a two year period, was followed by a fraudulent election which reclaimed 'power' for a US client regime. In Venezuela, the US continues to finance opposition parties who support violent street mobs, the sabotage of public services like electricity, while relying on local business elites to hoard basic goods and inflate prices. So far, these efforts to undermine the Venezuelan government have failed.

Conclusion

The Obama administration's empire builders have relied on a wider variety of interventions than their predecessor under President George W. Bush. They are much less prone to launch large-scale ground operations and more likely to turn to local client elites. They have shown a far greater sense of priorities in selecting targets for direct intervention.

Washington relies more on its imperial European allies, especially the French, to take the lead in Africa, without relinquishing its key interest in maintaining Egypt tightly under US-Israeli control. There is a shift in priorities toward the Far East, especially the countries bordering China, like Japan and South Korea, as part of the long-term US strategy to encircle and limit China's economic expansion. The US 'Pivot to Asia', under the Obama Administration, is characterized by alternating economic negotiations with growing military encirclement.

Controlling the Persian Gulf and undermining Iran continues to be a high priority for US empire builders, but the costly and disastrous invasion and occupation of Iraq under George W. Bush and its adverse domestic fallout has led Washington to rely less on military confrontation with Tehran and more on economic sanctions, military encirclement and now diplomatic negotiations to secure collaboration from the new Rouhani regime.

The principal strategic weakness in US empire building policy lies in the absence of domestic support. There is a growing demand for better paying jobs to reverse the decline of US living standards and greater protection for social services and livelihoods. The second strategic weakness is the incapacity of the US to create a viable economic "co-prosperity sphere", which would win allies in Asia and Latin America. The so-called "Pivot to Asia" is overly and overtly reliant on military(mostly naval) power, which functions in times of 'territorial conflicts' with China, but does not create stable, structural links with local productive elites—who rely on China for trade.

In the end the most serious obstacle to effectively adapting US foreign policy to the current realities is the influential Israel-linked Zionist Power Configuration embedded in the Congress, the Administration and the mass media.[6] Zionists are deeply committed to pushing the US into more wars for Israel. Nevertheless the shift to negotiations with Iran, the refusal to bomb Syria and the reluctance to get involved in the Ukraine are all indications that Washington is less inclined to launch more large-scale military intervention and more receptive to the public opinion constraints on the exercise of imperial power.

The Obama Regime's Military Metaphysics Rejects Diplomatic Opportunities

Introduction

Political and economic changes in recent years have opened *possibilities* for the end of international and national conflicts. Regime changes, pragmatic leaders and the promise of serious negotiations in the Middle East, North Africa, Russia, Southwest Asia, China and elsewhere provided the Obama regime an opportunity to end long-standing and costly wars, to access new markets and resources, and to reduce domestic deficits and external trade imbalances.

However, at every opportunity, with precise consistency, the Obama regime rejected fresh overtures from adversaries, choosing instead to rely on a now discredited "double discourse", of talking peace and engaging in war, of talking trade and increasing sanctions, of talking about greater Asian engagement and fomenting economic pacts which exclude the second biggest economy in the world.

The Obama regime's incapacity to take advantage of the favorable political and diplomatic conjuncture can be attributed to several structural causes:

1. His embrace of a "military metaphysic" which identifies violence as the key to empire building, independently of the context, correlation of forces and possibilities of victory.

2. His overweening commitment and submission to Israeli dictated Middle East policies transmitted and implemented by the domestic Zionist Power Configuration.

3. His overwhelming commitment to FIRE–capital (finance, insurance and real estate) over any long-term large scale commitment to rebuilding the productive sector and the welfare state.

4. His commitment to short term goals of "regime change"—destroying adversaries—over and against pursuing long-term economic linkages and incremental concessions.

Regime Dogmatism and Rigidity

The Obama regime's conception of empire building and its defense *is inflexible* in its reliance on strategic military intervention and *abysmally ignorant* of its short- and long-term negative consequences. Imbued with self-deluding moralizing as a "rational" justification for crude militarism, the regime is deaf, dumb and blind to the diplomatic openings and opportunities offered by adversaries. Even as it *proposes* negotiations and promises of "new beginnings" it announces at the same time plans to destabilize the same regime.

From the perspective of long term empire building and given the economic constraints of a stagnant economy, impending military defeats in Southwest Asia and the Middle East and the political debacles resulting from the global spy expose, the Obama regime's current diplomatic failures can only lead to further economic decline, greater political isolation and more explosive military conflicts.

Militarism Trumps Diplomacy: Seven Lost Opportunities

Over the past year at least *seven grand opportunities* emerged which offered the Obama regime a chance to crawl out from under long term costly wars and confrontations and to move ahead toward an era of relative economic expansion and peaceful coexistence.

The Case of Iran: Sacrificing a "Grand Bargain" to Serve the Israeli State

For over a decade the US has headed a Security Council coalition opposed, as it claims, to Iran developing a nuclear bomb. Rejecting the evaluation of all of its own intelligence agencies, which clearly specify that Iran is not engaged in weaponizing its nuclear program, the Obama regime and Congress chose or are forced to accept, Israeli propaganda to the contrary. Washington imposes harsh sanctions, threatens war and demands unilateral, unconditional surrender, citing the supposedly "extremist Islamist" character of the regime. Washington never engaged in serious negotiations. In mid-2013, Iran elected a new President (Rouhani) who by all accounts is a pragmatic, conciliatory and flexible political leader who early on emphasized the desire to end the nuclear stalemate and provide guarantees in exchange for an end to economic sanctions.

President Rouhani proposed to negotiate with the Obama regime with an 'open agenda' without conditions. He emphasized his priority was domestic economic recovery and development over and above any present or future nuclear weaponry or even high level uranium enrichment. He appointed a prominent Western oriented Foreign Minister, Mohammed Jawad Zarif who has a track record favorable to a "Grand Bargain".

Instead of welcoming these major political and diplomatic breakthroughs, the Obama regime supported a Congressional resolution drawn up and promoted by Zionist zealot David Cohen of Treasury and the Israel lobby (AIPAC) to *tighten oil sanctions even further*. Obama and Congress chose military confrontation, threats and regime change over and against pursuit of a grand diplomatic opportunity which could include: 1) securing an intrusive supervision of Iran's nuclear program; 2) reduced enrichment of uranium; 3) Iranian co-operation in securing the peace in Iraq, Afghanistan and Syria; and 4) access to a multi-billion dollar petroleum market.

Washington demands "negotiations" that require a surrender of Iran's sovereignty. The Obama regime disdains a favorable diplomatic solution with the elected Rouhani regime in favor of pleasuring the acolytes of the Netanyahu regime, by pursuing an impossible unattainable "regime change" via economic strangulation.

Palestine–Israel Peace Negotiations: Land Grabbing and Peace Negotiations

There is no political leadership more accommodating and financially dependent on US policymakers than that of the Mahmoud Abbas regime in occupied Palestine. Abbas' police force works in tandem with the Israeli occupation army in repressing popular protests. He has arbitrarily retained dictatorial powers, represses popular democratic movements and denies Palestinian citizens legal electoral rights. He has refused to organize or condone mass protests against Israeli land seizures.

In other words, he is the "perfect client" for Washington and the most pliant negotiator for the Israelis: one willing to accept an agreement with Israel, which accepts: 1) 500,000 Jewish colonial settlers in the West Bank and East Jerusalem; 2) "no return" of exiled Palestinians; 3) the continued imprisonment of over 6,000 political prisoners; and 4) a perpetual Israeli military presence in Galilee. Abbas is willing to accept and call "Palestine" a series of non-contiguous territorial islands, surrounded by a ten meter Wall and subject to colonial depredations and military intrusions. In entering negotiations, Abbas did not object, let along reject, to Kerry's appointment of Martin Indyk as the US mediator, despite his notoriety in Washington as a Zionist apologist and purveyor of confidential documents in the 1980s.

The stage was set for a US "brokered" peace agreement—except that Israel announced a grand land grab: a massive expansion of 3000 new housing settlements in the West Bank and East Jerusalem. Secretary of State Kerry and President Obama did nothing to restrain Israel; on the contrary Kerry acknowledged that the Obama regime had foreknowledge and clearly gave the green light. In effect the negotiations served as an Israeli pretext *to accelerate the annexation of the last 20%* of what was "historic Palestine". As it stands, the Abbas regime has lost the last shred of legitimacy as it bows its head and enters negotiations over a smaller and smaller remnant of Palestinian territory. It is clear that the Abbas regime is "putting in time" to cover the four hundred million payoff from Washington and to buy personal safety and protection from their Israel colonial overseers. By accepting peace negotiations as a pretext for colonization, Obama gratifies his wealthy Zionist bankers in the US and deepens the anger and alienation of Palestinians and tens of millions of their Muslim supporters around the world. Kerry's support for the Israeli land grab makes the perverse outcome a source for *continued armed strife*. Obama trashed a great "peace opportunity" by choosing Israeli annexation over a mini-state ruled by an iron fisted Palestinian stooge on the US payroll and willing to side with Washington in every Middle Eastern conflict.

US and Venezuela: Peaceful Co-Existence or Destabilization?

Since late 2001 and for the next twelve years, the US has engaged in a multifaceted destabilization campaign designed to overthrow the democratic-nationalist government of President Chavez. Threats, military coups, large scale funding of electoral opposition parties, violent street demonstrations and referendums are part of the imperial repertory that has been tried and failed to stem the tide of Venezuela's policy of expanding public ownership, social welfare and regional integration (ALBA). With the death of Hugo Chavez and the election of President Maduro, Washington refused to accept the electoral outcome, validated by international observers and governments the world over. Washington launched its defeated client candidate (Capriles) on a destabilization campaign first via violent street actions and then in a regional crusade, both of which made no headway and only further isolated the US in Latin America.

The Obama-Kerry regime, having failed to destabilize the Maduro regime, 'apparently' decided to try diplomacy, following the common sense precept; "if you can't defeat them by force entice them with peace". At a conference in Guatemala, Kerry called the Venezuelan Foreign Minister Elias Jaua for "a new relation, the re-opening of Ambassadorial ties and diplomatic negotiations" ... Venezuela's President Maduro responded favorably, eager to lessen tensions and reach a peaceful accommodation. Then Samantha Powers, Obama's nominee to be the US Ambassador to the UN, in testimony before Congress, declared that upon appointment she would prioritize "the fight against state repression in Venezuela", in other words intervene in Venezuela on behalf of the opposition. Kerry endorsed her positions, highlighting Washington's hostility to the Maduro government. Kerry's overtures were exposed as a phony ploy of no consequence. Peaceful reconciliation went out the window. No negotiations took place. In order to retain ties with its client opposition, Washington closed the book on ending its isolation in Latin America and eliminated prospects for any economic openings which might have benefited US business interests.

US and Russia: Obama's Snowden Caper Revives the Cold War

At the beginning of his second term, President Obama announced that he would seek to improve relations with Russia. President Putin responded favorably. President Putin backed 1) the US-NATO assault ("no fly zone") on Libya; 2) the US designed economic sanctions against Iran; 3) allowed the US to ship arms and military personnel through Russia to bolster the occupation of Afghanistan; and 4) convinced President Assad of Syria to participate in negotiations in Geneva with the Islamic terrorist led opposition backed by Saudi-Turkey-NATO. Putin went along with US policy on Israel-Palestine. Clearly Washington got most of all it wanted from Putin via this diplomatic relation. Ongoing peaceful cooperation was clearly working in Obama's favor. In exchange Obama offered to attend an OECD meeting in Russia and have a side meeting with Putin.

In the run-up, Russia granted asylum to US political refugee Edward Snowden seeking refuge from political persecution. Obama sharply denounced Putin. Washington ignored its ignominious record of giving refuge to and refusing extradition requests for Chechen terrorists, Russian oligarchical swindlers, as well as Cuban airline bombing terrorist Posada Carriles and Bolivian President Sanchez de Losada, accused of murdering dozens of protestors. The White House responded by snubbing Putin and threatening further reprisals and "dire consequences". In other words Obama put into question a favorable asymmetrical diplomatic relation, resorting to Cold War rhetoric and threats. The Russians responded by affirming their right to grant asylum to political refugees and pointed to the onerous restrictions they imposed on Snowden effectively curtailing any further revelations. Putin restricted Snowden's freedom to discuss US spy operations. In a word instead of deepening a favorable diplomatic policy, Obama put it into the deep freeze, ensuring the loss of an important ally in its ongoing wars and conflicts.

The Syrian Triangle: Secular Collaborator, Al Qaeda Terrorists
and Obama's Double Discourse

For years Bashar al-Assad worked closely with the US in 1) curbing Al Qaeda terrorists; 2) preventing cross border attacks in Israel; 3) denying sanctuary for Iraqi insurgents fighting against the US occupation of Baghdad; and 4) complying with US policy by withdrawing troops from Lebanon.

Syria was a "co-operative adversary", maintaining regional stability and a tolerant multi-ethno-religious state in a region riven by Islamic and Jewish sectarian violence. But Washington under Obama magnified their differences and prioritized the policy of establishing a submissive client-state. Instead of continuing a policy of diplomatic pressure and tactical collaboration, Obama joined with an unholy alliance of Gulf State Islamic autocracies, ex-colonial European powers (especially France and England), Israel's secret services (Mossad) and Turkey's Islamist President Erdogan in arming, financing, training and providing sanctuary to armed Islamic mercenaries led by Al Qaeda brigades. Syria was riven by conflict, the economy was destroyed, security was non-existent and millions of refugees fled to Iraq, Jordan, Turkey, and beyond. Thousands of Jihadists from afar journeyed to the neighboring countries, received arms, paychecks and terrorist training in pursuit of a "Taliban style" regime in Syria as a springboard to destabilizing pro-US client states in the region. Turkey and Egypt's (under Morsi) interventions on behalf of the Islamic uprising provoked internal mass popular protest, weakening the US collaborator regimes. Obama's "all or nothing" attempt to establish a Syrian client regime via violence has produced "no win" situations: either Assad retains power as a less co-operative adversary or the Islamic terrorists establish a regime that serves as a springboard for one, two, and many caliphates. In the midst of this negative scenario, through Russian mediation, Bashar al-Assad agreed to pursue negotiations with the opposition in Geneva.

The war continues and refugees destabilize neighboring clients while Obama's incapacity to recognize failures and seek diplomatic 'half way solutions' erodes imperial pretensions.

US-Afghanistan: Prolonging the Longest War and Sacrificing a Diplomatic Retreat

The US invasion of Afghanistan in 2001 was the prelude to (1) the longest war in US history; (2) a war costing hundreds of billions of dollars and tens of thousands of dead and wounded soldiers; (3) the incitement of major insurgencies in Pakistan and elsewhere. In the face of substantial majorities calling for the end of US warfare and in the face of rising fiscal deficits, the Obama regime promised to withdraw most combat troops by the end of 2014, providing the "security situation allows". Well, that is a very dubious condition. The 300,000 Afghan army is riven by nationalists, Islamists and other opponents of the corrupt Hamid Karzai puppet regime and US war atrocities, drone killings included .They will likely overthrow the pro-US regime, first chance.

In the face of a military retreat and with improbable collaborators in the state, who have their baggage packed and tickets in hand, the Obama regime seemingly has no option but to cut losses by opening negotiations with the Taliban. The opportunity for negotiations exists: the Taliban opened an office in Qatar (December 2011) and Washington seemed to be agreeable to talks … and then Washington chose to accommodate its corrupt puppet ruler Karzai by insisting on his presence in the process. Obviously, regime continuance excludes any meaningful recognition of the Taliban's minimum demands for regime change. To further undermine any settlement, the Obama regime rejected the Taliban's strategic demand of total US military withdrawal. Taliban closed their Qatar office in July 2013. In other words the Obama regime sacrificed the possibility of a peaceful settlement which would moderate Taliban foreign and domestic policies in order to prop up a corrupt puppet regime lacking popular support, based on armed forces of dubious loyalty and dependent on a continued US presence. Instead of accepting retreat, cutting losses and pursuing accommodation, Obama maximizes losses and ensures that the inevitable military withdrawal will prejudice relations for decades ahead.

US-China Containment in the Face of Impotence is a No Brainer

China has the second largest economy in the world and a growth rate three to four times that of the United States. China has become one of the most important investment sites for the top US multinational corporations and potentially a major source of investment capital for the US economy. Given China's growing demands for advanced technology, financial and IT services, agricultural, energy and other commodities and the US demand for manufactured goods, there is a high degree of economic "complementarity". US-China cooperation offers opportunities for greater integration and joint ventures which can exploit market opportunities.

Faced with the historic opportunity to forge an economic partnership with an emerging global power, Obama has instead opted to isolate China by: 1) actively promoting regional trade agreements (the Trans-Pacific Partnership) which pointedly exclude China; and 2) intervening and fomenting territorial and maritime disputes between China and its neighbors and supporting separatist ethno-religious groups in China.

The Obama regime raised illusions that Obama would turn from his losing and costly Middle Eastern military adventures toward the more lucrative and profitable Asian markets, when he announced a "pivot to Asia". Instead of a reasoned and balanced shift toward 1) expanding US economic bridgeheads in China; and 2) seeking to deepen financial penetration and technological links, Obama simply *transferred his failed militarist ideologically driven policies* to Asia. He sided with Japan in a South China Sea dispute. He is inciting the Philippines and Vietnam to contest China's maritime claims. He is securing new military base agreements with Canberra and Manila. The Obama regime has 1) fortified its forward bases aimed at China; 2) encouraged and supported separatist Tibetans; and 3) armed Uighur terrorists.

The Obama regime has attempted to undermine China's economic linkages in Asia without providing any comparable alternative. The end result is that China still *remains the pre-eminent trading partner* for most of the members of what Obama conceived of as a "US centered" Pan-Pacific trade alliance. Furthermore, by bluster and provocative military maneuvers, Obama has pushed China into a closer and deeper strategic economic and political alliance with Russia. Obama's "isolationist ploy" was dead in the water. Commodity exporters like Australia, Indonesia, Peru, Chile and Colombia can ill afford to shun China, for the simple fact that the US offers no alternative market! Nor can Taiwan, South Korea and Japan find an alternative market for their high tech exports. Nor can the US replace the massive infrastructure investments that China has made in Burma, Cambodia, Laos and Pakistan.

Obama's policy of mindless military posturing, accompanied by vacuous ideological sniping, has lessened US economic opportunities and heightened military tensions. Obama's belligerent policy toward Beijing in pursuit of a US centered and hegemonized Asia lacks economic substance and client states willing to sacrifice economic gain for the dubious "honor" of housing US military bases pointed at threatening their principal economic partner.

The grand historic opportunity of a declining empire coming to peaceful and profitable terms with a rising global economic power was missed.

Conclusion

The Obama regime has systematically rejected opportunities to resolve conflicts and move on to a more moderate and balanced foreign policy, one more in accord with the real capacity of the US economy and state. Current and recent foreign policy discussions and decision makers have been blinded by a 'military metaphysic' whose only 'calculus' is based on the capacity to project military power independent of the real consequences. Obama's diplomatic initiatives lack substance and most often are neutralized by parallel military moves and aggressive interventions. Even within the constraints of obsessive empire building, a dysfunctional legislature and incompetent executive advisers, recent political changes including the ascendancy of pragmatic adversaries provided the Obama regime with real options which clearly would have opened the door to political compromises and strategic gains.

The Obama regime's failure to pursue diplomatic solutions can be attributed to the structural links between the Presidency and the military-police state apparatus. The latter has gained a high degree of autonomy from the productive economy, as evidenced everywhere, from Obama's China containment policy to the economic losses resulting from economic sanctions on Iran, Syria and (previously) Libya.

Obama's deep, longstanding and pervasive links to the 1% of Americans affiliated with notorious Israeli ideologues and his pandering to their lobbies and wealthy fund raisers has led to a rigid adherence to colonial-military policies that eschew any diplomatic compromises which might dim the megalomaniacal vision of "Greater Israel". Obama's myopia is 'structural'. He follows the dictates of prestigious Ivy League advisers whose judgment is forever defined by "what's good for Israel" and whose academic expertise is clouded by pea-brained assessments of what 'others' want and how they will react to perpetual belligerency.

The world view of the Obama regime is one of mirror looking in an echo chamber: it cannot visualize and accommodate the interests of rivals, competitors or adversaries, no matter how absolutely central they are to any meaningful compromise. The give and take of real world politics is totally foreign to the world's Chosen People. They only know how to "seize power" and create military facts, even as they then spend a dozen years and billions of dollars and millions of lives in endless wars, bemoaning lost markets amidst serial diplomatic failures. The epitaph for the Obama regime will read:

They fought the Wars
They lost.
They turned friends
into enemies.
Who became
Friends of our enemies.
They stood alone, in splendid isolation,
And said it was their only choice.

THE DECLINE OF THE US (AND EVERYONE ELSE …)

The world political economy is a mosaic of cross currents: domestic decay and elite enrichment, new sources for greater profits and deepening political disenchantment, declining living standards for many and extravagant luxury for a few, military losses in some regions with imperial recovery in others.

There are claims of a unipolar, a multi-polar and even a non-polar configuration of world power. Where, when, to what extent and under what contingencies do these claims have validity?

Bubbles and busts come and go—but let us talk of 'beneficiaries': those who cause crashes and reap the greatest rewards while their victims have no say. The swindle economy and the criminal state prosper by promoting the perversion of culture and literacy. 'Investigatory journalism', or peephole reportage, is all the rage. The world of power spins out of control. As they decline, the leading powers declare: "It's our rule or everyone's ruin!"

Global Configurations of Power

Power is a relationship between classes, states, and military and ideological institutions. Any configuration of power is contingent on past and present struggles reflecting shifting correlations of forces. Structures and physical resources, concentrations of wealth, arms and the media matter greatly; they set the framework in which the principal power wielders are embedded. But strategies for retaining or gaining power depend on securing alliances, engaging in wars and negotiating peace. Above all, world power depends on the strength of domestic foundations. This requires a dynamic productive economy, an independent state free from prejudicial foreign entanglements and a leading class capable of harnessing global resources to 'buy off' domestic consent of the majority.

To examine the position of the United States in the global configuration of power it is necessary to analyze its changing economic and political relations on two levels: by region and by sphere of power. History does not move in a linear pattern or according to recurring cycles: military and political defeats in some regions may be accompanied by significant victories in others. Economic decline in some spheres and regions may be compensated by sharp advances in other economic sectors and regions.

In the final analysis, the question is not 'keeping a scorecard' or adding wins and subtracting losses, but translating regional and sectoral outcomes into an understanding of the direction and emerging structures of the global power configuration. We start by examining the legacy of recent wars on the global economic, military and political power of the United States.

Sustaining the US Empire: Defeats, Retreat, Advances and Victories

The dominant view of most critical analysts is that over the past decade US empire-building has suffered a series of military defeats, experienced economic decline, and now faces severe competition and the prospect of further military losses. The evidence cited is impressive: The US was forced to withdraw troops from Iraq after an extremely costly decade-long military occupation, leaving in place a regime more closely allied to Iran, the US' regional adversary. The Iraq war depleted the economy, deprived American corporations of oil wealth, greatly enlarged Washington's budget and trade deficits, and reduced the living standards of US citizens. The Afghanistan war had a similar outcome, with high external costs, military retreat, fragile clients, domestic disaffection, and no short or medium term transfers of wealth (imperial pillage) to the US Treasury or private corporations. The Libyan war led to the total destruction of a modern, oil-rich economy in North Africa, the total dissolution of state and civil society, and the emergence of armed tribal, fundamentalist militias opposed to US and EU client regimes in North and sub-Sahara Africa and beyond. Instead of continuing to profit from lucrative oil and gas agreements with the conciliatory Gaddafi regime, Washington decided on 'regime change', engaging in a war which ruined Libya and destroyed any viable central state. The current Syrian "proxy war" has strengthened radical Islamist warlords, destroyed Damascus' economy and added massive refugee pressure to the already uprooted millions from wars in Iraq and Libya. US imperial wars have resulted in economic losses, regional political instability and military gains for Islamist adversaries.

Latin America has overwhelmingly rejected US efforts to overthrow the Venezuelan government. The entire world—minus Israel and Washington— rejects the blockade of Cuba. Regional integration organizations, which exclude the US, have proliferated. US trade shares have declined, as Asia is replacing the US in the Latin American market.

In Asia, China deepens and extends its economic links with all the key countries, while the US 'pivot' is mostly an effort at military base encirclement of China involving Japan, Australia and the Philippines. In other words, China is more important than the US for Asian economic expansion, while Chinese financing of US trade imbalances props up the US economy.

In Africa, US military command operations mainly promote armed conflicts and lead to greater instability. Meanwhile Asian capitalists, deeply invested in strategic African countries, are reaping the benefits of its commodity boom, expanding markets and the outflow of profits.

The exposure of the US National Security Agency's global spy network has seriously undermined global intelligence and clandestine operations. While it may have helped privileged private corporations, the massive US investment in cyber-imperialism appears to have generated negative diplomatic and operational returns for the imperial state.

In sum, the current global overview paints a picture of severe military and diplomatic setbacks in imperial policies, substantial losses to the US Treasury and the erosion of public support.

Nevertheless this perspective has serious flaws, especially with regard to other regions, relations and spheres of economic activity. The fundamental structures of empire remain intact.

NATO, the major military alliance headed by the US Pentagon, is expanding its membership and escalating its field of operations. The Baltic States, especially Estonia, are the site of huge military exercises held just minutes from the principal Russian cities. Central and Eastern Europe provide missile sites all aimed at Russia. Until very recently, the Ukraine had been moving toward membership in the European Union and a step toward NATO membership.

The US-led Trans-Pacific Partnership has expanded membership among the Andean countries, Chile, Peru and Colombia. It serves as a springboard to weaken regional trading blocs like MERCOSUR and ALBA, which exclude Washington. Meanwhile, the CIA, the State Department and their NGO conduits are engaged in an all-out economic sabotage and political destabilization campaign to weaken Venezuela's nationalist government. US-backed bankers and capitalists have worked to sabotage the economy, provoking inflation (50%), shortages of essential items of consumption, and rolling power blackouts. Their control over most of Venezuela's mass media has allowed them to exploit popular discontent by blaming the economic dislocation on 'government inefficiency'.

Overall, the US offensive in Latin America has focused on a military coup in Honduras, ongoing economic sabotage in Venezuela, electoral and media campaigns in Argentina, and cyber warfare in Brazil, while developing closer ties with recently elected compliant neoliberal regimes in Mexico, Colombia, Chile, Panama, Guatemala and the Dominican Republic. While Washington lost influence in Latin America during the first decade of the 21st century, it has since partially recovered its clients and partners. The relative recovery of US influence illustrates the fact that 'regime changes' and a decline in market shares have not lessened the financial and corporate ties linking even the progressive countries to powerful US interests. The continued presence of powerful political allies—even those 'out of government'—provides a trampoline for regaining US influence. Nationalist policies and emerging regional integration projects remain vulnerable to US counter-attacks.

While the US has lost influence among some oil producing countries, it lessened its dependence on oil and gas imports as a result of a vast increase in domestic energy production via 'fracking' and other intensive extractive technologies. Greater local self-sufficiency means lower energy costs for domestic producers and increases their competitiveness in world markets, raising the possibility that the US could regain market shares for its exports.

The seeming decline of US imperial influence in the Arab world following the popular 'Arab Spring' uprisings has halted and even been reversed. The military coup in Egypt and the installation and consolidation of the military dictatorship in Cairo suppressed the mass national-popular mobilizations. Egypt is back in the US-Israel orbit. In Algeria, Morocco and Tunisia the old and new rulers are clamping down on any anti-imperial protests. In Libya, the US-NATO air force destroyed the nationalist-populist Gaddafi regime, eliminating an alternative welfare model to neo-colonial pillage—but has so far failed to consolidate a neoliberal client regime in Tripoli. Instead rival armed Islamist gangs, monarchists and ethnic thugs pillage and ravage the country. Destroying an anti-imperialist regime has not produced a pro-imperialist client.

In the Middle East, Israel continues to dispossess the Palestinians of their land and water. The US continues to escalate military maneuvers and impose more economic sanctions against Iran—weakening Teheran but also decreasing US wealth and influence due to the loss of the lucrative Iranian market. Likewise in Syria, the US and its NATO allies have destroyed Syria's economy and shredded its complex society, but they will not be the main beneficiaries. Islamist mercenaries have gained bases of operations while Hezbollah has consolidated its position as a significant regional actor. Current negotiations with Iran open possibilities for the US to cut its losses and reduce the regional threat of a costly new war but these talks are being blocked by an 'alliance' of Zionist-militarist Israel, monarchist Saudi Arabia and 'Socialist' France.

Washington has lost economic influence in Asia to China but it is mounting a regional counter-offensive, based on its network of military bases in Japan, the Philippines and Australia. It is promoting a new Pan Pacific economic agreement that excludes China. This demonstrates the US capacity to intervene and project imperial interests. However, announcing new policies and organizations is not the same as implementing and providing them with dynamic content. Washington's military encirclement of China is off-set by the US Treasury's multi-trillion dollar debt to Beijing. An aggressive US military encirclement of China could result in a massive Chinese sell-off of US Treasury notes and five hundred leading US multinationals finding their investments in jeopardy!

Power-sharing between an emerging and established global power, such as China and the US, cannot be 'negotiated' via US military superiority. Threats, bluster and diplomatic chicanery score mere propaganda victories but only long-term economic advances can create the domestic Trojan Horses need to erode China's dynamic growth. Even today, the Chinese elite spend hefty sums to educate their children in "prestigious" US and British universities where free market economic doctrines and imperial-centered narratives are taught. For the past decade, leading Chinese politicians and the corporate rich have sent tens of billions of dollars in licit and illicit funds to overseas bank accounts, investing in high end real estate in North America and Europe and dispatching billions to money laundering havens. Today, there is a powerful faction of economists and elite financial advisers in China pushing for greater 'financial liberalization', i.e. penetration by the leading Wall Street and City of London speculative houses. While Chinese industries may be winning the competition for overseas markets, the US has gained and is gaining powerful levers over China's financial structure.

The US share of Latin American trade may be declining, but the absolute dollar worth of trade has increased several-fold over the past decade.

The US may have lost right-wing regime clients in Latin America, but the new center-left regimes are actively collaborating with most of the major US and Canadian mining and agro-business corporations and commodity trading houses. The Pentagon has not been able to engineer military coups, with the pathetic exception of Honduras, but it still retains its close working relations with the Latin American military in the form of 1) its regional policing of 'terrorism', 'narcotics' and 'migration'; 2) providing technical training and political indoctrination via overseas military 'educational' programs; and 3) engaging in joint military exercises.

In sum, the structures of the US empire—corporate, financial, military and politico-cultural—all remain in place and ready to regain dominance if and when political opportunities arise. For example, a sharp decline in commodity prices would likely provoke a deep crisis and intensify class conflicts among center-left regimes, which are dependent on agro-mining exports to fund their social programs. In any ensuing confrontation, the US would work with and through its agents among the economic and military elite to oust the incumbent regime and re-impose pliant neoliberal clients. The current phase of post-neoliberal policies and power configurations is vulnerable. The relative 'decline of US influence and power' can be reversed even if it is not returned to its former configuration. The theoretical point is that while imperialist structures remain in place and while their collaborator counterparts abroad retain strategic positions, the US can re-establish its primacy in the global configuration of power.

Imperial 'roll-back' does not require the 'same old faces'. New political figures, especially with progressive credentials and faint overtones of a 'social inclusionary' ideology are already playing a major role in the new imperial-centered trade networks. In Chile, newly elected "Socialist" President Michelle Bachelet and the Peruvian ex-nationalist, President Ollanta Humala, are major proponents of Washington's Tran-Pacific Partnership, a trading bloc which competes with the nationalist MERCOSUR and ALBA, and excludes China. In Mexico, US client President Enrique Peña Nieto is privatizing the 'jewel' of the Mexican economy, PEMEX, the giant public oil company—strengthening Washington's hold over regional energy resources and increasing US independence from Mid-East oil. Colombian President Santos, the 'peace president', is actively negotiating an end to guerrilla warfare in order to expand multinational exploitation of mineral and energy resources located in guerrilla-contested regions, a prospect which will primarily benefit US oil companies. In Argentina, the state oil company, Yacimientos Petroliferos Fiscales (YPF) has signed a joint venture agreement with the oil giant, Chevron, to exploit an enormous gas and oil field, known as Vaca Muerte (Dead Cow). This will expand the US presence in Argentina in energy production alongside the major inroads made by Monsanto in the powerful agro-business sector.

No doubt Latin America has diversified its trade and the US share has relatively declined. Latin American rulers no longer eagerly seek 'certification' from the US Ambassador before announcing their political candidacy. The US is totally alone in its boycott of Cuba. The Organization of American States is no longer a US haven. But there are counter-tendencies, reflected in new pacts like the Trans-Pacific Partnership (TPP). New sites of economic exploitation, which are not exclusively US controlled, now serve as springboards to greater imperial power.

Conclusion

The US economy is stagnant and has failed to regain momentum because of its pursuit of 'serial' imperial wars. But in the Middle East, the US decline, relative to its past, has not been accompanied by the ascent of its old rivals. Europe is in deeper crisis, with a vast army of unemployed, chronic negative growth and few signs of recovery for the visible future. Even China, the new emerging global power, is slowing down, with its growth falling from over 11% to 7% in the current decade. Beijing faces growing domestic discontent. India and China are liberalizing their financial systems, opening them up to penetration and influence by US finance capital.

The main anti-imperialist forces in Asia and Africa are not composed of progressive, secular, democratic and socialist movements. Instead, the empire is confronted by religious, ethnic, misogynist and authoritarian movements with irredentist tendencies. The old secular, socialist voices have lost their bearings, and provide perverse 'justifications' for the imperialist wars of aggression in Libya, Mali and Syria. The French Socialists, who had opposed the Iraq war in 2003, now find their President Francois Hollande parroting the brutal militarism of the Israeli warlord, Netanyahu.

The point is that the thesis of the 'decline of the US empire' and its corollary, the 'crises of the US' are overstated, time bound and lack specificity. In reality, there is no alternative imperial or modern anti-imperial tendency on the immediate horizon. While it is true that Western capitalism is in crisis, the recently ascending Asian capitalism of China and India face a different crisis resulting from their savage class exploitation and murderous caste relations. If objective conditions are 'ripe for socialism', the socialists—at least those retaining any political presence—are comfortably embedded with their respective imperial regimes. The Marxists and Socialists in Egypt joined with the military to overthrow an elected conservative Islamist regime, leading to the restoration of imperialist clientelism in Cairo. The French and English 'Marxists' have supported NATO's destruction of Libya and Syria. Numerous progressives and socialists, in Europe and North America, support Israel's warlords and/or remain silent in the face of domestic Zionist power in the executive branches and legislatures.

If imperialism is declining, so is anti-imperialism. If capitalism is in crisis, the existing anti-capitalists are in retreat. If capitalists look for new faces and ideologues to revive their fortunes, isn't it time the anti-imperialists and anti-capitalists did likewise?

PART II

CYBER-IMPERIALISM

The Logic
behind Mass Spying:
Empire and Cyber Imperialism

Introduction

Revelations about the long-term global, intrusive spying by the US National Security Agency (NSA) and other allied intelligence apparatuses have provoked widespread protests and indignation and threatened ties between erstwhile imperial allies.

Allied regimes have uniformly condemned NSA espionage as a violation of trust and sovereignty, a threat to their national and economic security and to their citizens' privacy.

In contrast, Washington has responded in a contradictory manner: on the one hand, US officials and intelligence chiefs have acknowledged 'some excesses and mistakes'; on the other hand, they defend the entire surveillance program as necessary for US national security.

Interpretations vary about the US global spy apparatus—how it was built and why it was launched against hundreds of millions of people. 'Subjective' and 'objective' explanations abound, evoking psychological, social, economic, strategic and political considerations.

A multi-factorial explanation is required.

The Integrated Hypothesis of the Global Police State

One of the essential components of a police state is an all-pervasive spy apparatus operating independently of any legal or constitutional constraints. Spy operations include: 1) massive surveillance over text, video and audio communications and 2) the capacity to secretly record, store and use information secretly collected. This information strengthens political and economic leaders who, in turn, appoint and direct the spy chiefs. The political and economic rulers control the spy-lords by setting the goals, means and targets of the surveillance state. The US global spy apparatus is neither 'self-starting nor self-perpetuating'. It did not arise in a vacuum and it has virtually no strategic autonomy. While there may be intra-bureaucratic conflicts and rivalries, the institutions and groups function within the overall 'paradigm' established and directed by the political and economic elite.

The Global Spy Structure

The growth and expansion of the US spy apparatus has deep roots in its history and is related to the colonial need to control subjugated native and enslaved peoples. However, the global operations emerged after the Second World War when the US replaced Europe as the center of world imperialism. The US assumed the principal role in preventing the spread of revolutionary and anti-colonial movements from the Soviet Union, China, Korea, Vietnam and Cuba to war and crisis-burdened countries of Europe, North and Southeast Asia, and Latin America. When the collectivist states fell apart in the 1990s the US became the sole superpower and a unipolar world emerged.

For the United States, 'unipolarity' meant 1) an impetus toward total global domination; 2) a worldwide network of military bases; 3) the subordination of capitalist competitors in other industrial countries; 4) the destruction of nationalist adversaries; and 5) the unfettered pillage of resources from the former collectivist regimes as they became vassal states. The last condition meant the complete dismantling of the collectivist state and its public institutions—education, health care and worker rights.

The opportunities for immense profits and supreme control over this vast new empire were boundless while the risks seemed puny, at least during the 'golden period', defined by the years immediately after 1) the capitalist takeover of the ex-Soviet bloc; 2) the Chinese transition to capitalism; and 3) the conversion of many former African and Asian nationalist regimes, parties and movements to 'free-market' capitalism.

Dazzled by their vision of a 'new world to conquer' the United States set up an international state apparatus in order to exploit this world-historical opportunity. Most top political leaders, intelligence strategists, military officials and business elites quickly realized that these easy initial conquests and the complicity of pliable and kleptocratic post-Communist vassal rulers would not last. The societies would eventually react and the lucrative plunder of resources was not sustainable. Nationalist adversaries were bound to arise and demand their own spheres of influence. The White House feared their own capitalist allies would take on the role of imperialist competitors seeking to grab 'their share' of the booty, taking over and exploiting resources, public enterprises and cheap labor.

The new 'unipolar world' meant the shredding of the fabric of social and political life. In the 'transition' to free market capitalism, stable employment, access to health care, security, education and civilized living standards disappeared. In the place of once complex, advanced social systems, local tribal and ethnic wars erupted. It would be 'divide and conquer' in an orgy of pillage for the empire. But the vast majority of the people of the world suffered from chaos and regression when the multi-polar world of collectivist, nationalist, and imperialist regimes gave way to the unipolar empire.

For US imperialist strategists and their academic apologists the transition to a unipolar imperial world was exhilarating and they dubbed their unchallenged domination the 'New World Order' (NWO), deeming that the US imperial state then had the right and duty to maintain and police its 'New World Order'—by any means. Francis Fukiyama, among other academic apologists, celebrated the 'end of history' in a paroxysm of imperial fever. Liberal-imperial academics, like Immanuel Wallerstein, sensed the emerging challenges to the US Empire and advanced the view of a Manichean world of 'unipolarity' (meaning 'order') versus 'multipolar chaos'—as if the hundreds of millions of lives in scores of countries devastated by the rise of the post-collectivist US empire did not have a stake in liberating themselves from the yoke of a unipolar world.

By the end of its first decade, the unipolar empire exhibited cracks and fissures. It had to confront adversarial nationalist regimes in resource-rich countries, including Muammar Gaddafi in Libya, Bashar al-Assad in Syria, Saddam Hussein in Iraq and Khamenei in Iran. They challenged US supremacy in North Africa and the Middle East. The Taliban in Afghanistan and nationalist Islamist movements questioned US influence over the vassal rulers of Muslim countries— especially the puppet monarchs in the Persian Gulf.

On the other side of the imperial coin, the domestic economic foundations of the 'New World Order' were weakened by a series of speculative crises undermining the support of the US public as well as sectors of the elite. Meanwhile European and Japanese allies, as well as emerging Chinese capitalists, were beginning to compete for markets.

Within the US an ultra-militarist group of political ideologues, public officials and policy advisers, embracing a doctrine combining a domestic police state with foreign military intervention, took power in Washington. 'Conservatives' in the Bush, Sr. regime, 'liberals' in the Clinton administration and 'neo-conservatives' in the Bush, Jr. administration all sought and secured the power to launch wars in the Persian Gulf and the Balkans, to expand and consolidate the unipolar empire.

Maintaining and expanding the unipolar empire became the trigger for the White House's global police state apparatus. As new regimes were added to Washington's orbit, more and more surveillance was needed to make sure they did not drift into a competitor's sphere of influence.

The year 2000 was critical for the global police state. First there was the dot-com crash in the financial sector. The speculative collapse caused massive but unorganized disaffection among the domestic population. Arab resistance re-emerged in the Middle East. The cosmically corrupt Boris Yeltsin vassal state fell and a nationalist, Russian President Vladimir Putin, took power. The willing accomplices to the disintegration of the former USSR had taken their billions and fled to New York, London and Israel. Russia was on the road to recovery as a unified nuclear-armed nation state with regional ambitions. The period of unchallenged unipolar imperial expansion had ended.

The election of President Bush Jr. opened the executive branch to police state ideologues and civilian warlords, many linked to the state of Israel, who were determined to destroy secular Arab nationalist and Muslim adversaries in the Middle East. The steady growth of the global police state had been 'too slow' for them. The newly ascendant warlords and the proponents of the global police state wanted to take advantage of their golden opportunity to make US/Israeli supremacy in the Middle East irreversible and unquestioned via the application of overwhelming force ('shock and awe').

Their primary political problem in expanding global military power was the lack of a fully dominant domestic police state capable of demobilizing American public opinion largely opposed to any new wars. 'Disaster ideologues' like Phillip Zelikow and Condoleezza Rice understood the need for a new 'Pearl Harbor' to occur and threaten domestic security and thereby terrify the public into war. They lamented the fact that no credible regimes were left in the Middle East to cast as the 'armed aggressor' and as a threat to US national security. Such an enemy was vital to the launching of new wars. And new wars were necessary to justify the scale and scope of the new global spy apparatus and emergency police state edicts the warlords and neoconservatives had in mind. Absent a credible 'state-based adversary', the militarists settled for an act of terror (or the appearance of one) to 'shock and awe' the US public into accepting its project for imperial wars, the imposition of a domestic police state and the establishment of a vast global spy apparatus.

The September 11, 2001 explosions at the World Trade Center in New York City and in a wing (mostly vacant for repairs) of the Pentagon in Washington, DC were the triggers for a vast political and bureaucratic transformation of the US imperial state. The entire state apparatus became a police state operation. All constitutional guarantees were suspended. The neo-conservatives seized power, the civilian warlords ruled. A huge body of police state legislation suddenly appeared, as if from nowhere—the 'Patriot Act'. The Zionists in office set the objectives and influenced military policies to focus on Israel's regional interests and the destruction of Israel's Arab adversaries who had opposed its annexation of Palestine. War was declared against Afghanistan without any evidence that the ruling Taliban was involved or aware of the September 11 attack on the US. Despite massive civilian and even some military dissent, the civilian warlords and Zionist officials blatantly fabricated a series of pretexts to justify an unprovoked war against the secular nationalist regime in Iraq, the most advanced of all Arab countries. Europe was divided over the war. Countries in Asia and Latin America joined Germany and France in refusing to support the invasion. The United Kingdom, under a

'Labor' government, eagerly joined forces with the US, hoping to regain some of its former colonial holdings in the Gulf.

At home, hundreds of billions of tax dollars were diverted from social programs to fund a vast army of police state operatives. The ideologues of war and the legal eagles for torture and the police state shifted into high gear. Those who opposed the wars were identified, monitored and the details of their lives were 'filed away' in a vast database. Soon millions came to be labeled as 'persons of interest' if they were connected in any way to anyone who was 'suspect', i.e. opposed to the 'Global War on Terror'. Eventually even more tenuous links were made to everyone...family members, classmates and employers.

Over 1.5 million 'security cleared' monitors were contracted by the government to spy on hundreds of millions of citizens. The spy state spread domestically and internationally. For a global empire, based on a unipolar state, the best defense was judged to be a massive global surveillance apparatus operating independently of any other government—including the closest allies.

The slogan, 'Global War on Terror' (GWOT), became an open-ended formula for the civilian warlords, militarists and Zionists to expand the scope and duration of overt and covert warfare and espionage. 'Homeland Security' departments, operating at both the Federal and State levels, were consolidated and expanded with massive budgets for incarceration and repression. Constitutional protections and the Writ of Habeas Corpus were rendered 'quaint vestiges of history'. The National Security Agency doubled its personnel and budget with a mandate to distrust and monitor allies and vassal states. The targets piled upon targets, far beyond traditional adversaries, sweeping up the public and private communications of all political, military and economic leaders, institutions, and citizenry.

The 'Global War on Terror' provided the ideological framework for a police state based on the totalitarian conception that 'everybody and everything is connected to each other' in a 'global system' threatening the state. This 'totalistic view' informs the logic of the expanded NSA, linking enemies, adversaries, competitors and allies. 'Enemies' were defined as anti-imperialist states or regimes with consistently critical independent foreign and domestic policies. 'Adversaries' occasionally sided with 'enemies', or tolerated policymakers who would not always conform to imperial policies. 'Competitors' supported the empire but had the capacity and opportunity to make lucrative trade deals with adversaries or enemies. 'Allies' were states and leaders who generally supported imperial wars but might provide a forum condemning imperial war crimes (torture and drone attacks). In addition, allies could undermine US imperial market shares and accumulate favorable trade balances.

The logic of the NSA required spying on the allies to root out any links, trade, cultural or scientific relations with adversaries and enemies, which might have spillover consequences. The NSA feared that associations in one sphere might 'overlap' with adversaries operating in strategic policy areas and undermine ally loyalty to the empire.

The spy logic had a multiplier effect—who gets to 'spy on the spies?' The NSA might collaborate with overseas allied intelligence agencies and officials—but American spymasters would always question their reliability, their inclination to withhold vital information, the potential for shifting loyalties. 'Do our allies spy on us? How do we know our own spies are not colluding with allied spies, who might then be colluding with adversarial spies?' This justified the establishment of a huge national vacuum cleaner to suck up all transactions and communications—justified by the notion that a wide net scooping up everything might catch that big fish!

The NSA regards all 'threats to the unipolar empire' as national security threats. No country or agency within or without the reach of the empire was excluded as a 'potential threat'.

The 'lead imperial state' requires the most efficient and overarching spy technology with the furthest and deepest reach. Overseas allies appear relatively inefficient, vulnerable to infiltration, infected with the residua of a long-standing suspect 'leftist culture' and unable to confront the threat of new dangerous adversaries. The imperial logic regards surveillance of 'allies' as 'protecting allied interests' because the allies lack the will and capacity to deal with enemy infiltration.

There is a circular logic to the surveillance state. When an allied leader starts to question how imperial espionage protects allied interests, it is time to intensify spying on the ally. Any foreign ally who questions NSA surveillance over its citizens raises deep suspicions. Washington believes that questioning imperial surveillance undermines political loyalties.

Secret Police Spying as a "Process of Accumulation"

Like capitalism, which needs to constantly expand and accumulate capital, secret police bureaucracies require more spies to discover new areas, institutions and people to monitor. Leaders, followers, citizens, immigrants, members of ethnic, religious, civic and political groups and individuals—all are subject to surveillance. This requires vast armies of data managers and analysts, operatives, programmers, software developers and supervisors—an empire of 'IT'. The ever-advancing technology needs an ever-expanding base of operation.

The spy-masters move from local to regional to global operations. Facing exposure and condemnation of its global chain of spying, the NSA calls for a new 'defensive ideology'. To formulate the ideology, a small army of academic hacks is trotted out to announce the phony alternatives of a 'unipolar police state or terror and chaos'. The public is presented with a fabricated choice of its perpetual, 'well-managed and hi-tech', imperial wars versus the fragmentation and collapse of the entire world into a global war of 'all against all'. Academic ideologues studiously avoid mentioning that small wars by small powers end more quickly and have fewer casualties.

The ever-expanding technology of spying strengthens the police state. The list of targets is endless and bizarre. Nothing and no one will be missed!

As under capitalism, the growth of the spy state triggers crisis. With the inevitable rise of opposition, whistleblowers come forward to denounce the surveillance state. At its peak, spy-state over-reach leads to exposure, public scandals and threats from allies, competitors and adversaries. The rise of cyber-imperialism raises the specter of cyber-anti-imperialism. New conceptions of inter-state relations and global configurations are debated and considered. World public opinion increasingly rejects the 'necessity' of police states. Popular disgust and reason exposes the evil logic of the spy-state based on empire and promotes a plural world of peaceful rival countries, functioning under co-operative policies—systems without empire, without spymasters and spies.

THE DEEPER MEANING OF MASS SPYING IN AMERICA

Introduction

The *exposure* of the Obama regime's use of the National Security Agency to secretly spy on the communications of *hundreds of millions* of US and overseas citizens has provoked worldwide denunciations.

In the United States, despite widespread mass media coverage and the opposition of civil liberties organizations, there has not been any mass protest. Congressional leaders from both the Republican and Democratic Parties, as well as top judges, approved of the unprecedented domestic spy program. Even worse, when the pervasive spy operations were revealed, top Senate and Congressional leaders repeated their *endorsement* of each and every intrusion into all electronic and written communication involving American citizens. President Obama and his Attorney General Holder openly and forcefully defended the NSA's universal spy operations.

The issues raised by this vast secret police apparatus and its *penetration* into and *control* over civil society, infringing on the citizens' freedom of expression, go far beyond mere 'violations of privacy', as raised by many legal experts.

Most civil libertarians focus on the *violations* of *individual* rights, *constitutional guarantees* and the citizen's privacy rights. These *are* important legal issues and the critics are right in raising them. However, these constitutional-legal critiques do not go far enough; they fail to raise even more fundamental issues. They avoid basic political questions.

Why has such a massive police-state apparatus and universal spying become so central to the ruling regime? Why has the entire executive, legislative and judicial leadership come out in public for such a blatant repudiation of all constitutional guarantees? Why do elected leaders defend universal political espionage against the citizenry? What kind of politics requires a police state? What kind of long-term, large scale domestic and foreign policies are so illegal and unconstitutional as to require the building of a vast network of domestic spies and a hundred billion dollar corporate-state techno-espionage infrastructure in a time of budget 'austerity' with the slashing of social programs?

The second set of questions arises from the use of the espionage data. So far most critics have questioned the existence of massive state espionage but have avoided the vital issue of what *measures are taken* by the spymasters once they target individuals, groups, movements? The essential question is: *What reprisals and sanctions follow from the 'information' that is collected, classified and made operational by these massive domestic spy networks*? Now that the 'secret' of all-encompassing, state political spying has entered public discussion, the next step should be to reveal the secret *operations* that follow against those targeted by the spymasters as a 'risk to national security'.

The Politics Behind the Police State

The fundamental reason for the conversion of the state into a gigantic spy apparatus is the nature of deeply destructive domestic and foreign policies which the government has so forcefully pursued. The vast expansion of the police state apparatus is not a response to the terror attack of 9/11. The geometrical growth of spies, secret police budgets, and the vast intrusion into all citizen communications coincides with the wars across the globe. The decision to militarize US global policy requires vast budgetary re-allocation, slashing social spending to fund empire-building, shredding public health and social security to bail out Wall Street. These are policies which greatly enhance profits for bankers and corporations while imposing regressive taxes on wage and salaried workers

Prolonged and extended wars abroad have been funded at the expense of citizens' welfare at home. This policy had led to declining living standards for many tens of millions of citizens and rising dissatisfaction, carrying with it the potential of social resistance as evidenced by the brief "Occupy Wall Street" movement which was endorsed by over 80% of the population. The positive response alarmed the state and led to an escalation of police state measures. Mass spying is designed to identify those citizens who oppose both imperial wars and the destruction of domestic welfare; labeling them as 'security threats' is a means of controlling them through the use of arbitrary police powers. The expansion of the President's war powers has been accompanied by the growth and expanding scope of the state spy apparatus: the more the President orders overseas drone attacks, the greater the number of his military interventions, the greater the need for the political elite surrounding the President to increase its policing of citizens in anticipation of a popular backlash. In this context, the policy of mass spying is taken as 'pre-emptive action'. The greater the police state operations, the greater the fear and insecurity among dissident citizens and activists.

The assault on the living standards of working and middle class Americans in order to fund the endless series of wars, and not the so-called 'war on terror', is the reason the state has developed massive cyber warfare against the US citizenry. The issue is not only a question of a violation of individual privacy: it is fundamentally an issue of state infringement of the collective rights of organized citizens to freely engage in public opposition to regressive socio-economic policies and question the empire. The proliferation of permanent bureaucratic institutions, with over a million security 'data collectors', is accompanied by tens of thousands of 'field operators', analysts and inquisitors acting arbitrarily to designate dissident citizens as 'security risks' and *imposing reprisals* according to the *political needs* of their ruling political bosses. The police state apparatus has its own rules of self-protection and self-perpetuation; it has its own linkages and may occasionally compete with the Pentagon. The police state links up with and protects the masters of Wall Street and the propagandists of the mass media—even as it (must) spy on them!

The police state is an instrument of the Executive Branch, acting as a vehicle for its arbitrary prerogative powers. However on administrative matters, it possesses a degree of 'autonomy' to target dissident behavior. What is clear is the high degree of cohesion, vertical discipline and mutual defense, up and down the hierarchy. The fact that one whistle-blower, Edward Snowden, emerged from the hundreds of thousands of citizen spies is the exception, the lone whistle blower, which proves the rule: There are fewer defectors to be found among the million-member US spy network than in all the Mafia families in Europe and North America.

The domestic spy apparatus operates with impunity because of its network of powerful domestic *and overseas allies*. The entire bi-partisan Congressional leadership is privy to and complicit with its operations. Related branches of government, like the Internal Revenue Service, cooperate in providing information and pursuing targeted political groups and individuals. Israel is a key overseas ally of the National Security Agency, as has been documented in the Israeli press.[7] Two Israeli high tech firms (Verint and Narus) with ties to Mossad, the Israeli secret police, have provided the *spy software* for the NSA and this, of course, has opened a window for Israeli spying in the US against Americans opposed to the Zionist state. Writer and critic Steve Lendman points out that Israeli spymasters, via their software "front companies," have long had the ability to 'steal proprietary commercial and industrial data" with impunity. And because of the power and influence of the Conference of Presidents of the 52 Major American Jewish Organizations, Justice Department officials have ordered dozens of Israeli espionage cases to be dropped. The tight Israeli ties to the US spy apparatus serves to prevent deeper scrutiny into Israel's operations and political goals—at a very high price in terms of the security of US citizens. In recent years two incidents stand out: Israeli security 'experts' were contracted to advise the Pennsylvania Department of Homeland Security in their investigation and 'Stasi-like' repression of government critics and environmental activists (compared to 'al Qaeda terrorists' by the Israelis), the discovery of which forced the resignation of OHS Director James Powers in 2010. In 2003, New Jersey governor, Jim McGreevy appointed his lover, an Israeli government operative and former IDF officer, to head that state's 'Homeland Security Department and later resigned, denouncing the Israeli, Golan Cipel, for blackmail in late 2004. These examples are a small sample illustrating the depth and scope of Israeli police state tactics intersecting in US domestic repression.

The Political and Economic Consequences of the Spy State

The denunciations of the mass spy operations are a positive step, *as far as they go*. But equally important is the question of *what follows from the act of spying*? We now know that hundreds of millions of Americans are being spied on by the state. We know that mass spying is official policy of the Executive and is approved by Congressional leaders. But we have only fragmented information on the repressive measures resulting from the investigations of "suspect individuals". We can assume that there is a division of labor among data collectors, data analysts and field operatives following up "risky individuals and groups", based on the internal criteria known only to the secret police. The key spy operatives are those who devise and apply the criteria for designating someone as a "security risk". Individuals and groups who express critical views of domestic and foreign policy are "a risk"; those who act to protest are a "higher risk"; those who travel to conflict regions are presumed to be in the "highest risk" category, even if they have violated no law. *The question of the lawfulness of a citizen's views and actions does not enter into the spymasters' equation; nor do any questions regarding the lawfulness of the acts committed by the spies against citizens.* The criteria defining a security risk supersede any constitutional considerations and safeguards.

We know from a large number of published cases that lawful critics, illegally spied upon, have subsequently been arrested, tried and jailed—with their lives and those of their friends and family members shattered. We know that hundreds of homes, workplaces and offices of suspects have been raided in 'fishing expeditions'. We know that family members, associates, neighbors, clients, and employers of "suspects" have been interrogated, pressured and intimidated. Above all, we know that tens of millions of law abiding citizens, critical of domestic economic and overseas war policies, have been censored by the very real fear of the massive operations carried out by the police state. In this atmosphere of intimidation, any critical conversation or word spoken in any context or relayed via the media can be interpreted by nameless, faceless spies as a "security threat"—and one's name can enter into the ever growing secret lists of "potential terrorists". The very presence and dimensions of the police state is intimidating. While there are citizens who would claim that the police state is necessary to protect them from terrorists, how many others feel compelled to embrace their state terrorists just to fend off any suspicion, hoping to stay off the growing lists? How many critically-minded Americans now fear the state and will never voice in public what they whisper at home?

The bigger the secret police, the greater its operations. The more regressive domestic economic policy, the greater the fear and loathing of the political elite.

Even as President Obama and his Democratic and Republican partners boast and bluster about their police state and its effective "security function", the vast majority of Americans are becoming aware that fear instilled at home serves the interest of waging imperial wars abroad; that cowardice in the face of police state threats only encourages further cuts in their living standards. When will they learn that *exposing* spying is only the beginning of a solution? When will they recognize that *ending* the police state is essential to dismantling the costly empire and creating a safe, secure and prosperous America?

PART III

POLICE STATE: THE DOMESTIC FOUNDATION OF EMPIRE

FABRICATING TERROR CONSPIRACIES

Representative democracies and autocratic dictatorships respond to profound internal crises in very distinctive ways: the former attempts to reason with citizens, explaining the causes, consequences and alternatives; dictatorships attempt to terrorize, intimidate and distract the public by evoking bogus external threats, to perpetuate and justify rule by police state methods and avoid facing up to the self-inflicted crises.

An instance of such a bogus fabrication is the Obama regime's August 5, 2013 announcement of an imminent global "terrorist threat"[8] in the face of multiple crises, policy failures and defeats throughout the Middle East, North Africa and Southwest Asia.

Internet 'Chatter' Evokes a Global Conspiracy and Revives the Global War on Terror

The entire terror conspiracy propaganda blitz, launched by the Obama regime and propagated by the mass media on August 5, 2013, was based on the *flimsiest sources* imaginable, the most laughable pretext. According to White House sources, the National Security Agency, the CIA and other spy agencies claimed to have monitored and intercepted unspecified Al-Qaeda threats, conversations by two Al Qaeda figures including Ayman al Zawahiri.[9]

Most damaging, the Obama regime's claim of a global threat by al-Qaeda, necessitating the shutdown of 19 embassies and consuls and a worldwide travellers alert, flies in the face of repeated public assertions over the past five years that Washington has dealt 'mortal blows' to the terrorist organization crippling its operative capacity[10] and citing the US "military successes" in Afghanistan and Iraq, its assassination of Bin Laden, the drone attacks in Yemen, Pakistan, Somalia and the US-backed invasion of Libya. Either the Obama regime was lying in the past or its August 5, 2013 terror alert was a fabrication. If, as Obama and the NSA currently claim, Al Qaeda has re-emerged as a global terrorist threat, then twelve years of warfare in Afghanistan and eleven years of war in Iraq, the spending of $1.46 trillion dollars, the loss of over seven thousand US soldiers and the physical and psychological maiming of over a hundred thousand US combatants has been a total and unmitigated disaster, and the so-called war on terror is a failure.

The claim of a *global terror threat*, based on NSA surveillance of two Yemen-based Al Qaeda leaders, is as shallow as it is implausible. Every day throughout cyberspace one or another Islamist terrorist group or individuals discuss terror plots, fantasies and plans of no great consequence.

The Obama regime failed to explain why, out of thousands of daily internet 'conversations', this particular one, at this particular moment, represented an ongoing viable terrorist operation. One does not need a million spies to pick up jihadist chatter about "attacking Satan".

For over a decade, Al Qaeda operatives in Yemen have been engaging in a proxy war with Washington-backed regimes and over the same time the Obama regime has been engaged in drone and Special Forces assassination missions against Yemeni militants and opposition figures.[11] In other words, the Obama regime has *magnified commonplace* events, related to an *ongoing conflict* known to the public, into a *new global* terrorist threat as revealed by his spymasters because of their high powered espionage prowess!

It is more than obvious that the Obama regime was engaged in a global fabrication designed to distract world public opinion and, in particular, the majority of US citizens, from police state spying and violations of basic constitutional freedoms.

By evoking a phony "terrorist threat" abroad and its detection by the NSA, Obama hopes to *re-legitimize* his discredited police state apparatus.

More important, by raising the spectre of a global terrorist threat, the Obama regime seeks to cover-up the most disreputable policies, despicable "show trials" and harsh imprisonment of government whistle blowers and political, diplomatic and military defeats and failures which have befallen the empire in the present period.

The Timing of the Fabrication of the Global Terror Threat

In recent years the US public has grown weary of the cost and inconclusive nature of the 'global war on terror', or GWOT. Public opinion polls support the withdrawal of troops from overseas wars and back domestic social programs over military spending and new invasions. Yet the Obama regime, aided and abetted by the pro-Israel power configuration, in and out of the government, engages in constant pursuit of war policies aimed at Iran, Syria, Lebanon and any other Muslim country opposed to Israel's erasure of Arab Palestine. The "brilliant" pro-war strategists and advisers in the Obama regime have pursued military and diplomatic policies which have led to political disasters, monstrous human rights violations and the gutting of US constitutional protections guaranteed to its citizens. To continue the pursuit of repeated failed policies, a gargantuan police state has been erected to spy, control and represses US citizens and overseas countries, allies and adversaries.

The August 5th "terror threat" fabrication occurred at a time and in response to the deepening international crisis and the political impasse facing the Obama regime—a time of deepening disenchantment among domestic and overseas public opinion and increasing pressure from the Israel Firsters to continue to press forward with the military agenda. .

The single most devastating blow to the police state build up is the documents made public by the NSA contractor, Edward Snowden, which revealed the vast worldwide network of NSA spying in violation of US constitutional freedoms and the sovereignty of countries. The revelations have discredited the Obama regime, provoked conflicts within and between allies, and strengthened the position of adversaries and critics of the US Empire.

Leading regional organizations, like MERCOSUR in Latin America, have attacked 'cyber-imperialism'; the EU countries have questioned the notion of 'intelligence cooperation'. Several US Congress people have called for reform and cutbacks in NSA funding.

The "terror threats" are timed by Obama to neutralize the Snowden revelations and justify the spy agency and its vast operations.

The Bradley Manning "show trial", preceding which a soldier had been tortured, often with forced nudity, in solitary confinement for almost a year, imprisoned for three years and publically prejudged by President Obama, numerous legislators and mass media (precluding any semblance of 'fairness') for revealing US war crimes against Iraqi and Afghan civilians, evoked mass protests the world over. Obama's "terror threat" was trotted out to coincide with the pre-determined conviction of Manning in this discredited judicial farce and to buttress the argument that his exposure of gross US war crimes "served the enemy" (rather than the American public whom Manning repeatedly has said deserve to know about the atrocities committed in its name). By re-launching the "war on terror" and intimidating the US public, the Obama regime was trying to discredit Bradley Manning's heroic revelations of *documented US war crimes* in Iraq and Afghanistan by focusing on nebulous Al Qaeda terror *threats* over the internet!

In the international political arena, Obama has suffered a series of political and diplomatic defeats with far-reaching implications for his fanatical empire building project. The Obama-backed and Al Qaeda-led Islamist mercenary invasion of the sovereign nation of Syria has suffered a series of military defeats and his proxy jihadist 'freedom-fighters' have been denounced by most prestigious human rights groups for their massacres and ethnic cleansing of civilian populations in Syria (especially Christians, Kurds, Alawis and secular Syrians). Obama's Syrian 'adventure' has backfired, and is clearly unleashing a new generation of Islamist terrorists, armed by the Gulf States, especially Saudi Arabia and Qatar, trained by Turkish and NATO Special Forces and now available for global terrorist "assignments" against US client states, Europe and the US itself. In turn the Syrian debacle has had a major impact on Obama's NATO ally, Turkey, where mass protests are challenging Prime Minister Erdogan's military support for Islamist mercenaries, based along the Turkish border with Syria. Erdogan's savage repression of hundreds of thousands of peaceful protestors, the arbitrary arrest of thousands of pro-democracy activists and his own "show trials" of hundreds of journalists, military officials, students, intellectuals and trade unionists, has certainly discredited Obama's main "democratic Islamist" ally and undermined Washington's attempt to anchor its dominance via a triangular alliance of Israel, Turkey and the Gulf monarchies.

Further discredit of Obama's foreign policy of co-opting Islamist "electoral regimes" has occurred in Egypt and is pending in Tunisia. Obama's post-Mubarak policy in Egypt intended a "power sharing" arrangement between the democratically elected President Morsi of the Muslim Brotherhood, the Mubarak-era military and neoliberal politicians, like Mohamed El Baradei. However, using as pretext that Morsi had instead imposed an Islamist agenda, General El-Sisi grabbed power via the army, overthrowing and jailing the civilian President Morsi. The Egyptian army under El-Sisi has massacred peaceful Muslim Brotherhood protestors, whose ranks were then swelled with pro-democracy protestors and purged the parliament, press and independent voices. Forced to choose between the military dictatorship composed of the henchman of the former Mubarak dictatorship and the mass-based Muslim Brotherhood, US Secretary of State John Kerry backed the military take-over as a "transition to democracy" (steadfastly refusing to use the term 'coup d'état'). This has opened wide the door to a period of mass repression and resistance in Egypt and severely weakened a key link in the Islamist movements, dubbed the "axis of reaction" in North Africa (Morocco, Algeria, Tunisia, Libya and Egypt).

Obama's incapacity to deal with the new peace overtures by the recently elected President Rouhani in Iran was evident in the Administration's capitulation to a Congressional vote (420 – 20) on July 31, 2013 in favor of further and more severe sanctions designed, according to the bill's AIPAC authors, to "strangle the Iranian oil economy". Secretary of State Kerry's July 2013 offer to "negotiate" with Iran, under a US-imposed blockade and economic sanctions, was seen in Teheran, and by most independent observers, as an empty theatrical gesture, of little consequence. Obama's failure to check the Israeli-Zionist stranglehold on US foreign policy toward Iran and to strike a deal ensuring a nuclear-weapon-free Iran ensures that the region will continue to be a political and military powder keg. Obama's appointments of prominent Zionist zealots to strategic Middle East policy positions ensures that the US and the Obama regime have no options for Iran, Palestine, Syria or Lebanon—except to follow the options dictated by Tel Aviv directly to its US agents, **the Conference of 52 Presidents of the Major American Jewish Organizations, who along with their insider Zionist collaborators, co-author the Middle East policy script for the US Congress and the White House.**

The Obama regime's Israeli-Palestine peace negotiations are seen by most observers as the most distorted and bizarre efforts to date in that cruel farce. Washington has purchased the leaders of the Palestinian 'Authority' with multi-million dollar handouts and given way to Israel's accelerated land grabbing in the occupied West Bank and 'Jews only' settlement construction, as well as the mass eviction of 40,000 Bedouins within Israel itself.

To ensure the desired result—a total fiasco, Obama appointed one of the most fanatical of pro-Israeli zealots in Washington as its "mediator", the tri-national Martin Indyk, known in diplomatic circles as "Israel's lawyer" (and the first US Ambassador to be stripped of security clearance for mishandling documents).

The breakdown of the negotiations is foretold. Obama, caught in the web of his own long-term reactionary alliances and loyalties and obsessed with military solutions, has developed a knack for engaging in prolonged losing wars, multiplying enemies and alienating allies.

Conclusion

The result of prolonged unpopular wars of aggression has been the massive build up of a monstrous domestic police state, pervasive spying around the world and the commission of egregious violations of the US Constitution. This, in turn, has led to crudely concocted "terror plots" to cover up the repeated foreign policy failures and to slander and persecute courageous whistle blowers and threaten other decent American patriots. The recent declaration of another vast 'terror plot', which served to justify the illegal activities of US spy agencies and 'unify Congress', produced hysteria lasting *less than a week*. **Subsequently, reports began to trickle in, even in the obedient US mass media, discrediting the basis of the August 5, 2013 alleged global terror conspiracy. According to one report, the much-ballyhooed** 'Al Qaeda plot' turned out to be a failed effort to blow-up an oil terminal and oil pipeline in Yemen. According to regional observers: "Pipelines are attacked nearly weekly in Yemen"[12] And so an unsuccessful jihadist attack against a pipeline in a marginal part of the poorest Arab state morphed into President Obama's breathless announcement of a global terrorist threat! An outrageous joke has been played on the President, his Administration and his Congressional followers. But during this great orchestrated 'joke', Obama unleashed a dozen drone assassination attacks against human targets of his own choosing, killing dozens of Yemeni citizens, including many innocent bystanders.

What is even less jocular is that Obama, the Master of Deceit, just moves on. His proposed "reforms" are aimed to retrench NSA activities; he insists on continuing the "bulk collection" tens of millions) of US citizens' telephone communications.[13] He retains intact the massive police state spy apparatus, keeps his pro-Israel policymakers in strategic positions, reaffirms his policy of confrontation with Iran and escalates tensions with Russia, China and Venezuela. Obama embraces a new wave of military dictatorships, starting, but not ending, with Egypt.

In the face of diminishing support at home and abroad and the declining credibility of his crude "terror" threats, one wonders if the ever-active clandestine apparatus would actually stage its own *real-life bloody act of terror*, a secret *state supported 'false-flag' bombing*, to convince an increasingly disenchanted and sceptical public? Such would be a desperate act for the State, but these are desperate times facing a failed Administration, pursuing losing wars in which the Masters of Defeat can now only rely on the Masters of Deceit.

The Obama regime is infested with the "toxic politics of terrorism" and this addiction has driven him to persecute, torture and imprison truth seekers, whistle blowers and true patriots who strive (and will continue to strive) to awaken the sleeping giant, in hopes that the people of America will arise again.

THE RISE OF THE POLICE STATE AND THE ABSENCE OF MASS OPPOSITION

Introduction

One of the most significant political developments in recent US history has been the *virtually unchallenged rise of the police state*. Despite the vast expansion of the police powers of the Executive Branch of government, the extraordinary growth of an entire panoply of repressive agencies, with hundreds of thousands of personnel, and enormous public and secret budgets, and the vast scope of police state surveillance, including the acknowledged monitoring of over 40 million US citizens and residents, *no mass pro-democracy movement* has emerged to confront the powers and prerogatives or even protest the investigations of the police state.

In the early fifties, when the McCarthyite purges were accompanied by restrictions on free speech, compulsory loyalty oaths and congressional 'witch hunt' investigations of public officials, cultural figures, intellectuals, academics and trade unionists, such police state measures provoked widespread public debate and protests, and even institutional resistance. By the end of the 1950s mass demonstrations were held at the sites of the public hearings of the House Un-American Activities Committee (HUAC) in San Francisco (1960) and elsewhere, and major civil rights movements arose to challenge the racially segregated South, the compliant Federal government and the terrorist racist death squads of the Ku Klux Klan (KKK). The Free Speech Movement in Berkeley (1964) ignited nationwide mass demonstrations against the authoritarian-style university governance.

The police state incubated during the first years of the Cold War was challenged by mass movements pledged to retain or regain democratic freedoms and civil rights.

Key to understanding the rise of mass movements for democratic freedoms was their fusion with broader social and cultural movements: democratic freedoms were linked to the struggle for racial equality; free speech was necessary in order to organize a mass movement against the imperial US Indo-Chinese wars and widespread racial segregation; the shutting down of Congressional 'witch hunts' and purges opened up the cultural sphere to new and critical voices and revitalized the trade unions and professional associations. All were seen as critical to protecting hard-won workers' rights and social advances.

In the face of mass opposition, many of the overt police state tactics of the 1950s went 'underground' and were replaced by covert operations; selective state violence against individuals replaced mass purges. The popular pro-democracy movements strengthened civil society and public hearings exposed and weakened the police state apparatus, but it did not go away. However, from the early 1980s to the present, especially over the past 20 years, the police state has expanded dramatically, penetrating all aspects of civil society while arousing *no sustained or even sporadic mass opposition.*

The question is why has the police state grown and even exceeded the boundaries of previous periods of repression and yet not provoked any sustained mass opposition? This is in contrast to the broad-based pro-democracy movements of the mid to late 20th century. That a massive and growing police state apparatus exists is beyond doubt: one simply has to look up the published records of personnel (both public agents and private contractors), the huge budgets and scores of agencies involved in internal spying on tens of millions of American citizens and residents. The scope and depth of arbitrary police state measures taken include arbitrary detention and interrogations, entrapment and the blacklisting of hundreds of thousands of US citizens. Presidential fiats have established the framework for the assassination of US citizens and residents, military tribunals, detention camps and the seizure of private property.

Yet as these gross violations of the constitutional order have taken place and as each police state agency has further eroded our democratic freedoms, there have been no massive "anti-Homeland Security" movements, no campus 'Free Speech movements'. There are only the isolated and courageous voices of specialized 'civil liberties' and constitutional freedoms activists and organizations, which speak out and raise legal challenges to the abuse, but have virtually no mass base and no objective coverage in the mass media.

To address this issue of mass inactivity before the rise of the police state, we will approach the topic from two angles.

We will describe how the organizers and operatives have *structured* the police state and how that has neutralized mass responses.

We will then discuss the 'meaning' of non-activity, setting out several hypotheses about the underlying motives and behavior of the 'passive masses' of citizens.

The Concentric Circles of the Police State

While the *potential* reach of the police state agencies covers the entire US population, in fact, it operates on the basis of 'concentric circles'. The police state is perceived and experienced by the US population according to the degree of their involvement in critical opposition to state policies. While the police state theoretically affects 'everyone', in practice it operates through a series of concentric circles. The 'inner core' of approximately several million citizens is the sector of the population experiencing the brunt of the police state persecution. This includes the most critical, active citizens, especially those identified by the police state as sharing religious and ethnic identities with declared foreign enemies, critics or alleged 'terrorists'. These include immigrants and citizens of Arab, Persian, Pakistani, Afghan and Somali descent, as well as American converts to Islam.

Ethnic and religious "profiling" is rife in all transport centers (airports, bus and train stations and on the highways). Mosques, Islamic charities and foundations are under constant surveillance and subject to raids, entrapment, arrests, and even Israeli-style 'targeted' assassinations.

The second core group targeted by the police state includes African Americans, Hispanics and immigration rights activists (numbering in the millions). They are subject to massive arbitrary sweeps, round-ups and unlimited detention without trial as well as mass indiscriminate deportations.

After the 'core groups' is the 'inner circle' which includes millions of US citizens and residents, who have written or spoken critically of US and Israeli policy in the Middle East, expressed solidarity with the suffering of the Palestinian people, opposed US invasions of Iraq and Afghanistan, or have visited countries or regions opposed to US empire building (Venezuela, Iran, South Lebanon, Syria, the West Bank and Gaza, etc.). Hundreds of thousands of these citizens have their telephone, e-mail and internet communications under surveillance; they have been targeted in airports, denied passports, subjected to 'visits' and to covert and overt blacklisting at their schools and workplaces.

Activists engaged in civil liberties groups, lawyers, and professionals, leftists engaged in anti-Imperialist, pro-democracy and anti-police state activities and their publications are on 'file' in the massive police state labyrinth of data collecting on 'political terrorists'. Environmental movements and their activists have been treated as potential terrorists with their own family members subjected to police harassment and ominous 'visits'.

The 'outer circle' includes, community, civic, religious and trade union leaders and activists who, in the course of their activity interact with or even express support for core and inner circle critics and victims of police state violations of due process . The 'outer circle' numbering a few million citizens are 'on file' as 'persons of interest', which may involve monitoring their e-mail and periodic 'checks' on their petition signing and defense appeals. These 'three circles' are the central targets of the police state, numbering upward of 40 million US citizens and immigrants—who have *not committed* any crime. For having exercised their constitutional rights, they have been subjected to various degrees of police state repression and harassment.

The police state, however, has 'fluid boundaries' about whom to spy on, whom to arrest and when—depending on whatever arouses the apparatchiks 'suspicion' or desire to exercise power or please their superiors at any given moment. The key to the police state operations of the US in the 21st century is to repress pro-democracy citizens and pre-empt any mass movement *without undermining the electoral system*, which provides political theater and legitimacy. A police state 'boundary' is constructed to ensure that citizens will have little option but to vote for the two pro-police state parties, legislatures and executives *without reference* to the conduct, conditions and demands of the core, inner and outer circle of victims, critics and activists. Frequent raids, harsh public 'exemplary' punishment and mass media stigmatization transmit a message to the passive mass of voters and non-voters that the victims of repression 'must have been doing something wrong' or else they would not be under police state repression.

The key to the police state strategy is to not allow its critics to gain a mass base, popular legitimacy or public acceptance. The state and the media constantly drum the message that the activists' 'causes' are not *our* (American, patriotic) 'causes'; that 'their' pro-democracy activities impede 'our' electoral activities; their lives, wisdom and experiences do not touch our workplaces, neighborhoods, sports, religious and civic associations. To the degree that the police-state has 'fenced in' the inner circles of the pro-democracy activists, they have attained a free hand and uncontested reach in deepening and extending the boundaries of the authoritarian state. To the degree that the police state rationale or presence has penetrated *the consciousness* of the mass of the US population, it has created a mighty barrier to the linking of private discontent with public action.

Hypothesis on Mass Complicity and Acquiescence to the Police State

If the police-state is now the dominant reality of US political life, why isn't it at the center of citizen concern? Why are there no pro-democracy popular movements? How has the police state been so successful in 'fencing off' the activists from the vast majority of US citizens? After all, other countries at other times have faced even more repressive regimes and yet the citizens rebelled. In the past, despite the so-called 'Soviet threat', pro-democracy movements emerged in the US and even rolled back a burgeoning police state. Why does the evocation of an outside 'Islamic terrorist threat' seem to incapacitate our citizens today? Or does it?

There is no simple, single explanation for the passivity of the US citizens faced with a rising omnipotent police state. Their motives are complex and changing and it is best to examine them in some detail.

One explanation for passivity is that precisely the power and pervasiveness of the police state has created deep *fear*, especially among people with family obligations, vulnerable employment and moderate commitments to democratic freedoms. This group of citizens is aware of cases where police powers have affected other citizens who were involved in critical activities, causing job loss and broad suffering, and are not willing to sacrifice their security and the welfare of their families for what they believe is a 'losing cause'—a movement lacking a strong popular base and with little institutional support. Only when the protest against the Wall Street bailout and the 'Occupy Wall Street' movements against the '1%' gained momentum did this sector express transitory support. But as the Office of the President consummated the bailout and the police-state crushed the 'Occupy' encampments, fear and caution led many sympathizers to withdraw timidly back into passivity.

The second motive for 'acquiescence' among a substantial public is that they tend to *support* the police state, based on their acceptance of the anti-terror ideology and its virulent anti-Muslim/anti-Arab racism, driven in large part by influential sectors of pro-Israel opinion makers. The fear and loathing of Muslims, cultivated by the police state and mass media, was central to the post-9/11 build-up of Homeland Security and the serial wars against Israel's adversaries, including Iraq, Lebanon, Libya and now Syria, with plans for Iran. Active support for the police state peaked during the first five years post- 9/11 and subsequently ebbed as the Wall Street-induced economic crisis, loss of employment and the failures of government policy propelled concerns about the economy far ahead of support for the police state. Nevertheless, at least one-third of the electorate still supports the police state, 'right or wrong'. They firmly believe that the police state protects their 'security'; that suspects, arrestees, and others under watch 'must have been doing something illegal'. The most ardent backers of the police state are found among the rabid anti-immigrant groups who support arbitrary round-ups, mass deportations and the expansion of police powers at the expense of constitutional guarantees.

The third possible motive for acquiescence in the police state is *ignorance*: those millions of US citizens who are not aware of the size, scope and activities of the police state. Their practical behavior speaks to the notion that 'since I am not directly affected it must not exist'. Embedded in everyday life, making a living, enjoying leisure time, entertainment, sports, family, neighborhoods and concerned only about household budgets ... This mass is so embedded in their personal 'micro-world' that it considers the macroeconomic and political issues raised by the police state as 'distant', outside of their experience or interest: "I don't have time", "I don't know enough", "It's all 'politics'" ... The widespread apoliticism of the US public plays into its ignoring the monster that has grown in its midst.

Paradoxically as some people's concerns and passive discontent over the economy has grown, it has *lessened support* for the police state as well as having lessened opposition to it. In other words the police state flourishes while public discontent is focused more on the *economic* institutions of the state and society. Few, if any, contemporary political leaders educate their constituency by connecting the rise of the police state, imperial wars and Wall Street to the everyday economic issues concerning most US citizens. The fragmentation of issues, the separation of the economic from the political and the divorce of political concerns from individual ones, allow the police state to stand 'above and outside' of the popular consciousness , concerns and activities.

State-sponsored fear mongering on behalf of the police state is amplified and popularized by the mass media on a daily basis via propagandistic-'news', 'anti-terrorist' detective programs, and Hollywood's decades of crass anti-Arab, Islamophobic films. The mass media portrayal of the police state's naked violations of democratic rights as *normal* and *necessary* in a milieu infiltrated by 'Muslim terrorists', where feckless 'liberals'(defenders of due process and the Bill of Rights) threaten national security, has been effective.

Ideologically, the police state depends on identifying the expansion of police powers with the 'national security' of the passive 'silent' majority, even as it creates profound insecurity for an active, critical minority. The self-serving identification of the 'nation' and the 'flag' with the police state apparatus is especially prominent during 'mass spectacles' where 'rock', schlock and 'sports' infuse mass entertainment with solemn Pledges of Allegiance to uphold and respect the police state and busty be-wigged young women wail nasally versions of the national anthem to thunderous applause. Wounded 'warriors' are trotted out and soldiers rigid in their dress uniforms salute enormous flags, while the message transmitted is that the police state at home works hand in hand with our 'men and women in uniform' abroad. The police state is presented as a patriotic extension of the wars abroad and as such, both impose 'necessary' *constraints* on citizen opposition, public criticism and any real forthright defense of freedom.

Conclusion: What is to be done?

The ascendancy of the police state has benefited enormously from the phony bi-partisan de-politicization of repressive legislation, and the fragmentation of socio-economic struggles from democratic dissent. The mass anti-war movements of the early 1990s and 2001-2003 were undermined (sold out) by the defection of their leaders to the Democratic Party machine and its electoral agenda. The massive popular immigration movement was taken over by Mexican-American political opportunists from the Democratic Party and decimated while the same Democratic Party, under President Barack Obama, has escalated police state repression against immigrants, expelling millions of Latino immigrant workers and their families.

Historical experience teaches us that a successful struggle against an emerging police state depends on the *linking* of the socio-economic struggles that engage the attention of the masses of citizens with the pro-democracy, pro-civil liberty, 'free speech' movements of the middle classes. The deepening economic crisis, the savage cuts in living standards and working conditions and the fight to save 'sacred' social programs (like Social Security and Medicare) have to be tied in to the expansion of the police state. A mass social justice movement, which brings together thousands of anti-Wall Streeters, millions of pro-Medicare, Social Security and Medicaid recipients with hundreds of thousands of immigrant workers will inevitably clash with the bloated police-state apparatus. Freedom is essential to the struggle for social justice and the mass struggle for social justice is the only basis for rolling back the police state. The hope is that mass economic pain will ignite mass activity, which, in turn, will make people *aware* of the dangerous growth of the police state. A mass understanding of this link will be essential to any advance in the movement for democracy and people's welfare at home and peace abroad.

PRESIDENTIAL RULE BY DECEPTION: OBAMA, THE MASTER CON-MAN

Introduction

In an electoral system, run by and for a corporate oligarchy, deception and demagoguery are essential elements—entertaining the people while working for the wealthy.

Every US President has engaged, in one fashion or another, in 'play acting' to secure popular approval, neutralize hostility and distract voters from the reactionary substance of their foreign and domestic policies.

Every substantive policy is accompanied by a 'down home' folksy message to win public approval. This happened with President 'Jimmy' Carter's revival of large-scale proxy wars in Afghanistan in the post-Vietnam War period; Ronald Reagan's genocidal wars in Central America, George Bush Sr.'s savaging of Iraq in the First Gulf War; 'Bill' Clinton's decimation of social welfare in the US while bombing civilians in Yugoslavia and deregulating Wall Street; George Bush Jr.'s invasion and partition of Iraq and Afghanistan, the attempted coup in Venezuela and massive tax cuts for the rich; and Barack Obama's staggering bailout of the biggest Wall Street speculators, unprecedented launching of five consecutive wars, and arrest and deportation of millions of immigrant workers. Each President has elaborated a style in order to ingratiate himself with the public while pursuing his reactionary agenda.

In rhetoric, appearance and in public persona, it is *de rigueur* for US presidents to present themselves as an 'everyman' even as committing political actions—including war crimes worthy of prosecution.

Each president, in his 'play acting', develops a style suitable to the times. They constantly strive to overcome the public's suspicion and potential hostility to their overt and covert policies designed to build empire as domestic conditions deteriorate. However, not all play acting is the same: each president's 'populist' style in defense of oligarchic interests has its characteristic nuances.

The Carter Feint: 'Human Rights' Wars in the Post-Vietnam War Era

'Jimmy' Carter was elected President at a time of the greatest mass anti-war upheaval in US history. His campaign projected a soft-spoken, conciliatory President from humble roots reaching out to the anti-war electorate and solemnly pledging to uphold human rights against domestic militarists and their overseas despotic allies. To that end, he appointed a liberal human rights advocate, Pat Derian, to the State Department and a veteran Cold Warrior, Zbigniew (Zbig) Brzezinski, as National Security Advisor and foreign policy strategist.

Duplicity reared its head immediately: Carter *openly* criticized the Somoza dictatorship in Nicaragua—while privately telling the dictator to ignore the public criticisms and assuring him of continuing US support.[14] As the Sandinista revolution advanced toward victory, Carter convoked a meeting of Latin American leaders urging them to join in a joint military intervention with the US to 'save lives' and to prevent the popular Nicaraguan revolution from taking power and dismantling the dictator's army. It soon became clear to the leaders of Latin America that Carter's mission was a thinly- veiled 'humanitarian' version of 'gunboat diplomacy' and they declined. When Carter realized that, without the fig leaf of Latin American participation, a US-led invasion would arouse universal opposition, he abandoned the project. The political climate would not support a unilateral US invasion so soon after the end of the war in Indochina.

However, Carter soon re-launched the Cold War, reviving military spending and pouring billions of dollars into funding, arming and training tens of thousands of fundamentalist Jihadists from around the world to invade Afghanistan and overthrow its leftist, secular government.

Carter's policy of re-militarization and launching of large-scale and long-term secret CIA operations in alliance with the most brutal dictators and monarchs of Saudi Arabia and Pakistan was accompanied by sanctimonious speeches about human rights and token appeals to protect 'civilians'. In this regard, Carter became our founding father of the double discourse: a con man who publically condemned the jailing and torture by Pinochet of political opponents in Chile while orchestrating what would become a decade-long blood bath in Afghanistan with millions of victims.

Reagan: Geniality with Genocide

Up until the ascendancy of Barack Obama, the avuncular President Ronald Reagan was acknowledged as the 'master con-man', by virtue of his Hollywood acting experience. Reagan was and remained a disciplined and hardened backer of policies designed to concentrate wealth while smashing unions, even as he entertained the flag-waving hard hat construction workers with his jokes about 'limousine liberals' and Cadillac welfare queens. The knowing wink and clever two-liners were matched by an adaptation of morality tales from his cowboy films. Reagan, in his role as 'the righteous sheriff', backed the mercenary contras as they invaded Nicaragua and destroyed schools and clinics, and the genocidal military dictators in El Salvador and Guatemala who murdered hundreds of thousands of Indians and peasants. Uncle Reagan's friendly chats would describe how he had stopped the communist 'outlaws' (peasants, workers and Indians) of Central America from flooding across the Rio Grande and invading California and Texas. His tales resonated with mass audiences familiar with the racist Hollywood cowboy film version of unshaven Mexican bandits crossing the 'US' border. The clean-shaven, straight-talking, 'stand-up for America' President Ronald Reagan was elected and re-elected by a resounding majority in the midst of CIA-backed mujahedeen victories over the government and secular civil structure of Afghanistan, Pentagon-supported Israeli slaughter of Palestinian refugees in their camps in Lebanon and the mass genocide of scores of thousands of indigenous villagers in Guatemala. When news reports seeped out about the mass graves of poor villagers in Guatemala, Reagan resorted to colloquial language right out of a Hollywood film to defend General Rios Mont: "He's getting a bum rap". In defending the brutal dictator of Guatemala, Reagan replaced Carter's sanctimonious phrasing in favor of down-to-earth macho talk of a no-nonsense sheriff.

In substance, both Carter and Reagan were rebuilding the US war machine after the debacle of Vietnam; they were setting up a global network of client dictators, Muslim fundamentalists and hypocritical Anglo-American humanitarians interventionists.

Bush Senior: Uni-Polarity and the Ticket to Uncontested Imperial Conquests

Following the break-up of the Soviet Union, the US and Western Europe re-conquered, pillaged and neo-colonized Eastern Europe. West Germany annexed East Germany. And a predator-gangster oligarchy in Russia seized over a trillion dollars of public assets, impoverishing millions and laundering the illicit funds via elaborate banking operations on Wall Street and in London and Tel Aviv.

President George Bush Sr. embraced the doctrine of a unipolar world—free from rival superpower constraints and independent Third World resistance. 'Poppy' Bush believed the US could impose its will by force anywhere and at any time without fear of retaliation. He believed he was heir to a new imperial order of free markets, free elections and unrestrained plunder. The first war he would launch would be in the Middle East—the invasion, massive bombing and destruction of Iraq. It was followed by an unprecedented expansion of NATO bases in the countries of Eastern Europe. The spread of neoliberalism led to the naked pillage of public assets throughout Latin America and Eastern Europe. The Empire ruled the Muslim world through an arc of client dictators from Tunisia, Egypt, and Saudi Arabia to Pakistan.

Bush adopted the persona of the 'happy warrior'—the invincible American President who had triumphed over the Evil Empire. Meanwhile, the domestic economy deteriorated under the enormous costs of the massive military build-up and gave rise to a crisis that hurt the electorate. Bush's personal rigidity and lack of theatricality prevented him from playing the con-man—unlike his predecessor, the actor Reagan. Even as he extolled the prowess of the US military, his career as an 'insider' corporate operative and CIA director did not provide him with the demagogic skills necessary for a successful re-election.

While Bush celebrated his overseas victories, he failed to attract a popular following. His pinched face and wooden upper-crust smile was no match for 'Cowboy' Reagan's street corner geniality or even 'Jimmy' Carter's pious intonations of human rights and Christian values … Deception and demagoguery are crucial elements in a re-election campaign—and so Bush, Sr. gave way *for the next Presidential con-man-in-chief, Bill Clinton.*

The Clinton Con: Black Churches, Welfare Cuts and the Wall Street Warrior

Bill Clinton, like Ronald Reagan, turned out to be a Wall Street populist .With his folksy Arkansas intonations he preached messages of hope in black churches while diligently applying the free-market lessons he had learned from his Wall Street mentors. Tooting the saxophone and oozing compassion, Clinton told the poor that he could 'feel their pain', while inflicting misery on single mothers forced to leave their children and take minimum-wage jobs in order to retain any public assistance. He joined hands with labor union bosses at Labor Day festivities, while fast-tracking job-killing free-trade treaties (like NAFTA) that devastated the American working class. Bill Clinton enthusiastically sent bombers over Belgrade and other Yugoslav cities for several weeks, destroying its factories, hospitals, schools, power plants, radio and TV stations and bridges, as well as the Chinese Embassy, in support of the terrorist Kosovo Liberation Army and its separatist war against Belgrade. Clinton bombed civilians and their vital infrastructure, a war crime in the name of 'humanitarian intervention', to the ecstatic cheers of many Western liberals, progressives, social democrats and not a few Marxists as well as many Jihadists. On the home front, this self-proclaimed 'people's candidate' ripped to shreds all restraints on banking speculation by repealing the Glass-Steagall Act of 1933, New Deal legislation enacted to protect against massive banking swindles. This opened the floodgates to massive financial manipulation, which destroyed the pensions of many millions of workers.[15]

Clinton's policies laid the groundwork for the information technology and Stock Market crash of 2000-01. His appointee, Alan Greenspan, created the conditions leading to speculative financial frenzy and subsequent economic crash of 2008. Bill Clinton's stand-up comic performances in black churches, his back slapping encounters with labor bureaucrats and his embrace of feminists and others just raised the rhetorical bar for future aspiring Wall Street warlords in the White House. It would take eight years and the election of Barack Hussein Obama to finally surpass Bill Clinton as Con-Man-In Chief.

Bush Junior: A Yale Man with a Texas Drawl

President George Bush, Junior's regime launched two major wars and backed two Israeli assaults on Palestinian civilians trapped in Gaza—the world's largest open-air prison. He virtually eliminated taxes on billionaires while overseeing the geometrical growth of the domestic police state apparatus, and he unleashed the biggest speculative bubble and crash since the Great Depression. He lowered the living standards for all Americans except the top 10% of the population—*and despite these disasters and his lack-luster performance as a con-man, he was re-elected.*

His handlers and backers did their best to market their boy: his Ivy League credentials and New England background was replaced by a transparently phony Texas accent; tinny, whiney sound bites, reminiscent of his father's, were replaced by a Texas 'ranchers' homely drawl. His 'just-folks' grammatical mistakes may have been mocked by the liberals but they resonated deeply with fundamentalist Christians—who would never have recognized the Phillips Exeter Academy/Yale Skull and Bones boy in their Commander-in Chief. President Bush, Jr. was decked out in the uniform of a 'Top Gun' fighter pilot to polish his military credentials, tarnished by revelations that the millionaire-playboy had gone AWOL during his service in the National Guard. His silly 'Mission Accomplished' claim that the Iraq war had been won in the first months after the invasion was rudely corrected by the huge outbreak of Iraqi resistance against the occupier. Bush handed over foreign policymaking, especially pertaining to the Middle East, to a small army of Jewish Zionists, aided and abetted by notorious militarists like Cheney and Rumsfeld.

Most major political events were handled by his Cabinet thugs. Secretary of State Colin Powell shamelessly fabricated the 'evidence' of Saddam Hussein's weapons of mass destruction in his performance before the United Nations. Donald Rumsfeld and Paul Wolfowitz invented Afghanistan's ties to the planners of 9/11. Cheney and his Zionist troika of Paul Wolfowitz, Douglas Feith and 'Scooter' Libby trumpeted the 'global war on terror' while Michael Chertoff, Michael Mukasey and Stuart Levey conducted a domestic war against the Bill of Rights and US Constitutional freedoms, defending torture, jailing thousands of Muslims, punishing businesses trading with Iran, and labeling US opponents of Israel's war crimes as 'security threats'. Bush, Jr. just nodded his approval, letting the "big fellas have a piece of the action". With Junior, there was no peace demagoguery just plain talk to plain folks and "Let the bombs fall and the Capital flow". Bush did not have to go preaching to black churches (he had a black Secretary of State and National Security Adviser to do his dirty work without the cant). Bush never claimed that Israel got a 'bum rap' when it was charged with genocidal crimes. Under Bush, Jr., war criminals did not have to 'sugar-coat' their crimes. While occupying the White House, Bush signed off on the multi-trillion-dollar bailout for Wall Street and then just went off to tend his cows and chop wood at the Texas ranch.

Bush's 'style' was a combination of 'laid back' and 'straight forward': he simply committed war crimes, protected Wall Street swindles and expanded the police state, without claiming otherwise. As the endless wars dragged on, as the stock market flopped under its own fraud and manipulation and the increasingly repressive legislation provoked debate, Bush just shrugged his shoulders and finished out his term in office without flourish or fanfare: "Y'all can't win 'em all. Let the next guy try his hand".

Barack Obama: The Master of Deceit

From the beginning of his presidential campaign, Obama demonstrated his proficiency as the master of all cons. He spoke passionately against torture while consulting with the torturers; he condemned Wall Street speculators while appointing key Street operatives as economic advisers. He promised a new deal in the Middle East, especially for Palestinians and then appointed dual Israeli-US citizen, Rahm Emmanuel (son of an Israeli Irgun terrorist), to be his most intimate presidential advisor. Honolulu born and bred, Barack modulated his voice according to the audience, adopting a Baptist minister's cadence for the black audiences while assuming the professorial tone of an Ivy League lawyer for his Wall Street contributors. He hob-knobbed with Hollywood celebrities and Silicon billionaires, who bankrolled the fairy tale of his 'historic breakthrough' - the First African American President who would speak for all Americans—nay for the entire world! Millions of giddy camp followers, white, black, old and young, the trade unionists and community activists alike, were willingly deceived. They had chosen to disregard the fact that Barack Obama's key advisers were rabid militarists, big bankers, corporate CEOs, die-hard Zionists and Wall Street manipulators. Indeed Obama's supporters were enchanted by the phony rhetoric, the demagogy, the 'populist style', and the fake 'authenticities'. Here was the man who promised to end the wars, close the torture concentration camp in Guantanamo, bring Wall Street to heel, repeal the Patriot Act and restore the Bill of Rights. And he was 'their guy'—shooting hoops in an urban playground—something Bush had never done! In truth, Barack Hussein Obama did a lot that Bush never dared to do. He surpassed Bush by far in committing war crimes against humanity, pushing for more military adventures abroad and police state repression at home. He exceeded by far any President in US history in assuming dictatorial police powers, in waging multiple wars while directing the massive transfer of state revenues to Wall Street bankers. President Obama, hands down, will be regarded as the greatest con-man president in American history. The Carters, Reagans and Clintons all pale in comparison: the enormous gap between style and substance, promise and performance, peace and war, capital and labor, has never been greater.

It is President Obama's hollow eloquence that raised the hopes of millions at home and abroad only to condemn them to an inferno of endless wars. It is the perversity of his rhetoric which attracts the Latino vote with promises of immigrant citizenship while his policy has been to fill detention centers with hundreds of thousands of immigrant workers and their families. His soaring rhetoric promising justice for Muslims in Cairo was followed by the bloody bombing of Tripoli, the torture and slaughter of the Libyan patriot President Gaddafi. His broken promises to the Palestinians contrast with the embrace of the bloody Israeli warlords. Obama far out-paced President Bush's drone attacks in Pakistan, Yemen and Afghanistan, bombings which targeted farmers, whole families, and famished orphans in their schools. On the other hand, soaring moral and ethical pronouncements accompany Obama's arming and praising the 40,000 Muslim fundamentalist mercenaries sent to degrade and shatter the secular Syrian state. The pretexts for mass killing fall from his lips like maggots on a rotten corpse: his blatant lies about the use of poison gas in Syria as the government in Damascus confronts a foreign mercenary invasion; the lurid tales of fabricated massacres in Benghazi (Libya); and the false claims of stolen elections in Venezuela. Obama's rhetoric converts executioners into victims and victims into executioners.

President Barack Obama promised a comprehensive health care overhaul for America and then presented the electorate with a confusing series of obligatory payments for plans designed by for-profit private health insurance companies. Obama 'defended social security' by raising the age of retirement, ensuring that hundreds of thousands of workers in hazardous occupations would die before ever receiving any benefits after a lifetime of obligatory contributions. Obama solemnly promised to defend Medicare and then proposed to reduce its budget by a trillion dollars over a decade.

Obama claims a presidential prerogative of 'defending American interests' by ordering the assassination of whomever his million-member secret police state apparatus designates as a security threat—including American citizens—without trial, without recourse to habeas corpus.

In the White House Rose Garden President Barack Obama strolls arm-in-arm with his wife and children, a family man, true to his promises... while in Aleppo a young teen, a street vendor, is beheaded before his parents and neighbors by fanatical 'freedom-fighters' praised and supported by the President. The boy's alleged crime was blasphemy. The murdered teen has joined the scores of thousands of Syrians killed and the hundreds of thousands who will join them, as Obama has decided to openly arm the mercenaries.

Casual, open collar President Obama jokes as he walks and talks with Chinese President Xi Jinping at the sumptuous estate of a California billionaire, offering friendship and peace—shaking hands for the cameras with a scorpion in his palm. The smiling Obama has ceaselessly dispatched his envoys to Asia, Latin America, Oceana and Africa to incite claims and conflicts against Beijing. Obama mistakenly believes that his own 'personal magic' will blind the Chinese to the fact that China is being encircled by US air and maritime bases. He seems to believe that the Chinese will ignore his efforts to forge US-centered trade pacts which specifically exclude China.

The master 'confidence-man' sincerely believes in his power to move and mystify the American public, pick the pockets of his adversaries and make his victims believe they have been in the presence of a world-class statesman. In fact, Obama has been playing the role of a protection racketeer, living off the earnings and lives of his people while handing them over to his corporate bosses and toeing the line for Israel.

Obama fills internment camps with hundreds of thousands of Latino immigrant workers while promising a 'roadmap to citizenship' to the cheers of Mexican-American Democratic Party vote hustlers!

Obama received 95% of the African American votes, while the income gap between blacks and whites widens and unemployment and poverty figures soar. Obama, the first 'African American' president, has bombed and intervened in more African countries, backing mercenary armies in Libya and Somalia, and establishing more military bases throughout the black continent than the last five 'white' presidents ... So much for the self-proclaimed "historic breakthrough of a Black president ending centuries of racism".

It's enough for Obama to appoint other black police state thugs and foreign interventionists, like Eric Holder and Susan Rice, to win the cheers of liberals even as their own security files grow in the data warehouses of the world's biggest spying agencies.

One cynic, commenting on the longstanding love affair between Obama and white liberals, observed that 'the more he screws them the better they like him … Even as he marches them off to jail, they would take care to note on his behalf, that the barred windows have curtains—something Bush would never have allowed.'

Conclusion

For sheer *span* of broken promises, of systematic lies in pursuit of wars and financial manipulation in the name of peace and social justice, of consistent and bold aggrandizement of executive power over the life and death of US citizens in the name of security, Obama *has set the standard of political deception and demagogy far beyond past and probable future US presidents.*

The political context of his ascent to power and his deep links to the military-financial-Zionist networks insured his success as a premier confidence man.

President George Bush, Jr., the cringing, fading warmonger engaged in prolonged, costly wars and facing the collapse of the entire banking and financial sector, provided candidate Obama with an easy target. Obama exploited the mass revulsion of the American people, longing for change. Obama's con-game and political hustle shamelessly exploited the heroic civil rights struggle of consequential African American leaders who were jailed, beaten, and killed fighting for social justice. His soaring rhetoric and vacuous promise of 'change' attracted millions of young activists … The problem is that in their enthusiasm and blind adherence to 'identity politics' with its claims that all 'blacks' and 'women' are oppressed they mistakenly assumed, as they were intended to do, that a black leader would be guaranteed to promote peace and justice.

Obama, once in office, not only deepened and widened the scope of President Bush, Jr's wars, massive spy apparatus and corporate profiteering; he bamboozled the vast majority of his liberal-labor supporters in the Democratic Party! Barack Obama conned the Democratic Party Congressional liberals and they, in turn, conned their constituents into supporting this fraud.

The costs of President Obama's two-faced policies are enormous: democracy has given way to a police state openly defended by the President and Congressional leaders; the cost of Wall Street's recovery and corporate profiteering is fast destroying public health and social security. Barack Obama's multiple endless wars and interventions are destroying vast cities, infrastructure, entire cultures while and killing and impoverishing millions of people from Libya to Palestine, from Syria to Iran. The economic sanctions against Iran, the provocative encirclement and isolation of China, and the campaign to destabilize Venezuela are the centerpieces of Obama's 'pivot to empire'. These policies portend even greater world-shattering catastrophes.

Unmasking the con-man is a first step requiring that we expose the tricks of the con-game. The politics of deception and demagogy *thrives by directing popular attention to style* and *rhetoric*, not substance. The solemn and pious cant of 'Jimmy' Carter distracted from his launch of the rabid Jihadists against the secular administration of Afghanistan. Uncle Ronald Reagan's geniality and populist TV patter covered-up his blood baths in Central America and mass firing of the unionized air controllers and jailing of union leaders. 'Bill' Clinton's show of empathy for the poor and embrace of 'feel-good' politics neutralized opposition as he bombed Yugoslavia into a pre-industrial age while his domestic policies kicked vulnerable single mothers from welfare programs. They all paled before the grand con-master Obama, billed as the 'first black' President, a community organizer who disowned his sponsor into the black communities of Chicago, Rev. Wright, for his anti-war, anti-imperial stand, and has capitalized on his racial credentials to garner the vote of guilt-ridden, soft-headed liberals and marginalized blacks in order to serve the interests of Wall Street and Israel.

Disarming these conmen and women requires exposing the nature of their demagogic populist styles and focusing on substantive politics. The decisive criteria need to be class politics that are defined by fundamental class alignments, between capital and labor regarding budgets, income, taxes, social spending, financing and property rights. 'Shooting hoops' in ghetto playgrounds is a con-man's distraction while his budget cuts close hospitals and schools in black and poor neighborhoods.

The extravaganzas, featuring sports and entertainment celebrities to promote imperial wars, are the 'con' to undermine international solidarity for war victims and the unemployed. President Obama, the confidence man, is still performing while sowing destruction.

The Two Faces of a Police State: Sheltering Tax Evaders, Financial Swindlers and Money Launderers while Policing the Citizens

> "The rotten heart of finance"
> **The Economist**

> "There is a degree of cynicism and greed
> which is really quite shocking"
> **Lord Turner, Bank of England**
> **Financial Service Authority**

Introduction

Never in the history of the United States have we witnessed *crimes* committed on the *scale* and *scope* of the present day by both private and state elites.

An economist of impeccable credentials, James Henry, former chief economist at the prestigious consulting firm McKinsey & Company, has researched and documented tax evasion. He found that the super-wealthy and their families have as much as *$32 trillion (USD)* of hidden assets in offshore tax havens, representing up to $280 billion in lost income tax revenue![16] This study excluded such non-financial assets as real estate, precious metals, jewels, yachts, race horses, luxury vehicles and so on. Of the estimated $32 trillion in hidden assets, $23 trillion is held by the super-rich of North America and Europe.

A recent report by a United Nations Special Committee on Money Laundering found that US and European banks laundered over $300 billion a year, including $30 billion just from the Mexican drug cartels.

New reports on the multi-billion dollar financial swindles involving the major banks in the US and Europe are published each week. England's leading banks, including Barclay's and a host of others, have been identified as having rigged the LIBOR, or inter-bank lending rate, for years in order to maximize profits. The Bank of New York, JP Morgan, HSBC, Wachovia and Citibank are among scores of banks, which have been charged with laundering drug money and other illicit funds according to investigations from the US Senate Banking Committees. Multinational corporations receive federal bailout funds and tax exemptions and then, in violation of publicized agreements with the government, relocate plants and jobs in Asia and Mexico.

Major investment houses, like Goldman Sachs, have conned investors for years to invest in 'garbage' equities while the brokers pumped and dumped the worthless stocks. Jon Corzine, CEO of MF Global (as well as a former CEO of Goldman Sachs, former US Senator and Governor of New Jersey) claimed that he "cannot account" for $1.6 billion in lost client investors funds from the collapse of MF Global in 2011.

Despite the growth of an enormous police state apparatus, the proliferation of investigatory agencies, Congressional hearings and over 400,000 employees at the Department of Homeland Security, *not a single banker has gone to jail*. In the most egregious cases, a bank like Barclay's will pay a minor fine for having facilitated tax evasion and engaging in speculative swindles. At the same time, the principal 'miscreant' in the LIBOR swindle, Chief Operating Officer (COO) of Barclay's Bank, Jerry Del Missier, will receive a severance payout of $13 million dollars. JPMorgan Chase has paid or agreed to pay in fines during the past year a total of over $30 billion for its role in mortgage securities fraud and the Bernie Madoff swindle—among other claim settlements. As NPR reported, "To put it in perspective: JPMorgan Chase reported a revenue of $23.9 billion during the third quarter of 2013."[17]

In contrast to its 'lax' law enforcement with regard to the swindles of the banking, corporate and billionaire elites, the burgeoning police state has intensified political repression of citizens and immigrants who have not committed any crime against public safety and order.

Millions of immigrants have been seized from their homes and work-places, jailed, beaten and deported. Hundreds of Hispanic and African American neighborhoods have been the target of police raids, shootouts and killings. In such neighborhoods, the local and federal police operate with impunity—as was illustrated by shocking videos of the police shootings and brutality against unarmed civilians in Anaheim, California. Muslims, South Asians, Arabs, Iranians and others are racially profiled, arbitrarily arrested and prosecuted for participating in charities and humanitarian foundations, or simply for attending religious institutions. Over 40 million Americans engaged in lawful political activity are currently under surveillance, spied upon and frequently harassed.

The Two Faces of the US Government: Impunity and Repression

Overwhelming documentation supports the notion that the US police and judicial system has *totally broken down* when it comes to enforcing the law of the land regarding crimes among the financial, banking, and corporate elite.

Trillion-dollar tax-evaders, billionaire financial swindlers and multi-billionaire money launderers are almost never sent to jail. While some may pay a nominal fine, none have the bulk of their illicit earnings seized even though many are repeat criminals. Recidivism among financial criminals is rife because the penalties are so light, the after-penalty profits remain so high and the investigations are infrequent, superficial and inconsequential. The United Nations Office on Drugs and Crime (UNODC) reported that $1.6 trillion was laundered, mostly in Western banks, in 2009, one fifth coming directly from the drug trade. The bulk of income from the cocaine trade was generated in North America ($35 billion), two-thirds of which were laundered in North American banks.

The failure to prosecute bankers engaged in a critical link of the drug trade is not due to 'lack of information', nor is it due to the 'laxness' on the part of regulators and law enforcement. The reason is that the banks are too big to prosecute and the bankers are too rich to jail. Effective law-enforcement would lead to the prosecution of all the leading banks and bankers, which would sharply reduce profits. Jailing the top bankers would close the 'revolving door', the golden portal through which government regulators secure their own wealth and fortune by joining private investment houses after leaving 'public' service. The assets of the ten biggest banks in the US form a sizeable share of the US economy. The boards of directors of the biggest banks inter-lock with all major corporate sectors. The top and middle financial officials and their counterparts in the corporate sector, as well as their principal stockholders and bondholders, are among the country's biggest tax evaders.

While the Security and Exchange Commission, the Treasury Department and the Senate Banking Committee all make a public pretense of investigating high financial crimes, their real function is to protect these institutions from any efforts to transform their structure, operations and role in the US economy. The fines, which were recently levied, are high by previous standards but still only amount to, at most, a couple of weeks' profits.

The lack of 'judicial will', the breakdown of the entire regulatory system and the flaunting of financial power is manifested in the 'golden parachutes' routinely awarded to criminal CEOs following their exposure and 'resignation'. This is due to the enormous *political power* the financial elite exercise over the state, judiciary and the economy.

Political Power and the Demise of 'Law and Order'

With regard to financial crimes, the doctrine guiding state policy is 'too rich for jail, too big to fail' , which translates into multi-trillion dollar treasury bailouts of bankrupt kleptocratic financial institutions and a high level of state tolerance for billionaire tax-evaders, swindlers and money launderers. Because of the total breakdown of law enforcement toward financial crimes, there are high levels of repeat offenders in what one British financial official describes as 'cynical (and cyclical) greed'.

The current 'banner' under which the financial elite have seized total control over the state, the budget and the economy has been 'change'. This refers to the deregulation of the financial system, the massive expansion of tax loopholes, the free flight of profits to overseas tax havens and the dramatic shift of 'law enforcement' from prosecuting the banks laundering the illicit earnings of drug and criminal cartels to pursuing so-called 'terrorist states'. The 'state of law' has become a *lawless state*. Financial 'changes' have permitted and even promoted repeated swindles, which have defrauded millions and *impoverished hundreds of millions*. There are 20 million mortgage holders who have lost their homes or have been unable to maintain payments; tens of millions of middle class and working class taxpayers who were forced to pay higher taxes and lose vital social services because of upper class and corporate tax evasion. The laundering of billions of dollars in drug cartel and criminal wealth by the biggest banks has led to the deterioration of neighborhoods and rising crime, which has destabilized middle and working class family life.

Conclusion

The ascendancy of a criminal financial elite and its complicit, accommodating state has led to the breakdown of law and order, the degradation and discrediting of the entire regulatory network and judicial system. This has led to a national system of 'unequal injustice' where critical citizens are prosecuted for exercising their constitutional rights while criminal elites operate with impunity. The harshest enforcement of police state fiats are applied against hundreds of thousands of immigrants, Muslims and human rights activists, while financial swindlers are courted at presidential campaign fund raisers.

It is not surprising today that many workers and middle class citizens consider themselves to be 'conservative' and 'against change'. Indeed, the majority wants to 'conserve' Social Security, public education, pensions, job stability, and federal medical plans, such as MEDICARE and MEDICAID against 'radical' elite advocates of 'change' who want to privatize Social Security and education, end MEDICARE, and slash MEDICAID. Workers and the middle class demand stability of jobs, neighborhoods and prices against runaway inflation of medical care and education. Wage and salaried citizens support law and order, especially when it means the prosecution of billionaire tax evaders, criminal money-laundering bankers and swindlers, who, at most, pay a minor fine, issue an excuse or 'apology' and then proceed to repeat their swindles.

The radical 'changes' promoted by the elite have devastated life for millions of Americans in every region, occupation and age group. They have destabilized family life by undermining job security while undermining neighborhoods by laundering drug profits. Above all they have *totally perverted the entire system of justice* where the 'criminals are made respectable and the respectable treated as criminals'.

The first defense of the majority is to *resist* 'elite change' and to *conserve* the remnants of the welfare state. The goal of 'conservative' resistance will be to transform the entire corrupt legal system of 'functional criminality' into a system of 'equality before the law'. That will require a fundamental shift in political power at the local and regional level, from the bankers' boardrooms to neighborhood and workplace councils, from compliant elite-appointed judges and regulators to real representatives elected by the majority groaning under our current system of injustice.

PART IV

THE POWER OF ISRAEL
IN THE
UNITED STATES

Israel Buys the US Congress: Sabotaging the US-Iran Peace Negotiations

"Pro-Israel Policy groups such as AIPAC work with unlimited funding to divert US policy in the region (Middle East)."

Jack Straw, Member of Parliament and former Foreign Secretary of the British Labor Party

"The United States should drop a nuclear bomb on Iran to spur the country to end its nuclear program."

Sheldon Adelson, largest donor to the Republican Party and major fundraiser for pro-Israel political action committees, speech at Yeshiva University, New York City, October 22, 2013.

Introduction

The question of war or peace with Iran rests with the policies adopted by the White House and the US Congress. The peace overtures by newly elected Iranian President Rouhani have resonated favorably around the world, except with Israel and its Zionist acolytes in North America and Europe. The first negotiating session proceeded without recrimination and resulted in an optimistic assessment by both sides. Precisely because of the initial favorable response among the participants, the Israeli government escalated its propaganda war against Iran. Its agents in the US Congress, the mass media and in the Executive branch moved to undermine the peace process. What is at stake is Israel's capacity to wage proxy wars using the US military and its NATO allies against any government challenging Israeli military supremacy in the Middle East, its violent annexation of Palestinian territory and its ability to attack any adversary with impunity.

To understand more fully what is at stake in the current peace negotiations one must envision the consequences of failure: Under Israeli pressure, the US has announced that its 'military option' could be activated—resulting in missile strikes and a bombing campaign against 76 million Iranians in order to destroy their government and economy. Teheran could retaliate against such aggression by targeting US military bases in the region and Gulf oil installations resulting in a global crisis. This is what Israel wants.

We will begin by examining the context of Israel's military supremacy in the Middle East. We will then proceed to analyze Israel's incredible power over the US political process and how it shapes the negotiation process today, with special emphasis on Zionist power in the US Congress.

The Context of Israeli Military Supremacy in the Middle East

Since the end of World War II, Israel has bombed, invaded and occupied more countries in the Middle East and Africa than any previous colonial power, except the US. The list of Israel's victims includes: Palestine, Syria, Lebanon, Egypt, Iraq, Jordan, Sudan and Yemen. If we include countries where Israel has launched quasi-clandestine terrorist attacks and assassinations, the list would be greatly expanded to include a dozen countries in Europe and Asia—including the US through its Zionist terror network.

Israel's projection of military power, its capacity for waging offensive wars at will, is matched by its near-total impunity. Despite their repeated violations of international law, including war crimes, Israel has never been censored at an international tribunal with punitive powers or subjected to economic sanctions on the state level subsequent to the Arab oil embargo of 1973 because the US government uses its position to veto UN Security Council resolutions and pressure its NATO-EU allies. (However, Israeli General Yaron and Israel were found guilty of war crimes at the civil society War Crimes Tribunal held in Malaysia in August 2013. Further, the global Boycott, Divest, Sanction (BDS) movement has registered a wide range of successes,[18] topped most recently by the Association of American Studies vote on December 17, 2013, by a 2-1 margin, to boycott Israeli universities and academic associations.)

Israel's military supremacy has less to do with the native techno-industrial 'brilliance' of its warmongers and more to do with the transfers and outright theft of nuclear, chemical and biological technology and weapons from the US (this was addressed extensively by Grant Smith in "Ten Explosive US Government Secrets of Israel", IRMEP).[19] Overseas Zionists in the US and France have played a strategic (and treasonous) role in stealing and illegally shipping nuclear technology and weapons components to Israel, according to an investigation by former CIA Director Richard Helms.[20]

Israel maintains huge nuclear, chemical, and biological weapon stockpiles, refusing any access to international arms inspectors. It is not obliged to abide by the non-proliferation treaty, because of US diplomatic intervention. Under pressure from its domestic 'Zionist power configuration' (ZPC), the US government has blocked any action which might constrain Israel's production of weapons of mass destruction. In fact the US continues to provide Israel with strategic weapons of mass destruction for use against its neighbors—in violation of international law.

US military aid and technology transfers to Israel exceed $100 billion dollars over the past half century. US diplomatic and military intervention was crucial in rescuing Israel from defeat during the 1973 war. US President Lyndon Johnson's refusal to defend the unarmed American intelligence ship, the *USS Liberty* in 1967, after it had been bombed and napalmed by Israeli fighter planes and warships in international waters, constituted a tremendous victory for Israel, achieved thanks to Johnson's Zionist advisers. Because of its impunity, even in killing American servicemen, Israel has been given a free hand to wage aggressive wars to dominate its neighbors, commit acts of terrorism, and assassinate its adversaries throughout the world without fear of retaliation.

Israel's uncontested military superiority has converted several of its neighbors to quasi-client collaborators: Egypt (pre and post the "Arab Spring") and Jordan have served as de facto allies, along with the Gulf monarchies, helping Israel repress the region's nationalist and pro-Palestinian movements.

The most decisive factor in the rise and consolidation of Israel's power in the Middle East has not been its military prowess, the extent of which might be measured by its defeat against Lebanon in 2006, but its political reach and influence via its Zionist agents in the US, UK and France. Washington's wars against Iraq and Libya, and its current support of the mercenary assault against Syria, have destroyed three major secular nationalist opponents of Israel's hegemonic ambitions.

As Israel accumulates more power in the region, expanding its colonization of Palestinian territory, it looks eastward toward destroying the last remaining obstacle to its colonial policies: Iran.

For at least two decades, Israel has directed its overseas agents (the ZPC) to destroy the government of Iran by destabilizing its society, inciting internal uprising via its support for Jundallah,[21] assassinating its scientists, bombing its military establishments and laboratories, engaging in cyber sabotage, and strangling its economy.

After the ZPC successfully pushed the US into war against Iraq in 2003—literally shredding its complex secular society and killing over a million Iraqis—it turned its sights on destroying Lebanon (Hezbollah) and the secular government of Syria as a way to isolate Iran and prepare for an attack. While thousands of Lebanese civilians were slaughtered in 2006, Israel's attack of Lebanon failed, despite the support of the US government and the ZPC's wild propaganda campaign. Hysterical at its failure and needing to 'compensate' for its defeat at the hands of Hezbollah and 'boost morale', Israel invaded and destroyed much of Gaza (2008/9), the world's largest open air prison camp.

Lacking military capacity to attack Iran on its own, Israel directed its agents to manipulate the US government to start a war with Teheran. The militarist leaders in Tel Aviv have unleashed their political assets (ZPC) throughout the US to work to destroy Iran—the last formidable adversary to Israeli supremacy in the Middle East.

The Israeli-ZPC strategy is designed to set the stage for a US confrontation with Iran, using its agents in the Executive branch as well as its ongoing corruption, bribery and control of the US Congress. ZPC control over the mass media enhances its propaganda campaign: Every day *The New York Times* and the *Washington Post* publish articles and editorials promoting Israel's war agenda. The ZPC uses the US State Department to force other NATO states to likewise confront Iran.

Israel's Proxy War with Iran:
US Political Pressure, Economic Sanctions and Military Threats

Alone, Israel's 'war' with Iran would not amount to much more than its cyber sabotage, the periodic assassination of Iranian scientists using its paid agents among Iranian terrorist groups and non-stop brow-beating from Israeli politicians and their 'amen crowd'. Outside of Israel, this campaign has had little impact on public opinion. Israel's 'war' on Iran depends exclusively on its capacity to manipulate US policy using its local agents and groups who dominate the US Congress and through the appointments of officials in key positions in the Departments of Treasury, Commerce, and Justice, and as Middle East 'advisors'. Israel by itself cannot organize an effective sanctions campaign against Iran, nor could it influence any major power to abide by such a campaign. Only the US has that power. Israel's dominance in the Middle East comes entirely from its capacity to mobilize its proxies in the United States who are assigned the task of securing total submission to Israel's interests from elected and appointed government officials—especially in regard to Israel's regional adversaries.

Strategically placed 'dual US-Israeli citizens' have used their US citizenship to secure high security positions in the Government directly involved in making policies affecting Israel. As Israelis, their activities are in line with the dictates of Tel Aviv. In the Bush administration (2001-2008) such highly placed 'Israel Firsters' dominated the Pentagon (Paul Wolfowitz, Douglas Feith), Middle East Security (Martin Indyk, Dennis Ross), the Vice President's office ('Scooter' Libby), Treasury (Stuart Levey) and Homeland Security (Michael Chertoff). In the Obama administration the 'Israel Firsters' include Dennis Ross, Rahm Emanuel, David Cohen, Secretary of Treasury Jack "Jake the Snake" Lew, Secretary of Commerce Penny Pritzker and Michael Froman as Trade Representative, among others. Israel's Proxy Power within the Executive branch is matched by its dominance of the US Congress.

Contrary to some critics, Israel is neither an 'ally' nor a 'client' of the US. Evidence of the gross asymmetry of the relation abounds, accrued over the past half century. Because of these powerful proxies in Congress and the Executive branch, Israel has received over $100 billion dollars in tribute from the US over the past 30 years, or $3 billion plus a year. The US Pentagon has transferred the most up-to-date military technology and engaged in several wars on Israel's behalf. The US Treasury has imposed sanctions against potentially lucrative trading and investment partners in the Middle East (Iran, Iraq and Syria) depriving US agricultural and manufacturing exporters and oil companies of over $500 billion in revenues. The White House sacrificed the lives of over 4,400 US soldiers in the Iraq War—a war promoted by Israel's proxies at the behest of Israel's leaders. The State Department has rejected friendly and profitable relations with over 1.5 billion Muslims by backing the illegal settlement of over half a million Jewish colonists on military-occupied Palestinian land in the West Bank and Jerusalem.

The strategic question is how and why this one-sided relation between the US and Israel persists for so long, even as it goes counter to so many strategic and elite US interests? The more immediate and pressing question is how this historically lopsided relation affects contemporary US-Iran sanctions and nuclear negotiations?

Iran and the Peace Negotiations

Undoubtedly the newly elected Iranian president and his foreign minister are prepared to negotiate an end to hostilities with the US by making major concessions ensuring the peaceful use of nuclear energy. They have stated they are open to reducing or even ending the production of highly enriched uranium; reducing the number of centrifuges and even allowing intrusive, unannounced inspections, among other promising proposals. The Iranian government proposes a roadmap with end goals as part of the initial agreements. The European Union's Foreign Secretary, Lady Ashton, has commented favorably on the initial meeting.

The US Administration has given conflicting signals following the Iranian overtures and the opening meeting. Some individual comments are guardedly positive; others are less encouraging and rigid. Administration Zionists like Jack 'Jake' Lew, the Treasury Secretary, insist sanctions will remain until Iran meets all US (read 'Israeli') demands. The US Congress, bought and controlled by the ZPC, rejects the promising Iranian overtures and flexibility, insisting on military 'options' or the total dismantling of Iran's legal and peaceful nuclear program—ZPC positions designed to sabotage the negotiations. To that end, Congress has passed new, more extreme, economic sanctions to strangle Iran's oil economy.

How Israel's Political Action Committees Control the US Congress and Prepare War with Iran

The Zionist Power Configuration uses its financial firepower to dictate Congressional policy on the Middle East and to ensure that the US Congress and Senate do not stray one iota from serving Israel's interests. The instrument used by Zionists in the purchase of elected officials in the US is the political action committee (PAC).

Thanks to a 2010 US Supreme Court decision, Super PACs linked to Israel spend enormous sums to elect or destroy candidates—depending on the candidate's political work on behalf of Israel. As long as these funds do not go directly to the candidate, these Super PACs do not have to reveal how much they spend or how it is spent. Conservative estimates of ZPC- linked direct and indirect funds to US legislators run close to $100 million dollars[22] over the past 30-year. The ZPC channels these funds to legislative leaders and members of Congressional committees dealing with foreign policy, especially sub-committee chairpersons dealing with the Middle East. Unsurprisingly, the largest Congressional recipients of ZPC money are those who have aggressively promoted Israel's hard-line policies. Elsewhere around the world, such large scale payoffs for legislative votes would be considered blatant bribery and subject to felony prosecution and imprisonment for members of both parties. In the US, the purchase and sale of a politician's vote is called 'lobbying' and is legal and open. The legislative branch of the US government has come to resemble a high-price brothel or white slavers' auction—but with the lives of thousands at stake.

The ZPC has purchased the allegiance of US Congress people and Senators on a massive scale: Of 435 members of the US (*sic*) House of Representatives, 219 have received payments from the ZPC in exchange for their votes on behalf of the state of Israel. Corruption is even more rampant among the 100 US Senators, 94 of whom have accepted pro-Israel PAC and Super PAC money for their loyalty to Israel. The ZPC showers money on both Republicans and Democrats, thus securing incredible (in this era of Congressional deadlock), near unanimous ('bipartisan') votes in favor of the 'Jewish State', including support for its war crimes, like the bombing of Gaza and Lebanon as well as the annual $3 billion dollar plus US taxpayer tribute to Tel Aviv. At least 50 US Senators have each collected between $100 thousand and $1 million in ZPC money over the past decades. In exchange, they have voted for over $100 billion in tribute payments to Israel ... in addition to other 'services and payments'. The members of the US Congress are cheaper: 25 legislators have received between $238,000 and $50,000, while the rest got peanuts. Regardless of the amount, the net result is the same: Congressional members pick up their script from their Zionist mentors in the PACs, Super PACs and AIPAC, back all of Israel's wars in the Middle East and promote US aggression on behalf of Israel.

The most outspoken and influential legislators get the biggest chunk of Zionist payola: Senator Mark Kirk (Bombs over Teheran!) tops the 'pigs at the trough' list with $925,000 in ZPC payoffs, followed by John McCain (Bomb, bomb, bomb Iran!) with $771,000, while Senators Mitch McConnell, Carl Levin, Robert Menendez, Richard Durban and other Zionophilic politicos are not shy about holding out their little begging bowls when the pro-Israel PAC bagmen arrive! Florida Congresswoman Ileana Ros-Lehtinen tops the 'House' list with $238,000 for her 100% pro-Israel record as well as for being more warmongering than even Netanyahu! Eric Cantor got $209,000 for championing 'wars for Israel' with American lives while cutting Social Security payments to US seniors in order to increase military aid to Tel Aviv. House Minority Whip Steny Hoyer, got $144,000 for 'whipping the few wobbly' Democrats back into Israel's 'camp'. House Majority Leader John Boehner was paid $130,000 to do the same among the Republicans.

The ZPC has spent huge amounts to punish and destroy a dozen or so dissident legislators who had stood up to Israel's wars and grotesque human rights record. The ZPC has poured millions into individual campaigns, not only financing opposition candidates who pledged allegiance to Israel but mounting scurrilous character assassinations of Israel's critics in office. These campaigns have been mounted in the most obscure parts of the US, including in majority African American districts, where local Zionist interests and influence are otherwise absolutely nil.

There are no comparable PACs, Super PACs, party leaders, or civic organizations that can contest the power of Israel's Fifth Column. According to documents archived by the courageous researcher, Grant Smith of IRMEP, when it comes to Israel, the US Justice Department has adamantly refused to enforce its own federal laws requiring the prosecution of US citizens who fail to register as foreign agents while working for a foreign country—at least since 1963. On the other hand, the ZPC, through the so-called 'Anti-Defamation League', has successfully pressured the Justice Department, the FBI and NSA to investigate and prosecute law-abiding, patriotic US citizens critical of Israel's land grabs in Palestine and the Zionist corruptors of the US political system on behalf of their foreign master.

The corruption and degradation of US democracy is made possible by the equally compromised and corrupted 'respectable press'. Media critic

Steve Lendman has pointed out the direct link between Israel and the mass media in his investigation of *The New York Times*. The leading ('fair and balanced') journalists reporting on Israel have strong family and political ties to that country and their articles have been little more than propaganda. *Times* reporter Ethan Bronner, whose son served in the Israel Defense Forces, is a long-time apologist for the Zionist state. *Times* reporter Isabel Kershner, whose 'writing' seems to come straight out of the Israeli Foreign Office, is married to Hirsh Goodman, an adviser to the Netanyahu regime on 'security affairs'. The *Times* bureau chief in Jerusalem, Jodi Rudoren, lives comfortably in the ancestral home of a Palestinian family dispossessed from that ancient city.

The *Times* unflinching pro-Israel posture provides a political cover and justification for the corrupted US politicians as they beat the war drums for Israel. It is no surprise that *The New York Times*, like the *Washington Post*, is deeply engaged in disparaging and denouncing the current US-Iran negotiations—and providing ample space for the one-sided rhetoric of Israeli politicians and their US mouthpieces, while studiously excluding the more rational, pro-rapprochement voices of experienced former US diplomats, war-weary military leaders, and representatives of the US business and academic communities.

To understand Congress' hostility to the nuclear negotiations with Iran and its efforts to scuttle them through the imposition of ridiculous new sanctions, it is important to get to the source of the problem, namely the statements of key Israeli politicians, who set the line of march for their US proxies.

In late October, 2013, former Israeli Defense Intelligence Chief, Amos Yadlin, spoke of "having to choose between 'the bomb' or the bombing"—a message which immediately resonated with the Conference of 52 Presidents of the Major American Jewish Organizations.[23] On October 22, 2013, Israel's Intelligence Minister Yuval Steinitz, called for harsh new sanctions on Iran and insisted that the US use them as leverage to demand that Iran agree to entirely abandon its peaceful nuclear energy and enrichment program. Defense Minister Moshe Ya'alon affirmed that "Israel will not accept any deal that allows Iran to enrich uranium". It is Israel's position to threaten war (via the US) if Iran does not submit to unconditional surrender of its nuclear program. This defines the position of all the major pro-Israel PACs, Super PACs and AIPAC. They in turn proceed to dictate policy to their 'lick-spittles' in the US Congress. As a result, Congress passes even more extreme economic sanctions on Iran in order to sabotage the ongoing negotiations.

Those who have received the biggest Zionist pay-offs from the pro-Israel PACs are the most vociferous: Senator Mark Kirk ($925,379), author of a previous sanctions bill, demands that Iran end its entire nuclear and ballistic missile program (!) and declared that the US Senate "should immediately move forward with a new round of economic sanctions targeting all remaining Iranian government revenue and reserves".[24] The US House of Representatives (*sic*) has already passed a bill sharply limiting Iran's ability to sell its main export, oil. Once again, the Israel- ZPC-Congressional axis seeks to impose Israel's war agenda on the American people! In late October 2013, Secretary of State Kerry was 'grilled' for 7 hours by Israeli Prime Minister Netanyahu, with the craven Kerry promising to promote Israel's agenda on dismantling Iran's nuclear enrichment program.

To counter the campaign to strangle Iran's oil economy, promoted by Israel's flunkeys in the Congress, the Iranian government has offered generous contracts to the US and EU oil companies.[25] Existing nationalist provisions are being removed. Under the new terms, foreign companies book reserves or take equity stakes in Iranian projects. Iran hopes to attract at least $100 billion dollars in investments over the next three years. This stable country boasts the world's largest gas and the fourth largest oil reserves. Because of the current US (Israel)-imposed sanctions, production has fallen from 3.5 million barrels per day in 2011 to 2.58 million barrels per day in 2013. The question is whether 'Big Oil', the giant US and EU companies, have the power to challenge the ZPC stranglehold over US-EU sanction policy. So far, the ZPC has dominated this critical policy and marginalized 'Big Oil', using threats, blackmail and coercion against US policymakers. This has effectively shut out US companies from the lucrative Iranian market.

Conclusion

As the US and the 5 other countries attempt to negotiate with Iran, they face enormous obstacles in overcoming Israel's power over the US Congress. Over past decades Israel's agents have bought the loyalties of the vast majority of Congress people, training them to recognize and obey the whistles, signals and script from the warmongers in Tel Aviv.

This 'Axis of War' has inflicted enormous damage on the world resulting in the deaths of millions of victims of US wars in the Middle East, Southwest Asia and North Africa. The gross corruption and widely recognized bankruptcy of the US legislative system is due to its slavish submission to a foreign power. What remains in Washington is a debased vassal state despised by its own citizens. If the ZPC controlled Congress succeeds once again in destroying the negotiations between the US and Iran via new war-like resolutions, we, the American people, will have to pay an enormous price in lives and treasure.

Americans must stand up and expose the role played by the Israeli PACs, Super PACs and the 52 Major American Jewish Organization in corrupting Congress and turning "our" elected representatives into flunkeys for Israel's wars. There has been a deafening silence from our noted critics—few alternative media critics have attacked Israel's power over the US Congress. The evidence is openly available, the crimes are undeniable. The American people need real political leaders with the courage to root out the corrupted and corruptors and force their elected members in the House and Senate to represent the interest of the American people.

Obama with Israel and Against the World

Introduction

As President Obama announced plans to attack Syria, adding Syria to the recent and ongoing wars in Afghanistan, Iraq, Libya, Yemen and elsewhere, a *profound* gap emerged between the highly militarized state and US public opinion.

A Reuters/IPSOS poll taken August 19-23 (2013) revealed that 60 percent of Americans surveyed were against the United States intervening in Syria, while 9 percent said President Obama should act. Even when the question was 'loaded' to include Obama's bogus and unsubstantiated claim that Syrian President Bashar al-Assad's forces 'used nerve gas to massacre civilians', almost *twice as many Americans opposed* US military intervention (46 percent to 25 percent). In panic several pro-Administration media outlets hastily conducted new polls to try to 'improve the results' in 'favor' of the White House desire to attack Syria. What is striking about these finding is that, despite the mass media and the Obama spokespeople's saturation of the airwaves with lurid images of 'victims', the US public has become more vehemently opposed to another imperialist war. A Reuters/IPSOS poll of August 13 had found 30.2 percent of Americans supported intervention in Syria if it were proved that nerve gas had been used by President Assad against civilians, while 41.6 percent wanted no part of the conflict. In other words, as the Obama regime intensified its preparations for war, American public opposition *increased by over 16 percent.*

A growing number of polls and studies show that a substantial well-entrenched majority of Americans are opposed to the current war in Afghanistan, even as the President and Congress continue to finance and dispatch US troops and engage in aerial assaults in Pakistan, Yemen and elsewhere.

Across the world huge majorities oppose Obama's war. Two thirds of the French and German public oppose the US bombing Syria, not to mention the hundreds of millions of Roman Catholics responding to Pope Francis's passionate anti-war message delivered on September 7 to over 100,000 worshipers in St. Peter's Square. It is only in Israel that a majority—of Jewish Israelis—support Obama's push to war.

If, as some scholars argue, militarism and 'national security' (and the police state) have become the secular religion of the State, it is clear that the majority of civil society are 'non-believers'. The 'true believers' of militarism as the road to empire building are firmly ensconced in Washington's political establishment, especially among the powerful lobbies and propaganda mills known as 'think tanks'. Militarist beliefs are widely embraced by strategically-placed officials with deep and *longstanding ties to the Israeli power structure*.

The two major *myths* propagated by cynical political pundits, that "the US public opinion gets the elected officials it deserves" and that "Congress and the President reflect the values and sentiments of the electorate", are contradicted by the divergent attitudes and interests showing up in repeated public opinion polls. The vast majority of Americas are concerned with domestic economic issues, such as unemployment, the steep decline in living standards, growing inequalities, the growing concentration of wealth (the 'Wall Street 1% versus the 99%' issue of the 'Occupy Movement'), the grotesque and inescapable debt among students and graduates, the savage cuts in social programs (education, health, housing and infrastructure) in the face of soaring military expenditures and stratospheric government subsidies to bailout the banks and speculators. In other words, the values, attitudes and interests of the vast majority of Americans diverge sharply from those of the Washington establishment, the mass media and the power brokers who penetrate and surround the political elite.

War and Peace: Oligarchy and Democracy

This divergence raises fundamental questions about the nature of the American political system, the role and influence of the mass media and the power of minorities against the interests of the majority. Divergences and deep differences between rulers and ruled have become the norm in the United States on all the major domestic and foreign issues of our day.

As the differences accumulate, deepen and fester, they 'grind' on our public. Political 'differences' turn into outright personal animosities, citizen disagreement is transformed into anger and even hatred of the 'O-man'. Obama's deceptions, the very words he mouths, are repeated and mocked. Nothing is more irritating than to have to listen to an unmasked confidence man as he still tries to bamboozle a disenchanted public. Americans are not fooled anymore. Obama's newly recruited Cabinet members of all genders and ethnicities are viewed as mere peddlers of toxic lies trying to justify ongoing war crimes via moral ejaculations that resonate in their own echo chambers and with their president, but not very far beyond the palace grounds.

Executive Prerogatives as Dictatorial Rule

The Presidential declarations of war against the will and opinion of the vast majority of citizens; the decision to finance massive bank bailouts with public funds behind the backs of 'the 99%'; the shallow proclamations 'ending' ongoing wars which still continue under other guises; and the transparent fabrications serving as pretexts for dragging the country into new wars by trotting out the *same lies recycled from the previous wars...* all undermine any notion of a constitutional democracy in the United States.

It's a dictatorship, stupid! There is nothing 'constitutional' here. That abused document has become presidential toilet paper! Legal hacks and whores scratch their backsides and regurgitate the previous illegal executive orders in order to 'legitimize' new arbitrary powers to declare war.

The voters of thousands of local, state and federal officials are ignored. Who even bothers to describe the US as a democracy except during the theater of elections? War has become the 'prerogative' of the President, we are told by the propagandists. Waging sequential wars is the favored alternative to building a national health system for the scores of millions of Americans without access to adequate medical care. When the President mouths his moral platitudes most Americans ignore him, while others jeer, curse and wish he would choke on his rank hypocrisy.

The Case for Impeachment

When in the course of human history an elected US President perpetuates and extends his power beyond the restraints of the constitutional order, and willfully commits the American people to endless suffering, emptying the public treasury of its citizens' wealth, the question of impeachment must be addressed. And it ill behooves the 'climbers and clamorers' serving foreign lands, to flatter, manipulate and blackmail the President whose own imperial pretensions further fuel the ambitions of their 'Chosen State'.

Profound and lasting divisions between the rulers and the ruled, burdened by long-standing hardships at a time when they lack redress in petition and protest, will eventually lead the American people to demand their President's impeachment—for high crimes and misdemeanors against the constitution and citizenry. What they demand would be a trial by jury, conviction and incarceration for multiple and grave violations against the constitutional order and dereliction of the President's duty to safeguard the nation from enemies, foreign and domestic. When the executive has usurped the constitutionally-guaranteed rights of the American people at the service of an empire and their foreign and domestic collaborators, with traitorous intent, he must be impeached and brought to justice.

Why and How the American Public Was Disenfranchised: The Tyranny of the Minority

It is not the members of the US military who choose to disenfranchise and ignore the vast majority of Americans overwhelmingly opposed to new Middle East wars. The usurpers are mostly civilians, some of whom had formerly carried weapons for a foreign nation and still carry dual citizenship while plying our President with calls for military expansionism. Nor is the exclusion of the majority of Americans part of some hidden conspiracy by the oil companies; in fact, these have lost hundreds of billions in potential profits to wars, which were not of their making and which now disrupt their access to oil fields, trade, production and shipping.

Idle chatter, flowing from 'leftist' or 'progressive' monthlies, liberal weeklies and a multitude of pundits, academics and 'critical' public intellectuals, decry the 'military-industrial complex' as the movers behind the wars in the Middle East. True, their lobbyists seek fat military contracts, but they were not the ones to formulate 'position papers' for the invasion of Iraq, nor secure sanctions and bellicose Congressional resolutions against Iran.

If we want to identify and understand the minority, which secures its own militarist agenda in the White House and Congress against the majority of Americans, it is clearly marked by its swaggering, consistent and intrusive presence. It is a smaller, more cohesive new version of the' 1%'—and best described as the Zionist Power Configuration (ZPC).

One can be 99% sure that among the scant 11% of Americans who 'support' US military intervention in Syria, the 'pro-Israel crowd and its acolytes' are overwhelmingly represented. The evidence is clear: they are the most actively engaged in propagandizing and pushing for war with Syria at the national and local levels throughout the country. They are the ever-present bullying pundits and news commentators lying about the Syrian government's exclusive use of chemical 'weapons of mass destruction' in a horrific civil war riddled by foreign mercenaries. They and other mass media pimps, pundits and publishers have totally buried a major Associated Press report from Syria which quotes members of the armed Syrian opposition who admit they had 'accidentally released stores of chemical weapons, supplied by Saudi Arabia' (their sponsor).

Israel's semi-official website, 'Ynet.com', published a lead article by Yitzhak Benhorin, entitled "AIPAC to Lobby Congress for Syrian Strike". The article reveals the leading role of the Israeli-directed Zionist war effort:

"After Israel's ambassador to Washington, Michael Oren and AIPAC noted that military action would send a message to Assad's supporters ... some 250 Jewish leaders and AIPAC activists ... intend to storm the halls on Capitol Hill beginning next week [September 9-13] to persuade [*sic*] lawmakers that Congress must adopt the resolution authorizing US strikes against Syria".[26] To counter Pope Francis' plea to the world for peace and opposition to Obama's threats to bomb Syria before 100,000 people of faith in front of St. Peter's Basilica, the *Cleveland Jewish News* reported that, "leading rabbis covering the religious and political spectrum [*sic*] urged lawmakers in Congress to support President Obama's plans to strike Syria."[27]

Every day since Obama called for a Congressional vote, the *Daily Alert*, publication of the Conference of 52 Presidents of the Leading American Jewish Organizations, has published only articles and statements promoting war and urging its supporters to round up Congressional votes for Obama to counter and undermine the pro-peace sentiments of the majority of Americans.

To the degree that we have moved from democracy to oligarchy, from a democratic republic to a militarist empire engaged in foreign wars of occupation, the Zionist Power Configuration (ZPC) has accumulated enormous influence in the government and, in turn, has furthered the tyranny of the minority over the majority. They are not alone, but certainly domestic tyranny against the majority of the citizens has been to their advantage; the ZPC has marginalized Americans of all creeds, races and religions (including the majority of American Jews and the secular)—especially those who would oppose their agenda.

The nature of oligarchy facilitates the minorities' access to power against the majority of citizens: it is far easier for them to buy and blackmail a handful of venal, wealthy legislators and a coterie of narcissistic senior administration officials, than peddle their agenda to the millions of citizens suffering the double onus of perpetual foreign wars and sharply declining domestic living standards.

Limits of Mass Media Manipulation

The arbitrary power of the oligarchy, with its domestic and foreign collaborators, and their growing distance from the ruled, is no longer bridged by mass media propaganda. The Obama regime and the Washington 'think tanks' have repeatedly saturated print and electronic media with the lurid images of little children suffering from the Syrian government's 'war crimes' in order to browbeat the American people into supporting another US military intervention. There are daily reports in *The New York Times, Washington Post, Financial Times*, and all the major and minor television networks, which endlessly repeat the 'need for war' and 'our humanitarian obligation to bomb Damascus'—to no avail. The mass media and the high powered propaganda campaign, run by and for the warmongers in Washington and Tel Aviv, have failed to gain the approval of more than 10% of the US citizenry—despite a near-total blackout of any alternative news or debate.

For years we have been told by 'media experts' about the power of the mass media to manipulate the US public, as if the people were a blank sheet of paper with the media writing the script for the oligarchy and the masses repeating it on 'blind faith and the flag'. In fact, time and time again, a majority of US citizens have rejected 'the line' peddled by the mass media, especially on questions of peace and war, their living standards, and the grotesque bankers' bailouts. The credibility of the US mass media is now minus zero!

The public's rejection of the Obama's push for war against Syria is another example of the growing limits of mass propaganda. In the wake of the destruction of the World Trade Center on September 11, 2001, the US public supported the invasion of Afghanistan and, to a lesser extent, the war in Iraq—once troops were sent. But as the costly, endless wars and occupation ground on, and new wars spread, and as the police state (and abuses) expanded and domestic living standards plunged, the public drew back and became wary. The domestic economic and social crisis drove the message home: *domestic decay results from imperial wars*. No amount of empty rhetoric or high powered Zionist lobbying for more wars on behalf of the state of Israel will convince Americans to continue sacrificing their lives and treasure and their children's and grandchildren's future living standards to this endless bloodletting, spiraling costs and devastating political and economic consequences.

The Quiet Rebellion of the Democratic Majority

It has been hard to black out all the news. Throughout Europe, vast majorities reject their rulers' participation in more imperial wars, particularly the push for war in Syria. Even the usually servile British Parliament rose up on its hind legs and bleated 'no' to bombing Damascus. Only the decrepit French regime under the 'socialist-imperialist' President Hollande, a most 'humanitarian' colonial whoremaster, has expressed unconditional support for Obama—at least for a few days until the French Parliament had a chance to finally bark out its disapproval. The editorial writers of the imperial 'mass media' smell 'trouble in the empire'. They have started to quote skeptical military officers and experts... who have posed a few rather timid questions, including retired generals who ask, "What will be the consequences of bombing the al-Assad government and aiding al Qaeda in the region?"

Chastened by the opposition, Obama now has to face the jeers of his Zionist backers … "not to back down from the Administration's 'red line' …" The White House Propaganda Office parrots Israeli reports of 'intercepted Syrian military directives ordering the use of chemical weapons' and those provided by 'rebel' sources based in Turkey and Saudi Arabia—but no credible documents have been given to the UN or the skeptical world public.

When Obama declares his 'red line', the American public senses the 'big lie'! Deception by the mass media and White House is losing its force. The majority of Americans are fed up with the fabrication of 'weapons of mass destruction' that provided a pretext for the invasion of Iraq, the phony 'mass rapes (the obscene and racist reports of Gaddafi handing out tons of Viagra to his black "African mercenaries") and other fake atrocities' in Libya and the blatant cover-up of Israeli land grabs and ethnic cleansing against the native Palestinian population.

The specter of economic insecurity, of lifelong debts and precarious employment stalks the cities and towns of America. A whole generation will be lost. There is anger and fear at home directed against the current push for new wars abroad and their most visible propagandist: President Barack Obama. The Obama regime is facing 'a fall' in this groundswell of disgust among the people. Will Obama's handlers and willing accomplices crawl back to their Washington think tanks? Will the oligarchs decide the Obama 'product' has exceeded its 'shelf life', is no longer useful, has lost its appeal to the public, and is too narcissistic? Will the oligarchs decide that there have been … one too many 'wars for Israel'? (Oh, my god, how did that one slip in?) Will they realize that their puppet has not focused enough attention on 'rebuilding America'? Soon there will be a new election. All aboard! The people have spoken! It's time to trot out the special new presidential product—one less effusive and more mainstream—on order from the oligarch's puppet factory!

With Obama's fall, we learn that the mass media are not all powerful and that Israel's smiling well-wishers among the elite will not cool their insatiable appetite for power even though they comprise a tiny 1% minority. The majority can bring down the regime. The question is: Can they create an alternative?

Fifteen Minutes
an American President

Introduction

Obama's rhetorical exercise in 'peace talk' at the United Nations General Assembly impressed few delegations and even fewer Americans: Far more eloquent are his five years of wars, military interventions, cyber-spying, drone murders, military coups and the merciless prosecution of patriotic truth tellers.

If his 'peace message' fell flat, the explicit affirmations of imperial prerogatives, threats of military interventions, and over two dozen (25) references to Israel as a 'strategic ally', confirmed the suspicions and fears that Obama was preparing for even more deadly wars.

Playing the 'War Card' in the Face of Massive Opposition

Obama's UN speech took place at a time when his war policies have hit rock bottom both at home and abroad. After suffering at least two major diplomatic defeats and a string of negative polls, which revealed that a strong majority of Americans rejected his entire approach to foreign policy, Obama made an overture to Iran. Up to that point few delegates or citizens were impressed or entertained by his 'new vision for US diplomacy'. According to many experts, it was vintage Obama, the con-man: talking peace while preparing new wars.

Nothing in the past six years warranted any hope that Obama would respond to new overtures for peace emanating from Iran, Syria or Palestine; his habitual obedience to Israel would lead him to push for new wars on behalf of the Jewish State. At no point did Obama even acknowledge the sharp and outraged criticism by leading heads of state regarding his policy of cyber colonialism (massive spying) and his pursuit of imperial wars.

Obama's Double Discourse: Talking Peace While Making War

At his 2009 inauguration, Barak Obama proclaimed, "We are going to have to take a new approach with a new emphasis on respect and a new willingness to talk." And then he proceeded to launch more wars, armed interventions, clandestine operations and assassination campaigns in more countries than any US president in the last fifty years.

Obama's record over the past five years reads:

1. Continued war, slaughter and military bases in Iraq.

2. A 40,000 plus US "troop surge" in Afghanistan.

3. An unprovoked assault against Libya, devastating the country, reducing oil production by 90%, throwing millions into chaos and poverty, and allowing a multitude of terrorist groups to divide the country and distribute its huge arsenal of weapons.

4. Over 400 unmanned aerial drone attacks, murdering over 4,000 civilians in Pakistan, Yemen, Afghanistan and Somalia.

5. Cross-border ground and air attacks in Pakistan and counter-insurgency warfare forcing over 1.5 million refugees to flee the war zones.

6. The arming and financing of 'African Union' mercenaries to invade and occupy Somalia, sending hundreds of thousands of Somalis into refugee camps.

7. Unconditional support for Israel, including the 'sale' of advanced weapons and an annual $3 billion dollars 'aid' package to a racist regime intent on more land grabs in the occupied West Bank and East Jerusalem, as well as the displacing, killing, arresting and torturing of thousands of Palestinians and Bedouins.

8. The sending of the US naval armada to the Persian Gulf while imposing even more brutal economic sanctions drafted by Israeli-Firsters in order to strangle the Iranian economy and starve its over 70 million citizens into submission.

9. Maintaining the notorious Guantanamo torture camp where hundreds of prisoners languish without trial (despite early promises to close it).

10. Arming and training Islamist terrorists and 'pro-Western' mercenaries to invade Syria, killing over 100,000 Syrians and driving over one million refugees from their homes. Obama's plans to bomb Syria are on hold, as of October 2013, thanks to Russian President Putin's peace initiative.

11. Engaging in grotesque global cyber-spying and the massive theft of highly confidential military, economic and political communications within allied nations (from Germany to Brazil) at the highest levels.

12. Unleashing a violent destabilization campaign in democratic Venezuela, following the defeat of the US candidate. Obama was the only leader in the world to refuse to recognize the election.

Altogether, Obama's five years in office have been marked by his relentless pursuit of imperial power through arms and domination. This has come at enormous economic cost to the American people in the form of huge fiscal deficits and significant overseas and domestic political losses.

As a result, Obama's rising tide of militarism has had the opposite effect of provoking a countercurrent of peace initiatives to challenge the assumptions and prerogatives of the war-mongers in the White House. The dynamics of this immense clash between the global war and peace forces will be played out in the next several months.

The Dynamics of Obama's Foreign Policy

Obama's future policy reflects the interplay between a highly militarized past and the tremendous current pressure for peace and diplomacy. The changes emerging from these powerful conflicting forces will have a decisive impact on the global configuration of power, as well as on the trajectory of the US economy for the foreseeable future.

We have proceeded by outlining in telegraphic form the principal events and policies defining Obama's embrace of a militarist policy over the past five years. We will now proceed to highlight the current countervailing forces and events pressuring the White House to adopt a diplomatic and peaceful resolution of conflicts. We will identify the leading pro-war power configuration acting as an obstacle to peace. In the final section we will spell out the policy resulting from these conflicting forces.

The Dynamics of Peace against the Legacy of War

By the early fall 2013, powerful tendencies emerged which seemed to *undermine* or at least *neutralize* Washington's drive to new and more deadly wars. Eight major events constrained Washington's empire builders to temporarily rethink their immediate steps to war:

1. President Vladimir Putin's proposal for Syria to destroy its chemical weapons under UN supervision, denying the US its current pretext for bombing Damascus. The subsequent UN Security Council resolution, which was unanimously approved, did not contain the UN Charter's 'war clause' (Chapter 7), thereby removing Washington's pretext to bomb Syria for 'non-compliance' to the tight timetable for disarming its chemical arsenal.

2. Iran's President Rouhani's calls for peace and reconciliation, his offer to start prompt and consequential negotiations regarding Iran's nuclear program, has isolated Israel and its Zionist agents in the international arena and forced Obama to reciprocate, resulting in a move toward US-Iranian negotiations.

3. Brazilian President Dilma Rousseff's powerful denunciation of US cyber spying against her government, economy and citizens before the General Assembly resonated with the vast majority of political leaders. Coming from the most powerful economy in Latin America, the sixth largest economy

in the world and a leading member of the BRICs, Rousseff's rejection of US cyber-colonialism and its IT and telecommunication corporations, and her call for national development, control and ownership of these communication networks, set a clear anti-colonial tone to the proceedings. Washington's response—its affirmation of its 'right' to spy on allies and their private citizens, as well as foes—has isolated Washington and found few supporters for such global cyber-imperial pretensions. To accommodate Brazil, Washington will be forced to enter into negotiations and acknowledge (if not comply with) Brazil's demands.

4. US domestic public opinion in the run-up to Putin's diplomatic solution of the Syrian crisis was overwhelmingly opposed to Obama's moves to bomb Syria. By a margin of two to one, the American electorate opposed any new war; and Congress was prepared to heed its constituents, as letters were running nine to one against war. In other words, Obama lacked domestic support for attacking Syria and was under strong pressure to accept Putin's diplomatic solution. The mass involvement of American citizens, at least temporarily, pushed back the war-mongers among Israel's wealthy and influential backers in Washington.

5. Obama's militarist foreign policy faces pressure from the Congressional deadlock over the budget and debt ceilings. Lacking a federal budget and with government offices closing, the White House has been forced to layoff millions of military and civilian employees. Obama is not in a position to launch a costly new war, even if his Zionist patrons are "storming" Congress and clamoring for one. The 'fiscal crisis of the state', which exploded in September 2013, is turning into a powerful political antidote to the policy of serial wars Obama undertook during his first five years in office. The debt-ceiling crisis and its aftermath further weaken the White House's capacity and willingness to pursue an extended war agenda in the Middle East. Congress's refusal to raise the debt ceiling, without budget reductions, could foreshadow a crisis in financial markets spreading to the world economy and leading to profound recession. The White House has its hands full trying to stabilize the domestic economy and placate Wall Street, thus weakening its willingness to engage in a new war.

One caveat: It is possible that, facing political divisions and an economic crisis, political adventurers and pro-Israel advisers might convince Obama to launch a war to 'unify the country' and 'divert attention' from his domestic debacle. A military distraction, of course, could backfire; it could be seen as a partisan ploy and deepen domestic divisions, especially if a US attack on Iran or Syria led to a wider war.

6. The Snowden revelations of the National Security Agency's global spying have weakened the White House's ties to its allies and heightened antagonism with its adversaries. Trust and co-operation, especially with

regard to intelligence, have been weakened in Asia, Latin America and, to a lesser degree, in Europe. Several countries are discontinuing the use of US-IT companies which had collaborated with the NSA. By losing access to the communications of top officials in targeted countries, these revelations may have undermined Washington's global reach. Obama and Kerry's outrageous justifications for spying on their allies and private citizens and their defense of intervention in cyberspace have stirred up powerful political currents of anti-imperialism among major trade partners. At the UN General Assembly Bolivian President Evo Morales asserted, "The US is mistaken if it thinks it is the owner of the world". His attack on US military imperialism— "...terrorism is combated through social policy not with military bases"— resonated with the vast majority of UN delegates. In stark contrast, Prime Minister Netanyahu's bellicose speech received a hostile reception among those heads of state who didn't simply walk out in disgust.

The Snowden disclosures of cyber-imperialism have seriously weakened the US capacity for war by exposing its intelligence operations and discrediting the warmongers associated with the NSA, making war planning more difficult.

The domestic and foreign forces, as well as world conditions for peace, would be overwhelming in any normal imperial system. But there is a 'special factor', a powerful 'undertow', which opposes the forces for peace, i.e. Israel and its US-based, billionaire funded, 300,000 member-strong national and local Zionist Power Configuration (ZPC) deeply embedded in government and civil society.

Against the Winds of Peace: The Zionist Power Configuration

On September 29, 2013, Israeli Prime Minister Netanyahu landed in New York, as part of an Israeli campaign to undermine worldwide support for a peaceful resolution of the war against Syria and the US-Iranian conflict. On September 30, Netayanhu met with President Obama and addressed the United Nations General Assembly the next day. Israel and Netanyahu represent the biggest and most powerful obstacle to the growing "tide of peace". Given its status as a pariah state and the global community's negative view of Israel and its bullying prime minister, Netanyahu has to rely almost exclusively on the US to maintain its monopoly of nuclear weapons in the region, its vast stockpile of chemical weapons and its military supremacy in the Middle East. The White House and the US Congress are crucial institutions backing Israel's ambition for uncontested hegemony in the Middle East. And the Zionist Power Configuration is decisive in setting US policy throughout the region.

Media analyst Steve Lendman describes, in his article entitled, "Israel Launches Anti-Rouhani Media Blitz", Netanyahu's repeated lies on questions pertaining to Iran's nuclear program and how the major US news media parrot Israel's bellicose propaganda. *The New York Times, Washington Post, Wall Street Journal* and *Bloomberg* back Netanyahu's demand for harsh economic sanctions and threats of aggression against Iran. *The Daily Alert,* mouthpiece of the Conference of 52 Presidents of the Major American Jewish Organization, reproduces and circulates scores of libelous polemical diatribes denigrating President Rouhani, and slavishly praises each and every bellicose eruption out of the mouths of Israeli politicians and generals. For example, leading Zionist propagandist, Jeffrey Goldberg calls President Rouhani a "dishonest warmonger" dismissing his peace overtures because he is not "ready to shut down his country's nuclear program". Aaron David Miller, another one of Israel's Washington intellectuals, echoes Netanyahu's "concerns about wily Iranian mullahs bearing gifts" while demanding that the US government "take care of Israel's concerns". The Zionist demand that the US "secure Israel's concerns" is a no brainer because the Jewish state is determined to strip Iran of its sovereignty, demanding that it surrender its entire medical and civilian nuclear program and submit to Israeli regional hegemony...

The US and British press reported that the American Israel Public Affairs Committee (AIPAC) has launched its own 'full- scale invasion' of the US Congress, sending over 300 full-time lobbyists to sabotage any form of rapprochement between the US and Iran. Just prior to the UN General Assembly meeting, AIPAC militants were writing legislation for the US Congress, which imposed new additional sanctions to further undermine Iranian oil exports; their efforts secured "bi-partisan" support of over 300 members of Congress. While President Obama faces a divided Congress, the Israel-Firsters from AIPAC easily *secure a near unanimous* vote to scupper any diplomatic dialogue between Washington and Teheran. These new extremist sanctions were dictated by the Israeli Foreign Office and are designed to sabotage any White House negotiations.

While some mainstream newspapers, like the *Financial Times*, describe the "suspicions in Congress which raise the bar for a deal", they fail to mention the extraordinary intervention and influence of AIPAC in sowing these "suspicions"—*and authoring all anti-Iran legislation* over the past two years! The mass media covers up the central role of the ZPC in opposing a US dialogue with Iran, and in subverting the push for peace favored by the vast majority of war-weary and economically-battered Americans. Even 'progressive and leftist' weeklies, monthlies and quarterlies are silent on the overwhelming role of the ZPC. Leading left journalists systematically skirt around any in-depth discussion of the AIPAC and the 52 pro-Israel Jewish organizations in manipulating the US Congress, the mass media and the Executive branch.

Any writer who attends US legislative committee hearings on the Middle East or observes Congressional debates, or interviews Congressional staff-members and lobbyists, or reads AIPAC reports, can compile ample public documentation of the major role that Israel, through its US Zionist organizations and agents, plays in dictating US-Iran relations. Nothing illustrates the extreme power the ZPC exercises over US policy toward Iran than the thundering silence of 'progressives' over the central ZPC role in policymaking. Is it simply cowardice or fear of being slandered as an 'anti-Semite'? Or is it fear of being excluded or blacklisted by major media and publications? Or is it complicity: being 'critical of privileges and power' while selectively excluding mention of Zionist access and influence?

So we have the situation in the US today where Israeli Prime Minister Netanyahu dictates the 'negotiating terms' to the Presidents of the 52 Major American Jewish Organizations. According to Netanyahu's dictates, the Islamic Republic of Iran must stop all uranium enrichment—including that for medical, research and energy use, close the enrichment facilities at Qom, remove all enriched uranium and halt the production of plutonium. Having set these ridiculous, sovereignty-killing conditions on Iran and having the unconditional support of the entire ZPC, Netanyahu proceeds to sabotage the peaceful, diplomatic process via the lap-puppies in the US Congress. As one Washington pundit noted, the Obama regime "is very conscious of the fact that Israeli views on Iran have a large influence [*sic*] on opinion in the US Congress".

No country on any continent would or could accept the terms dictated by Israel and its Fifth Column in the US—terms that undermine national sovereignty. In fact, all countries with nuclear power facilities and advanced medical and research institutions engage in some or all of these activities. By setting these extremist terms, Netanyahu is in effect dooming the negotiations from the start and setting the stage for war, the so-called "military option" that both he and Obama agree would follow from a collapse in negotiations.

In a rational democratic world, most experts would argue that given the new alignment of forces for peace, including the vast and growing domestic opposition to new wars, and world public opinion in favor of President Rouhani's overtures for negotiations, the US could easily ignore Israel's war mongering. But a more realistic and reflective analysis, however, would argue that the negotiations will only proceed with great difficulty, especially in the face of ZPC sabotage in adding new sanctions rather than a good-faith act of cutting or reducing the current sanctions.

The Israeli-ZPC 'war offensive' went into high gear precisely at the moment when world public opinion, the UN and even the White House enthusiastically welcomed the peace overtures from newly elected Iranian President Rouhani.

The purpose was to sabotage any dialogue with Iran before they even began. The ZPC took the following measures:

1. AIPAC and its clients in the US Congress have circulated new harsh sanctions and rapidly signed up dozens of Congressional supporters. The entire Zionist apparatus, led by the '52 Presidents of the Major Jewish American Organizations', backed the latest and most severe sanctions against the Iranian oil industry. They followed Netanyahu's dictate to make the Iranian economy collapse. The purpose of the ZPC is to create the worst possible conditions for negotiations—undermining the 'goodwill' following Obama's gestures (the phone conversation with Rouhani) and sure to provoke widespread opposition among the sanction-weary Iranian population against a US-Iran dialogue.

2. The notorious Israeli spy outfit, Mossad, was most probably involved in the brutal assassination of Iran's official in charge of cyber-defense, Mojtaba Ahmadi. Most experts agree that since 2007, Israel's intelligence agency has been behind the horrific assassinations of five Iranian nuclear engineers and scientists, as well as the head of their ballistic missile program. The timing of the current Mossad outrage is designed to further poison the climate for US-Iranian negotiations, even though the victim this time is not directly linked to Iran's nuclear program.

3. Netanyahu's speech to the General Assembly was pure corrosive vitriol, character assassination and fabrication. He made constant reference to Iran's 'nuclear weapons program', although on-site reports from the International Atomic Energy Agency and sixteen US intelligence agencies have repeatedly shown that no such program exists. Nevertheless, thanks to the power and influence of the ZPC, Netanyahu's venomous message was relayed by all the major media and picked up and repeated by influential pro-Israel think tanks, academics and pundits. Netanyahu unleashed the Zionist pro-war propaganda machine to energize Jewish powerbrokers to 'put the squeeze' on the White House. The effect was immediate: Obama rushed out to parrot Netanyahu's lies that Iran had a nuclear weapons program. Secretary of State Kerry obediently pledged to keep 'the military option' for dealing with Iran 'on the table'—in other words, the threat of a unilateral attack. UN Ambassador Samantha Power demanded the newly elected President Rouhani make immediate concessions in order to prove his "seriousness".

Conclusion: World Peace or Zionist War?

Recent political and diplomatic changes provide the world community with a measure of optimism regarding the prospects for peace. Under intense pressure from US public opinion, Obama temporarily went along with Russian President Putin's diplomatic approach over chemical weapons in Syria.

The UN General Assembly's favorable response to Iranian President Rouhani's call for dialogue has compelled Obama to openly consider direct negotiations with Teheran over its nuclear program.

World public opinion, favorable interlocutors in Iran, bold diplomatic initiatives from Russia, and cooperative behavior from Damascus, all events pointing to a peaceful resolution of current Middle East conflicts, face a formidable enemy embedded in the very centers of power in the United States, the ZPC, which acts on behalf of the ultra-militarist Israeli state.

Over the years, the ZPC has successfully pushed for crippling sanctions and wars against a number of Israel's regional opponents. Leading Zionists in the Bush regime fabricated the myth of Saddam Hussein's 'weapons of mass destruction' leading the US to invade, occupy and destroy Iraq, despite massive opposition from the US public on the eve of the invasion. Zionists in US Treasury and in the White House slapped broad economic sanctions on Iraq, Iran and Syria –*preventing the biggest US oil companies* from investing and trading with these resource-rich nations, which cost 'Big Oil' close to $500 billion in lost revenues. An empirical study of congressional committees, legislative debates, resolutions and voting behavior demonstrates that the ZPC co-authored the sanction legislation and administrators linked to the ZPC implemented the measures.

The popular notion that 'Big Oil' was responsible for these wars and sanctions, as part of some scheme to take over the oil production facilities of Iraq and Iran, lacks empirical basis. The ZPC defeated 'Big Oil': Exxon, Mobil and Chevron were no match for the ZPC when it came to penetrating Congress, authoring legislation, mobilizing billionaires to fund Congressional campaigns, organizing thousands of zealous militants or influencing the mass media—including the *Wall Street Journal*. The governments of billions of poor people in Africa, Asia and Latin America can only dream of the annual $3 billion dollar tribute that the ZPC secures for Israel from the American taxpayers over the past 30-plus years.

The UN Security Council and its Human Rights Commission are powerless to sanction Israel for its war crimes because the ZPC guarantees a US veto of any resolution. Despite the opposition of the entire Muslim world, the ZPC ensures that Washington will continue to support Israel's colonial expansion and land grabs in the occupied Palestinian territory, and its bombing of Gaza, Lebanon, Syria, Iraq and Sudan. In other words, the ZPC has successfully undermined the interests of the biggest US multinational corporations, the position of the UN Security Council and the needs of billions of poor in the Third World. The ZPC induces the US to start prolonged brutal wars costing the US economy over a trillion dollars and totally destroying six sovereign countries (Iraq, Libya, Syria, Afghanistan, Yemen and Somalia). Today Israel and the ZPC set the terms for US-Iran negotiations—dooming them to failure. The mass media echo Netanyahu's scurrilous (and infantile) characterization of President Rouhani as 'untrustworthy', and a 'wolf in sheep's clothing'. And US Secretary of State John Kerry parrots Netanyahu's lies about Iran's nuclear arms program. Shortly after his talk with Rouhani,

US President Obama dutifully made his report of the entire conversation to Netanyahu—seeking Israel's approval. Obama then met with his Israeli 'handlers' and pledged fealty to the interests of Israel, bleating out that the 'military option (to attack Iran) is still on the table'. For the one hundred and ninety-first time (over the past year) President Obama pledged unconditional US support to defend Israel. Like a broken record (or broken political hack), Obama repeated that "Israel must [*sic*] reserve the right to take military action against Iran if it feels threatened by Iran".

The Zionist propaganda apparatus has set the terms for the US government with regard to Iran. Tel Aviv orders and the ZPC demands that Obama 'negotiate' under Israeli terms. Iran, the ZPC insists, must provide detailed information on its military bases and defenses, end its legal enrichment of uranium for civilian use, turn over its existing stockpiles, end the production of plutonium at the Arak facility, dismantle the underground research facilities at Fordow and cease the conversion of first generation centrifuges to more efficient second generation ones.

President Obama might then permit the Iranians to enrich uranium to about 3.5 percent, operate a few primitive centrifuges and maintain a tiny stock of enriched uranium—for medical purposes.... These are conditions which Israel and the ZPC know that no free and independent country or national leader would ever accept. The Zionists seek to sabotage diplomacy in order to push the US into another Gulf war which they believe will establish Israel as the un-challenged regional hegemon.

It is essential for the peace camp in the United States to expose the role of the ZPC in dictating the US negotiating terms with Iran and to publicly repudiate its control over the US Congress and the White House. Otherwise the majority of Americans who favor peace and diplomacy will have no influence in shaping US-Iran relations. The problem is that the majority of anti-war Americans and the international community cannot match the billionaire Jewish Zionists in buying and controlling the members of the US Congress. AIPAC has no rival among Christians, Muslims or even anti-Zionist Jews. The pro-peace Pope Francis from his pulpit in the Vatican cannot match the power of the Presidents of the 52 Major Jewish American Organizations whose militants can literally "storm Washington" and push the US into war!

Until the 99% of non-Zionist Americans (of all ethnicities and persuasions) organize as a coherent force to push back the tiny 1%—Israel's Fifth Column—all the hopes for peace awakened by President Putin's initiative on Syria and President Rouhani's diplomatic opening at the United Nations will collapse. Worse, Israeli Prime Minister Netanyahu will again lead an American President, Obama, by the nose, from sabotaged diplomacy into another costly Gulf War, one in which thousands of US soldiers (not a single Zionist among them) and tens (if not hundreds) of thousands of Iranians will perish!

Israel's Willing Executioners: AIPAC Invades Washington

When a country, like the United States, is in decline, it is not because of external competition: declining competitiveness is only a symptom. It is because of internal rot. Decline results when a nation is betrayed by craven leaders, who crawl and humiliate themselves before a minority of thuggish mediocrities pledged to a foreign state without scruples or moral integrity

Introduction: A Week of National Humiliation:

From March 4th to March 9th, 2012, 13,000 militant Israel Firsters, took over "political Washington"[28] and imposed a foreign regime's (Israel's) political agenda to the rousing applause and appreciation of their captive vassal US legislators and executives who crowded the halls and platforms groveling for the imperious nods of their visiting Israeli overlords.[29]

The annual meeting of the American (*sic*) Israel Public Affairs Committee (AIPAC) is the most outrageous public display of Zionist-Jewish power as it shapes US foreign policy. The sole purpose of AIPAC is to ensure Israel's unchallenged military and political power over a huge region from North Africa to the Persian Gulf. Over three quarters of the US Congress members paraded themselves before the AIPAC, as well as President Obama and Vice President Biden and any high ranking Cabinet members in any way related to US foreign policy (Secretary of State Clinton, Secretary of Defense Panetta included). They all loudly parroted the political agenda and military priorities that the AIPAC has imposed on the United States.[30]

AIPAC: A Launch Pad for Israeli Leaders

The AIPAC gathering is clearly not a meeting of "just another lobby":[31] it is the launch pad used by Israel's top political and military leaders to drag the US into another major war in the Middle East—this time against Iran.[32] Shimon Peres, Israel's President, opened the conference, setting the militarist tone and political framework for US President Obama who followed, slavishly echoing the language and substance of the Israeli leader.[33] The following day Israeli Prime Minister Netanyahu, spoke, and forcefully laid out the line for a US war against Iran[34] with thousands of prominent and respectable Jewish Americans, *Israel Firsters*, leaping to their feet dozens of times in fanatic support for a US war—a war, in which few, if any, of them, their children, relatives or friends will suffer loss of life or limb.[35]

This was the same Bibi Netanyahu who once opined that the 9/11 attack on the US benefited Israel because it linked the US closer to Israeli interests.

Not since the War of 1812, which saw the British occupation and burning of Washington, has the US capital been so utterly humiliated by a foreign power. Unlike the British crown, which then negotiated a peace settlement, allowing the US to regain its sovereignty and capital, the Israeli leaders and their rabid "fifth column" demand a military agreement in which Israel dictates the terms under which the US goes to war with Iran.

Israeli leaders have not secured the submission of the US because of Israel's military, economic or political superiority: they have a puny economy, a fraction of the US nuclear weapons, few allies and even less public approval in the international community. But they do have at least a half million fanatical, unconditional Zionist militants in the United States, including thousands of loyal multi-millionaires and billionaires who fund the campaign of both Democrat and Republican parties.[36] AIPAC is the *vanguard* of Israel's shock troops in the US.

Highly disciplined and organized, AIPAC lobbyists invade the offices of every Congressperson armed with a legislative script carefully prepared by and for the State of Israel.[37] They have secured the full commitment of most members of Congress for Israel's agenda waving both dollar signs and stars (of David). As past history has amply demonstrated, Congressional staff or legislators who dare hesitate or ask for time to reflect, rapidly find themselves on the receiving end of AIPAC's political bullying and threats which usually secure acquiescence. Refusal to capitulate to AIPAC means the end of a political career in Washington.

The Israeli agenda (*and therefore AIPAC's*) is to pursue an unprovoked war, either initiated by the US or as part of a US-backed Israeli sneak attack, against the sovereign Islamic Republic of Iran.[38] Iran is targeted today because the other opponents of Israel's colonization of Palestine have been destroyed in previous Zionist-backed US wars, namely Iraq, Afghanistan and Libya while there is an ongoing proxy war against the Assad regime in Syria.[39]

Today Israeli leaders insist that Iran should be violently denied what over 120 other nations practice freely: the legal enrichment of uranium for medical, commercial and scientific purposes. Past Israeli propaganda, echoed by the 52 Presidents of the Major American Jewish Organizations, falsely claimed Iran possessed nuclear weapons or ... was in the process of manufacturing them and therefore posed an *'existential'* threat to Israeli. Even the mere *'capacity'* to enrich uranium for medical purposes (many times below the level needed for a weapon) is presented as a major threat to the Jewish State. Meanwhile, the 17 US intelligence agencies[40] (in their yearly 'findings') and even the US-influenced International Atomic Energy Agency have found no such evidence of an ongoing weapons program—thus the need for bizarre terms like *'existential threat'*.

Israel's high command has now come up with a new flimsy pretext for war. Now Iran's *potential* (through its advanced scientific and technical manpower and research centers) for acquiring a *'nuclear weapon capability'* may constitute a sufficient cause for war.[41] In other words, Israel has ordered its 13,000 AIPAC militants, to demand every US Congress person vote for a war resolution on the basis of Iran's *current uranium enrichment program* geared to medical uses and on its sophisticated scientific and intellectual potential! Meanwhile, the Mossad has launched a not-so-secret program of terrorist assassinations of Iranian *scientists*—in their homes, offices and universities; with nary a protest from the 'Zionized' US press.

Israel's Willing Executioners

Netanyahu's newest criterion for war (Iranian capability) has the blind support of the major Jewish organizations in the US.[42] American Zionists are willing executioners promoting an aggressive, unprovoked, military attack against the homeland (and homes) of 75 million Iranians. Let us be clear, there are naked genocidal impulses permeating some of the pronouncements of leading US Jewish religious leaders. The executive vice president of the Orthodox Rabbinical Council of America, Rabbi Herring, suggested that Israel should consider *"the use of tactical nuclear weapons in areas that aren't so populated or in the open desert ...to show the Iranians that their lives are on the line, that Israel won't go quietly"*.[43] The rabbi did not specify whether population centers of a quarter of a million inhabitants or less qualify under his definition of *"not so populated"* and therefore are suitable targets for this educational display of thermo-nuclear destruction, *"just to show the Iranians"*...

Let us keep in mind that among the Zionist fundamentalists, *"not a few organizational leaders ... wanted to use tactical nuclear weapons right now"*.[44]

When Netanyahu gave the command to the AIPAC delegates to invade the US Congress and secure a *war commitment* on the basis of Iran's 'capacity' (for uranium enrichment), there was no debate and no dissention among the 'shock troops'—only blind unanimous approval among Jewish American citizens for their foreign master. These respectable Jewish-Americans marched lock-step in platoons right up to the Congress members on their lists, canned arguments in one hand and Israeli-ghost-written legislation in the other. They boast of having rounded up a substantial majority of elected US representatives—for war!

If Israel's power in the US depends on AIPAC's tight control over the US Congress, the lobby, for its part, depends on the power of the wider Zionist power configuration permeating strategic political and administrative offices, political party structures and the electoral process itself. This, in turn, depends on Zionist media influence linked back to economic and financial power. The democratic and representative process has been totally crushed under this narrow-focused juggernaut for war on behalf of Israel.

AIPAC's Congressional and Executive Collaborators

While much has been made of the influence AIPAC exercises over the US Congress and Executive via '*lobbying*', better termed intimidation and pressure tactics, a great part of its success is based on the larger Zionist matrix of power operating within the government, civil society and the economy. When AIPAC lobbyists approach Congress members with Israeli-dictated foreign policy priorities in hand, they coordinate and are given a major platform by the forty-plus elected Zionist legislators who *just happen* to occupy strategic positions, such as the chairpersons of Congressional committees dealing with foreign policy, especially policy related to the Middle East.

In other words, AIPAC's conquest of Congress is 'by invitation'. The relation is 'reciprocal'. AIPAC and the 52 Presidents of the Major American Jewish Organizations and various fundraisers mobilize money and activists to help elect the reliable Zionists to office. Once in place, they openly collaborate in writing pro-Israel legislation and ensuring that 'majorities' vote the 'right way'.[45]

Mark Dubowitz, executive director of "Foundation for Defense of Democracies" helped write the latest (Iran) sanctions bill ...[46] The "Foundation" is better known as an unconditional and unquestioning promoter of Israel's agenda. Dubowitz is one of many *un-elected 'legislators* who write and promote laws at Israel's behest. The legislation to impose sanctions on Iran, co-authored by Dubowitz, is designed to brutalize and starve 75 million Iranian citizens into submission to further Israel's goal of unquestioned supremacy in the Middle East.

AIPAC's operations are not confined to Congress or to the electoral process. From the Reagan Administration to the Obama Administration, AIPAC has supplied committed Zionists to key positions in the Treasury,

State Department, National Security Council and the President's inner circle of advisors on the Middle East.[47] AIPAC pressure ensures the appointment of Zionists to the executive branch and has led to the creation of special administrative posts designed specifically to pursue Israel's agenda. A good example of AIPAC's success is the post of Undersecretary of Treasury for Terrorism and Intelligence. The position was first held by Stuart Levey, a Zionist zealot, whose whole purpose was to design and implement US (and later EU) sanctions against Iran. His replacement, David Cohen, a clone also from AIPAC, is the author of legislation pushing for punitive sanctions against Syria.[48]

Dennis Ross, widely known as 'Israel's lawyer' and a former AIPAC leader, was appointed senior adviser to Presidents Clinton, Bush and Obama, was the architect of US support for Israel's starvation blockade and criminal bombing of Gaza (1999), and the murderous invasion of Lebanon (2006). He has provided 'cover' for Netanyahu's massive building of Jews only settlements on occupied Palestinian lands and his cynical 'peace negotiations' ploy.[49]

Jeffrey Feltman, the current AIPAC front man in the State Department, is the key official in charge of Middle East affairs, especially Lebanon, Syria and Iran.[50] Obama's own inner circle of advisers is dominated by unconditional Israel supporters, including David Axelrod as chief confidant and the former Presidential Chief of Staff, dual US-Israeli citizen and current Mayor of Chicago, Rahm Emanuel.[51] What is striking is the *constant cycle* from leadership and activity in Zionist (Israeli-front) organizations, entry into powerful government post, return to one or another pro-Israel think tank, 'civic organizations', electoral office or lucrative private practice—all promoting the interests of Tel Aviv.

AIPAC and the 52 *Grassroots* Organizations

AIPAC's power in Washington depends on the activism of hundreds of thousands of American Zionists affiliated with organizations under the Conference of 52 Presidents of the Major American Jewish Organizations (CMAJO). While there is considerable overlap of membership, CMAJO leaders openly serve as a transmission belt for Israel: transmitting the political line from Tel Aviv to their membership, including activist doctors, dentists and stock brokers in New York, Miami, Kansas City, Los Angeles and San Francisco and all points north, south, east and west. When AIPAC has 'trouble' securing an elected representative's sign-on to legislation for sanctions against whichever country is currently targeted by Israel, the reluctant legislator becomes a prime target for local Zionist notables and 'fund raisers', who pay them a 'visit' to persuade, if possible, threaten retaliation, if necessary. If a legislator still refuses to hew to Israel's line, or considers service to a foreign power to be harmful to United States, he/she will soon find that AIPAC has raised millions of dollars to fund a campaign of slander and electoral defeat.[52]

Along with these upper middle class 'grass roots' activists there are the numerous highly politicized Zionist mega-millionaires and billionaires, like Adelson, Saban and scores of others, who make no bones about being fanatical Israel Firsters and donate millions to Congress people willing to subordinate US interests to Israel's quest for Middle East supremacy.[53]

Besides this *legal* corruption of the political process, there is the issue of *illegal* espionage and thuggery on AIPAC's part, most recently evidenced by the ongoing lawsuit by one of two former top AIPAC officials, Steven Rosen caught spying for Israel (passing classified documents on US military policy towards Iran). Rosen, who was acquitted in a highly manipulated 'trial', maintains that AIPAC routinely encouraged its officials to secure confidential US government documents for Israel.[54]

And then there are the prominent *freelance* Zionists, who engage in vicious, highly publicized, political thuggery, physical assaults and blackmail against critics of Israel.[55] The most prominent defamers, like Abraham Foxman of the Anti-Defamation League, Harvard Law Professor Alan Dershowitz, Daniel Pipes and David Horowitz, manipulate legions of *respectable and wealthy* thugs to pressure schools, universities and other employers to censor and fire critics of Israel. These Zionist organizations far exceed the reach and effective blacklisting of an earlier generation of witch hunters, like Senator Joseph McCarthy, who were rank amateurs in comparison. The recent antics of Israel-Firster, Andrew Adler, editor of the *Atlanta Jewish Times*, whose call for the Israeli Mossad to assassinate President Obama[56] led merely to his resignation as editor after several weeks of nervous outrage (but no federal investigation or charges).

What is striking here is that while most respectable Zionists dissociate themselves from AIPAC spies and verbal assassins, the power of the Israel Firsters ensures that such goons and thugs are rarely charged for their crimes and have never gone to jail.[57]

The wider impact of Zionist influence and thuggery is evident in the timorous self-censorship of the majority of Americans who privately express fear and loathing at the confrontational, strident and abusive Zionist-Americans pushing a foreign agenda.[58]

Israel, Zionism and the Mass Media

The mass media is a key political resource, which the pro-Israel power configuration exploits to the full. Not a single major print, television, film or radio outlet is willing to provide a balanced account of the Israel-Palestine conflict.[59] Israel's dispossession of thousands of Arab families from their homes and the daily terrorist Zionist settler and military assaults against Palestinians protesting land seizures go unreported.[60]

The hundreds of nuclear weapons in Israel's arsenal are never mentioned while the Jewish State's hysterical claims that non-nuclear Iran represents an *existential threat* are repeated and magnified, ad nauseam. The leaders of the 52 know their Goebbels: *A lie repeated often enough becomes an accepted truth.*

Zionism and Leveraging Power

What is crucial in understanding the Zionist Power Configuration's stranglehold over our government is how it *leverages* power. For example, a tiny minority falsely claims to speak for all American Jews, who represent about 3%[61] of the US population. However, based on this claim, they mobilize and raise funds to elect the committed Zionists who hold about 10% of the seats in the US Congress and Senate. These representatives, in turn, enjoy the support of a tiny cadre of super rich Zionists, whose promotion allows them to gain control over key committees dealing with Middle East policy and security.

Domestic security has been deeply influenced by the Zionist-Israeli agenda: Former US Attorney General, Michael Mukasey and Homeland Security Czar, Michael Chertoff, have been among the most prominent officials orienting US domestic security to focus on critics of Israel and the entrapment of Muslim citizens in bizarre webs of phony terrorist plots, while real domestic security has suffered and civil rights have been shredded. The over-representation of Zionists on the US Supreme Court (3 out of 9) and the careful selection of recent justices, like Justice Sotomayor, underscore the profound nature of the process as it extends to the judiciary.[62]

The Zionist Power Configuration controls the Mid-East policies of both the Democratic and Republican Party and their presidential nominees through their Congressional and political party power bases. The US president, in turn, is leveraged, in order to secure key policy appointments for Zionists in the State Department, Treasury and Pentagon. Their leverage in the foreign policy establishment allows Zionist officials to put pressure on allies and clients in the United Nations and European Union to support policies, such as Israel's boycott and punishment of the elected Hamas government in Gaza and the wars in Iraq, Afghanistan and Libya.

Leverage is how Israel, an exceedingly small and insignificant state with less than 1% of world GNP, exports and market shares, and occupying .001% of the world's territory, can play such a disproportionate role in the reconfiguration of power in the Middle East. Through its American-Zionist influentials, Israel has manipulated the US into a quagmire of wars in the Middle East, costing the world's consumers of oil untold billions of dollars and pushing the world economy into recession.

Israel's "Petroleum Tax": War Threats and the Price of Gas

During the first 3 months of 2012, the price of oil rose 15% (over 30% since the summer of 2011) largely due to Israel's warmongering and threats to launch an offensive war against Iran. Israeli Prime Minister Netanyahu, President Peres and Foreign Minister Lieberman have all repeatedly demanded that the US bomb Iran, or failing that, they warn, Israel would launch its own offensive war against the Iranian people and drag the US into another war.

Almost all oil experts and political analysts agree that the spike in oil prices is a result of Israel's warmongering, as major international oil speculators bet that an Israeli assault on Iran will provoke a major disruption in production and transportation of petroleum in the Middle East and provoke a global shortfall.[63]

The 52 Presidents of the Major American Jewish Organizations have added to the war hysteria by echoing and embellishing on Israel's claims of an Iranian nuclear threat (or Iran's "growing capacity" to threaten Israel in the future).[64]

During the first three months 2013 alone, the increased price of gasoline—or more accurately Israel's *war tax* on the American consumers and drivers—costs an additional 60 cents a gallon, or $9 dollars more to fill a 15 gallon tank. This represents *tribute* the Zionist power configuration has imposed on the American consumers in their push for a new war on Israel's behalf. No US politician would dare discuss this issue, let alone speak up and tell the Zionist chattering classes and their "beloved leaders" to stop pimping for war or else risk the cutting off of Israel's $3 billion dollar annual handout from the US taxpayers.

Leading economists have stated that the price hike in petroleum (caused by a bellicose Israel) is stunting growth and pushing the US and EU back into recession ... costing millions more job losses.[65] If we add the consumer losses caused by high gas prices to the losses in world economic output, the mere *war chants* of Netanyahu, Lieberman, Peres and the AIPAC will cost the global economy hundreds of billions over the course of the year.

Any mention of Israel's gas tax on the American family's budget will elicit outraged accusations of *anti-Semitism* from respectable Zionists and ugly threats from their thug accomplices. When Obama performed his infamous annual belly crawl to pleasure the AIPAC delegates and their Israeli guests, in the midst of cheers over his re-affirmation of America's unconditional loyalty to the state of Israel, he also quietly asked Israel to lower the war cries, at least until after the November elections because of its effects on the price of gasoline on the American voter.[66]

The high price of oil might have damaged Obama's chances for re-election. The American electorate might not understand the real cost of

Obama's submission to Israel and may not be aware of Israel's gas tax, but they are holding their putative President responsible for their *pain at the pump!* There is only one thing that Obama cherishes more than Zionist support and that is the votes of an economically squeezed American electorate, who are turning against him in droves as the price of gasoline soars.

Conclusion

The week of March 4 to 11, 2012 will go down in history as a week of national humiliation: a time when legions of fanatical American Zionists took over Washington; when the entire Cabinet, led by President Obama, groveled before the officials of a foreign state—in the heart of Washington, DC. When the President and Prime Minister of Israel directed their foreign legionnaires to march on the US Congress and shove their flimsy pretexts for war with Iran into the faces of cringing legislators, the simplistic and idiotic message was: *Bomb Iran because it may soon have … a nuclear 'capacity'.* If asked what constitutes capacity, they quote their beloved leaders in Tel Aviv, including the semi-literate (former nightclub bouncer) Foreign Minister Avi Lieberman, the morally corrupt Bibi Netanyahu and the quietly diabolic Shimon Peres that Iranians can 'enrich uranium'—a capacity long held by 125 other countries.

It is with supreme arrogance that the followers of AIPAC and the 52 Presidents penetrate the US government in order to serve a foreign government. None bother to hide their past, present or future affiliations with the state of Israel. They are backed by prestigious Zionist academics, whose tendentious justifications for war have already sent tens of thousands of US soldiers to an early grave or to the wards of military and veteran hospitals and clinics across the country: *They have sold us the argument that by serving the interests of the State of Israel we serve the United States.* From this, it only follows that to break the law and act as an unregistered agent for a foreign power, to transfer highly classified government documents to Mossad agents at the Israeli embassy and to threaten Americans who criticize or oppose Israel is a patriotic act.[67] Naval analyst Jonathan Pollard, the convicted US master-spy for Israel, is widely celebrated in Israel as an honorary Colonel in the IDF and a hero; the leaders of the major Zionist organizations are again pressuring Obama to release this traitor.

The documented performance of the leading Zionists in public office in the United States over the past two decades has been an unmitigated disaster. The self-proclaimed best and brightest have led the country into the worst economic and military catastrophes in a century. It was Alan Greenspan, as head of the Federal Reserve, who de-regulated the financial sector and optimized conditions for the mega-swindles and speculative frenzy bringing down the entire financial system. It was his replacement, Ben Bernanke, who pushed for trillions of US taxpayer dollars in bail-out funds to save his cronies on Wall Street and set them back on course, in the last 2 years, to repeat their speculative orgy (and allow such tribal compatriots as Stephen Schwartzman to reap $213 million in earnings in 2011).[68]

It was Fred Kagan, Paul Wolfowitz, Doug Feith, Libby, Abrams and Ross, as well as their less prominent lieutenants, who pushed the US into wars on Israel's behalf in Afghanistan and Iraq, all the while confidently predicting 'low cost, quick victories' (even slam-dunks). Never has such a cohort of Ivy League mediocrities collectively produced so many disastrous policies in such a brief historical time while never being held in any way, shape or form responsible or accountable for their performance. It is obvious that these policy disasters did not result from faulty intellect or lack of an elite education. Their apparent ignorance of historical, political, economic and military realities was a result of their blinding Zionist loyalties to the Israeli state whose real interests they embraced. This lack of accountability guarantees that this process will continue until the US, as a republic, is destroyed for the masses of its misled citizens.

In order to justify a war against Israel's regional adversaries, these blind mediocrities have distorted the realities of Arab nationalism. It was with supreme tribal arrogance and racism that they assured themselves that *Arabs* could never sustain prolonged resistance to their imperial juggernaut. They believed precisely what their tribal religion/ideology told them: They were a *chosen* people (genetic studies aside). They were the most financially successful investors or speculators. They attended and taught at the most prestigious universities. When, on occasion, a leading Zionist philanthropist, like Bernard Madoff, fell afoul—and actually went to jail—it was because, like his fellow tribalists, Milken, Boesky and Pollard—he didn't buy his one-way ticket to Israel soon enough.

When a country, like the United States, is in decline, it is not because of external competition: declining competitiveness is only a symptom. It is because of *internal rot*. Decline results when a nation is betrayed by craven leaders, who crawl and humiliate themselves before a minority of thuggish mediocrities pledged to a foreign state without scruples or moral integrity.

THE GREAT
TRANSFORMATION OF
JEWISH AMERICAN CHARITIES

Introduction

During the first half of the 20th century, socially conscious Jews in the United States organized a large network of solidarity and charity associations financed mostly through small donations, raffles and dues by working and lower middle class supporters. Many of these associations dealt with the everyday needs of Jewish workers, immigrants and families in need. Some were linked to labor unions, social democratic and leftist parties. Their leaders were, in many cases, individuals who worked long hours engaged in resolving problems and intervening in local crises. They drew a modest paycheck (when funding was available) comparable to that of a skilled worker. A few women's groups like the Hadassah went door to door in predominantly Jewish commercial districts, hitting up Jewish and non-Jewish storekeepers with raffle tickets to purchase beds in Hebrew hospitals in Palestine/Israel. The predominant ethic was improving the livelihood of Jews in America, joining with the America left and labor groups in united fronts against fascism and domestic, ethnic and racial supremacist organizations. Up until the establishment of Israel, Zionist organizations were a small minority in the Jewish community, especially among working class Jews.

When I was growing up in a multi-ethnic working class community (Lynn, Massachusetts) most of our Jewish friends and neighbors were workers and small shopkeepers: house painters, bookkeepers, carpenters, truck drivers (Gatso Feldman), window repairers (a long white bearded rabbi), junk collectors (Mr. Stone) on a horse drawn wagon calling for business with his whiskey hoarse voice (*"Rax, Rax, Rax"*! (Rags!)), butchers, bakers, drug store owners, tailors (*"Sam, you made the pants too long"*), fur and leather workers (Goldie Goldstein), warehousemen and a few owners. On the shady side there were poolroom hustlers (Marty Z), prostitutes (Sophie K) and gangsters (Louie F). In the mid-1950s, Jews and non-Jews were engaged in a punch-out with the reactionary, anti-Semitic Feeneyites on Boston Common.

But by the late 1940s changes began to take place under the pressure of events. As my Jewish college friend, Paul L, tells it, "One day the photo of Karl Marx, at the front of my Yiddish classroom, was taken down and replaced by one of Theodore Herzl, the founder of Zionism". The reasons were two-fold: Joseph McCarthy the anti-communist was coming to town to interrogate and blacklist the leaders of United Electrical Workers at the local giant General Electric plant in Lynn. Secondly, the founding of Israel converted the Yiddish social democratic directors from leftists to Zionists—and Zionists were not on McCarthy's agenda. By the mid-1950s, the right turn among the Jewish labor associations was visible—literally! One night after our studies, I met up with two Jewish friends and we walked to Peter's bar (10-cent beers with a rancid after-taste). On our way, my friends argued leftwing politics—Paul was for social democracy, Lenny for Trotskyism—I was the audience and potential adherent. As we passed the store window of the Workingman's Circle (a Yiddish pro-labor organization) Lenny stopped and triumphantly pointed to a sign in the window—a US Marine recruitment poster! Paul was crushed: the Circle had embraced Cold War militarism.

At 14 years of age, I went to work at my father's fish store in neighboring town of Revere, where the vast majority of our customers were Jews, many immigrants from Vilnius. Though there were several fish markets with Jewish owners, my father competed successfully because of his daily trek to the Atlantic Avenue piers in Boston to provide his customers with the freshest fish, caught the night before by Italian fishermen from the North End.

Of the thousands of customers, I recall only a couple of cases of Jewish ethnocentrism One well-known "*yenta*" (disagreeable woman) came in the store, saw our prices and then announced, "For those prices I could buy from a Jew!" Needless to say, she was sent on her way with a shower of Greek and Yiddish invectives from my father and his part-time fish-cutter Julius, 'the Bolshevik from Vilnius'!

Big Bucks: The Israel First Industry

Over the past fifty years a far-reaching transformation has taken place within Jewish organizations, among its leaders and their practices and policies. Currently Jewish leaders have converted charities, social aid-societies and overseas programs for working class Jews into money machines for self-enrichment; converted charities funding health programs for Jewish refugees fleeing Nazism into the funding of colonial settlements for armed Zionist zealots intent on uprooting Palestinians; and organized a powerful political machine which buys US Congress people and penetrates the Executive in order to serve Israeli military aims. The leaders of the principal Jewish organizations have changed from defending human rights and fighting fascism to defending each and every Israeli violation of Palestinian human rights—from arbitrary arrests of nonviolent dissidents to the detention of children in 'cages'. Israel's Kafkaesque prolonged administration detention without trial is approved by contemporary leaders. In the past Jewish leaders, especially labor and socially-engaged activists, had joined forces with Leftists in opposition to political bigots, McCarthyite purges and blacklists. Today's leaders practice the very same McCarthyite bully, blackmail and blacklist politics against critics of Israel and its Zionist appendages.

In the past Jewish leaders of social aid organizations received modest salaries, not any more than those of skilled workers. Today the leaders of the major Jewish "nonprofit" organizations are millionaires drawing between $200,000 and $800,000 a year plus lucrative allowances for "business expenses" (travel, housing, meals, etc.) which add another 30% to their income.

The moderately social liberal Jewish weekly, *The Jewish Daily Forward*, recently completed a survey of the salaries of Jewish *"not-for profits"* leaders, with the aid of a professor from the Wharton School of Business, University of Pennsylvania. Among the leading profiteers was Abraham Foxman of the Anti-Defamation League (ADL), earning $688,280; Howard Kohr of the American Israel Public Affairs Committee (AIPAC), $556,232; David Harris of the American Jewish Committee (AJC), $504,445; Morton Klein of the Zionist Organization of America (ZOA), $435,050; Janice Weinman of Hadassah, $410,000; Malcolm Hoenlein of the Presidents of Major Jewish Organizations (PMJO)- $400,815, Mark Helfield of the Hebrew Immigration Aid Society, $268,834; and Ann Toback of the Workmen's Circle/Arbeter Ring, $185,712. [69] These salaries and perks put the Jewish leaders of nonprofits in the upper 10% of US incomes—a far cry from the not-too-distant past. According to the analysis by *The Forward* and the Wharton team, *'most leaders (CEOs) are vastly overpaid—earning more than twice what the head of an organization of their size would be expected to make"* (italics added).

While the membership has declined in many organizations, especially among working and lower middle class Jews, the funding has increased, and most important, the plutocratic leaders have embraced a virulent militarist foreign policy and repressive domestic policies. Forward describes Abraham Foxman as "diverting the ADL from its self-described mission of fighting all forms of bigotry in the US and abroad to putting the ADL firmly on the side of bigotry and intolerance". We can add that the ADL was convicted of spying on political groups in the US and has been active in bullying academic institutions to fire professors and civic organizations to cancel events critical of Israel and the "Israel First Industry" in the US.

The overwhelming response of the Jewish readers to *Forward's* survey was one of indignation, disgust and anger. As one reader commented,

"The economic disconnect between their (CEOs) salaries and the average incomes of those who contribute to their charities is unacceptable". Another indignant reader remarked succinctly: "Gonifs! (Thieves!)". Many announced they could cut off future donations. One formerly orthodox reader stated, "I would rather give to a street beggar than to any of these".

The drop-off of donations from lower-middle class Jews, however, will have little effect in reducing the salaries of the 'nonprofit' CEO's or changing the politics of their 'nonprofits' because they increasingly depend on six and seven digit contributions from Jewish millionaires and billionaires. Moreover, the contributions by big donors are linked to the politics of repression at home and securing multi-billion dollar military aid and trade programs for Israel from the US Treasury. The billion- dollar donors have no objection to funding the millionaire leaders—as long as they concentrate their efforts on buying the votes of US Congress members and aligning their politics with Israel's war aims. Foxman will continue to be "overpaid" for running an organization with a rapidly declining membership, which does not fight bigotry, so long as he secures big bucks from rightwing Zionist donors who value his success in sabotaging the White House-Iran interim agreement and securing new Senate sanctions against Iran.

Likewise in 2013, AIPAC Executive Director Howard Kohr pocketed $556,232 in salary plus $184,410 for "expenses"($740,647 in total) for dedicating most of his budget and lobbyists to fighting for US sanctions against Iran, supporting US wars for Israel in the Middle East, funding Jews-only settlements in Palestine and securing US vetoes of UN resolutions critical of Israeli war crimes.

David Harris, Executive Director of the American Jewish Committee ($504,445 plus expenses) has devoted most of the AJC's time and resources to pressuring Congress and the Executive to follow Netanyahu's demand for harsher sanctions on Iran. According to the *Forward*, "On July 1 (2013), a few weeks after Hassan Rouhani was elected as Iran's new President, Harris charged that Rouhani was implicated in the 1994 bombing of the AMIA Jewish Center in Buenos Aires. This was a week after Alberto Nisman, the Argentine prosecutor (and an ardent Jewish Zionist) had informed the *Times of Israel* editor, David Horvitz, that Rouhani was neither under indictment nor accused of any involvement". It's inconceivable that Harris could have been unaware of this. So he lied, outright.

Conclusion

The Great Transformation among American Jewish charitable organizations is marked by the shift 1) from social aid for working Jews, poor immigrants and elderly Holocaust victims to political influence peddling at the service of the highly militarized state of Israel; 2) from engaging in social welfare for American Jews to political lobbying for military transfers to Israel; 3) from grassroots leaders sharing life styles and struggles with their rank and file donors to millionaire CEOs entertaining Zionist billionaires and banging tables for Israel at the White House while paying off the Congressional influential; and 4) from reaching out and aligning with Americans working for peace with justice in the Middle East to embracing every tin horn monarch and dictator who signs off on Israeli annexation of Palestinian land.

The key to the transformation is located in the ideological and structural transformation among the leaders of the Jewish organizations. The rise to prominence—indeed the centrality—of billionaire/millionaire Zionist donors has put in place leaders who mirror their *Israel-First* outlook and have similarly enriched themselves. The Great Transformation of Jewish charitable organizations has resulted from the ascendancy of an ethnic supremacist ideology which views 'others' as inferior subjects to be ruled by the superior intelligence of Jewish political and business leaders and which orders that the 'disobedient' and 'dissident' be castigated as 'anti-Semites' and punished by jail, media ostracism, censorship, overt threats and, most commonly, loss of employment. A key consequence of the rise to political power of the once socially conscious Jewish organizations is the shedding of their popular mass base. Jewish members have resigned in protest over the CEOs manipulative authoritarian leadership style. Expulsions and harassment have forced others to retire. But most of all the leadership's blind political submission to Israeli state policy and self-enrichment has alienated growing numbers of young socially active as well as middle age Jews who are disenchanted with their *Gonif leaders.*

As disenchantment grows, the organized groups and leaders act with greater discipline and aggression to preserve *their false image as "representatives of the Jewish community"*. Jewish dissidents are silenced or isolated. The CEO "leaders" and their rabbinical allies fuse ethno-supremacy, the menorah, the Israeli flag and the politics of Israel-First into a powerful instrument of internal control. Lucrative salaries and personal enrichment at the service of Israel are not seen as morally reprehensible: They are viewed as virtues, at least among respectable ... gonifs.

I remember the older brother of a boyhood Jewish friend, who joined the Lincoln Brigade and fought on the Republican side in the Spanish Civil War. It is linked to a contrary more recent memory—a young student at Binghamton University telling me, that he was going to Israel to serve with the Israeli Defense Forces after graduation. No doubt this young American's Zionist "militancy" will translate into breaking the legs of protesting Palestinian school children. How will he feel about it, then? Yes, a 'transformation' has taken place but I must confess that I prefer Izzy Levine's candy and comic book store where neighborhood school kids socialized, including the descendants of Sicilians, Odessa Jews, African Americans and Spartan Greeks, over the current Judeo-centric CEOs who run the 'Israel-First' industry. Izzy was a far greater American than Abe Foxman, political blackmailer, police informer and millionaire *gonif*.

PART V

IMPERIAL AND ZIONIST WARS AND TERROR IN THE MIDDLE EAST:

PALESTINE, IRAN, SYRIA AND YEMEN

ISRAELI TERROR:
THE "FINAL SOLUTION"
TO THE PALESTINE QUESTION

Introduction

For the past forty-five years the state of Israel has been dispossessing millions of Palestinians living in the Occupied Territories, confiscating their lands, destroying homes, bulldozing orchards and setting up 'Jews-only' colonial settlements serviced by highways, electrical systems and water works for the exclusive use of the settlers and occupying soldiers.

The process of Israeli territorial expansion throughout the West Bank and East Jerusalem has greatly accelerated in recent years, converting Palestinian-held territory into non-viable isolated enclaves—like South Africa's Bantustans—surrounded by the Israeli soldiers who protect violent settler-vigilantes as they assault and harass Palestinian farmers at work in their fields, beat Arab children on their way to school, pelt Palestinian housewives as they hang their laundry, and then invade and defecate in Palestinian mosques and churches.

The Rage and Rape of Gaza and its Apologists

Israel's strategic goal is to impose 'Greater Israel' on the region: to take over all of historical Palestine, expel the entire non-Jewish population and subsidize 'Jews-only' settlements (for settler-immigrants, often from the US and former USSR). While bulldozers and tanks have dispossessed Palestinians in the West Bank for decades, the launching of thousands of missiles and bombs have become the 'weapons of choice' for uprooting and eliminating the Palestinians in Gaza. In just eight days, Israel's November 2012 blitzkrieg resulted in the killing of 168 Palestinians (42 children and 100 civilians), the wounding of 1,235, the destruction of over 1,350 buildings and the further traumatizing of over 1.7 million children, women and men fenced in the world's largest concentration camp. According to the Israeli Defense Minister, the Jewish State dropped "a thousand times more bombs onto Gaza" than the Palestinians fired back into Israel.

The November 2012 Israeli offensive began with the gruesome assassination of a prominent Hamas leader, Ahmed Jabari, and immediately escalated into an assault on the entire Palestinian population of Gaza. Secure in the knowledge that the Palestinians had no capacity to retaliate with similar weaponry, the Israeli High Command ordered the systematic destruction of civilian life, workplaces and densely populated neighborhoods. Over 75% of the casualties have been non-combatants; almost half are children, women and elders.

The Israeli propaganda machine and its fifth column in the US fabricated and repeated the Big Lie: that the Jewish state was 'defending itself'... with only six (mostly military) deaths and 280 wounded (the majority non-threatening) versus the mostly civilian slaughter of Palestinians that was 25 orders of magnitude greater. The US Zionist power configuration (ZPC), embedded in the policy centers of the US Executive, the Congress and both political parties, parroted this line. All the major US TV networks and print media reproduced verbatim Israeli Foreign Office press handouts about Israel's 'defensive' ... genocide ... while entire Palestinian families were being buried under the rubble of their bombed apartments.

Death and destruction, planned and executed with the unanimous support of all the major Israeli political parties and leaders, enthralled the mass of its Jewish citizens: Indeed, over 80% of Israeli Jews supported the terror blitz against Gaza. As the Russian media outlet (RT) reported: "A new wave of hatred towards Palestinians is sweeping through Israel from public figures to the man (person) in the street". The Israeli Interior Minister declared that "Gaza should be bombed into the Middle Ages". Israeli demonstrators in Tel Aviv shouted; "They [the Palestinians] don't deserve to live, they must die", "May your children die" and "Now we must go back there (to Gaza) and kick out all Arabs". The prominent Israeli Rabbi Yaakov Yosef, the son of a former chief rabbi, made a speech in the Cave of the Patriarchs in occupied Hebron where he blessed the Israeli soldiers and urged them "to slaughter their enemy".

Even more to the point, Israel Katz, Israel's Transport Minister, demanded that "Gaza be bombed so hard the population will have to flee into Egypt (the Sinai desert)". Avi Dichter, the Minister of Home Front Defense, incited the Israeli military to "re-format" Gaza—that is, to erase its population with bombs.

Almost half of Israeli Jews considered Netanyahu's terror bombing of Gaza insufficient: According to the independent Israeli Maagar Mohot poll,[70] effectively half of Israelis (49%) opposed the cease fire and demanded the bloody assault against the Palestinian population of Gaza continue. The same poll reported that almost a third of Israeli Jews thought their government should have sent ground forces into Gaza, an invasion which would have led to tens of thousands of Palestinian casualties and total destruction of their vital infrastructural life-lines. Netanyahu and his allies in power now confront a new, totalitarian mass opposition that openly embraces a genocidal 'Final Solution' to the Palestinian problem.

Genocide at the Service of Greater Israel

The parallels between the pronouncements and actions of Nazi Germany and Zionist Israel are overwhelming. The bloodlust in Israel goes far beyond psychopathic raving of a few deranged rabbis and marginal politicians: it extends from the top Cabinet members to the average citizen.

In Israel, almost an entire people—over 80% of Jews—support, with varying degrees of intensity, the terror bombing and slaughter of the people of Gaza. Setting aside the profound sociopathic disorders of the raging and racist multitude in Israel, what is politically more significant are the totalitarian rants of leading Israeli public figures, and the fact that they have been published as editorials, in such newspapers as the respectable *Jerusalem Post*: "We need to flatten all of Gaza. There should be no electricity in Gaza, no gasoline or moving vehicles, nothing,"[71] writes Gilad Sharon while a prominent Knesset member Michael Ben-Ari , wrote, "There are no innocents in Gaza ... mow them (all) down".[72] These outbursts reveal Israel's strategic tool to achieve its goal: genocide at the service of Greater Israel—the bloody purge of 5 million Palestinians, the creation of a 100 percent 'pure' Jewish State. Overseas (mostly US) Zionist-Jewish media moguls, Ivy League university academics, billionaires, US Congress people and government officials finance, underwrite, propagandize for and promote with single-minded perseverance the defense of Israel's most heinous war crimes, its violations of international law and its ongoing crimes against humanity.

During the entire period of the recent Israeli blitzkrieg, Israel's fifth column, the Presidents of the 52 Major American Jewish Organizations, *The New York Times* and the rest of the major US press rose to the dirty task of giving unconditional support for Israel's war crimes. Vocal support from the US White House and by extension the leaders of the European Union echoed Netanyahu's lies. In order to grasp the media white wash of these ongoing crimes against humanity one could compare the US press reports on Israel's bombing of Gaza to those which would have appeared in the leading fascist newspapers at the time of Hitler's 'defensive' attacks on Poland and Belgium and the bombing blitz of civilians in London.

The true purpose of Israel's terror bombing raids and assassinations in Gaza and the cutting up of the West Bank is *to make these territories uninhabitable for the Palestinians*. The daily humiliation and destruction of the basic conditions for normal life are designed to force young, educated, ambitious Palestinians to abandon their land, homes and families for less grotesquely barbaric sites, where they might achieve a normal civilized existence, free from foul-mouthed Jewish settlers, unending military incursions, and Israeli soldiers pistol-whipping their fathers or breaking the legs and arms of stone-throwing Arab school kids.

Following the Logic of Public Flogging

This obscene Israeli-Jewish behavior is *intentionally open and flagrant*: Flaunting Jewish military superiority over the defenseless Arabs is a vital part of the psychological war reinforcing the idea of Arab inferiority and of Palestinians as aliens in their own country. Israel's underlying slogan "Arab Raus!" (Arabs Get Out!) echoes the Nazi screed, "Juden Raus!" (Jews Get Out!). The message is clear: "If you are not a Jew then you do not exist! Your very alien presence is an abomination in the eyes of the Zionist God. So if you won't leave politely we will hasten your departure with a few thousand bombs, missiles and a rain of white phosphorous." That is the deeper meaning of Israel's rape of Gaza.

The Impact of Israel's Genocide on US Society

Leading journalists in the politically most influential US newspapers, academics from the most prestigious universities and 'experts' from the leading research institutes have systematically defended each and every Israeli war crime, including the rape of Gaza, the demolition of Palestinian civil society and the cruel blockade of 1.7 million Palestinians in the biggest 'open air concentration' camp in the world.

As usual, the Uber-Zionist Harvard law professor, Alan Dershowitz and his acolytes provide a legal gloss on the savage bombing of essential public services and private communication and media centers. Not to be outdone by the loudmouths in Harvard Square, Yale and Princeton professors, with tribal loyalties to the Jewish state, describe the Israeli killing machine as a righteous citizen army defending its eternally victimized people. "Experts" at the Brookings Institute, Hudson Institute and dozens of other 'research' (read propaganda) centers provide 'scientific' explanations regarding Israel's unique right to dispossess millions of Palestinians. The experts' justifications of Israeli war crimes permeate the mass media, penetrate the homes of millions of Americans and fill the heads of elected officials. Meanwhile they 'convince' and/or browbeat thousands of non-tribal school teachers and educators into complicity or silence, thus perverting and hollowing out what residual humane and democratic values remain embedded in the citizenry. It is precisely the much-vaunted 'high achievements' of so many Israel-Firsters that has led to their rise to the most influential positions in US society and state and makes their support of terror bombings, ethnic cleansing and genocide so deeply destructive to the US political culture. In spite of this, some of the same expert-academic apologists for Israel's terror against the Arab civilians are the most vociferous defenders of human rights *everywhere else in the world—including in the US* (piously condemning US war crimes whenever and wherever they are not explicitly aligned with the interest of the Jewish State). These 'experts' have perverted the concept of universal human rights in the minds of the US public.

As the US mass audience and political class watches the smoke, debris and wreckage of Gaza—and even catch glimpses of a child's dismembered small body—they are told by the tribal loyalists that this destruction is morally justified, that the target is really "Hamas"—even over the piercing cries of Palestinian mothers for their slaughtered children. US citizens are told that Israel's aggressive aerial bombing and mass shelling from warships offshore is really a "defensive" maneuver against a "terrorist" regime—one which just happens to lack a single airplane, warship, tank or missile capable of hitting a single major Israeli military or civilian installation.

The Zionist Academic–Journalist Propaganda Complex

The Israeli academic-journalist propaganda complex in the US has pushed the entire US political narrative even further to the fascist right. It has perverted our political vocabulary, equating mass slaughter with national defense; equating the 'anxiety' of Israeli Jewish civilians with the homeless, jobless and traumatized widows and children emerging from their devastated densely-populated urban neighborhoods.

The tribal scholars and mass media pundits excel in transforming executioners into victims and victims into executioners. The Liberal-Zionists, peace-time critics of Israel, remove their peace buttons and pick up scripts defending 'just wars', as soon as Israel starts bombing another Arab population or adversary. For the liberal (human-rights-spouting) Zionists, bombing civilians is always illegal—except when it is Israel launching the missiles. Propaganda zealots for Israel saturate the media attacking any human rights activist critical of Israel with charges of "anti-Semitism". They smear, threaten and blackmail each and every dissenting voice daring to oppose their narrative.

The entire mass media and the most prestigious universities censor any mention of Israeli crimes against humanity. As bombs rained on Gaza not one single Congressional voice denounced the odious American President Obama when he defended Israel's eight-day "Guernica" against a defenseless population. Unlike the citizens in Nazi Germany, we in the US and Western Europe cannot claim that we did not know about Israeli war crimes as they were happening. On the other hand, how can the mass of semi-literate TV viewers in the US really 'know' what is going on when Israel-Firsters have so thoroughly 'framed the context'—claiming it's all defensive, that only Hamas "terrorists" are targeted ... despite the images of children being frantically pulled from the wreckage of their homes.

However, the educated classes in the US *do know* about Israel's tradition and practice of mass civilian bombings; they do remember Lebanon 2006 as well as Gaza 2008-2009 (and countless Israeli massacres in the late 20th century). At the same time, they also "remember" the vicious reprisals and vitriolic attacks the Zionist ideological attack-dogs launched against their critics. Having 'learned their lessons' from the Zionist 'thought-cops' they conveniently remember ... to forget and walk away... from the whole 'Middle East mess'. Worse still, they sanctimoniously blame the Palestinians for their efforts to retaliate in the face of Israel's blatant murders of their most prestigious leaders as well as their stubborn refusal to surrender.

There are a few Left-Zionists who actually praise the 'resilience' of the Palestinians and their refusal to surrender to the dictates of Israel and its occupying army. They note how the Gazans 'celebrate' their 'victory' amidst the rubble after having secured a very tenuous cease fire. Any reasonable observer could reply to this sentimental nonsense: Is survival in an open air concentration camp for another day, the daily prospect of Israeli drone flights overhead and a brutal land and sea blockade any "victory"? There is no cause for celebration. Transforming Israeli war crimes into Palestinian virtues is a cheap liberal Zionist sideshow. An eight-day Israeli assault, which had successfully destroyed every major and minor public office responsible for providing the people of Gaza with essential services, and the savaging of the water and sewage system, power and electrical grids and media offices (not to mention perishable food and medicine) is nothing to celebrate. In fact the underlying strategic goal of the Jewish state—to make the remains of historical Palestine uninhabitable (a modern 'howling wilderness') for its people—has been advanced by leaps and bounds. Surviving another day in order to bury loved ones and scrounging among the burnt ruins of a home for a birth certificate or photograph is hardly the noble "Hamas victory" proclaimed by Norman Finkelstein and Uri Avneri.

Why NATO/Washington Support Israel's Genocidal War

Unlike in the past, where some international organizations and European states raised tepid objections to Israel's military assaults against Palestine or Lebanon, after the November 2012 assault nothing took place. The White House immediately embraced Israel's terror bombing as did the governments of Western Europe. Meanwhile, Turkey, the Gulf States, the Arab

League and the pan-Islamic organizations did nothing concrete, offering no arms, no boycotts, no oil embargos—only shallow symbolic gestures.

Netanyahu timed his assault to take advantage of the western imperial offensive against independent countries and leaders who had historically supported the Palestinian liberation struggle for decades. Since NATO states had invaded and bombed the sovereign nation of Libya back into the Stone Age, Netanyahu's Cabinet Ministers must have reasoned, "Why can't we send the Gazans back to the Middle Ages with our bombs"? When NATO and the Gulf States now arm, finance and support a prolonged terrorist-led assault against the secular regime, people and infrastructure of Syria, Netanyahu reasons, "Why don't we do the same to the Palestinians"?

With the EU, Washington and the Gulf States engaged in covert and overt wars against all of Palestine's staunchest allies (Iraq, Afghanistan, Libya, Syria, Iran and the Sudan) and against the people's movements in Yemen, Bahrain and Pakistan, Netanyahu's plan to ethnically purge Palestine has advanced with total impunity—indeed with overt Western approval, and without concern for any international 'humanitarian' sanctions or even protest.

Netanyahu's murderous war on Gaza, with full US complicity, has unmasked a collaborationist tendency of Egypt's Islamist President Morsi. Morsi, together with US Secretary of State Hillary Clinton, secured a cease fire only after Netanyahu had accomplished his immediate goal of destroying the public institutions of civil society and undermining the vital public functions of the Hamas government.

Against the protests of the blood-thirsty Israeli public, who wanted their bombers and army to 'finish the job', Israeli Prime Minister Netanyahu negotiated and signed an agreement on a cease fire where Israel will *pay no indemnity to the devastated civilians of Gaza while confirming the Mubarak-era Israeli– Egyptian treaty and starvation blockade of Gaza.*

Conclusion

The people of the Middle East, especially the Palestinians, are in their worst position ever. Palestinians have lost the political, financial and military support of the independent, secular regimes of Libya, Syria and Iraq. And Iran, the principle source of arms for the Palestinians, faces a US naval armada off its coast. Israel is accelerating its naked land grabs in the West Bank. The PLO continues to be Israel's frontline 'cop on the block'—jailing resistance fighters and dissidents by the hundreds. Israel's Fifth Column in the US ensures unconditional support for Israel's ethnic cleansing of its non-Jewish population. Above all, as the terror bombing of Gaza reveals, Israel as a state and as a people, is free to bomb and destroy Gaza in order to force a mass exodus of the Palestinians so that they may establish a 'pure' and unadulterated Jewish state on historical Palestine.

Epilogue

Less than 24 hours after the so-called "cease fire" Israeli soldiers murdered an unarmed Palestinian protestor and wounded dozens with live ammunition on the Gazan side of the border. Israel storm troopers raided West Bank homes and arrested 55 Palestinians accused of supporting Hamas. Scores more Palestinians in the Beit Lahia area of the West Bank were summarily arrested and jailed as suspected Hamas members. Jewish vigilante settlers near occupied Hebron uprooted 400 olive trees belonging to Palestinian farmers from the village of Hawara. As the missile murderers take their break, the bulldozers rev up their engines: Israel's leaders pursue their strategic objective of a "pure" Jewish state with their inexorable and destructive juggernaut. The 'cease fire' merely changed the *methods* and the *terrain* of *dispossession* for the time being.

Israel's assault on Gaza has totally demolished its vibrant recovery and growth since the previous war of destruction. In 2011 the economy of Gaza grew by 20%; after the recent Israeli attack who would dare consider Gaza as a place to live and invest?

Obama at the General Assembly: Sacrificing Palestine for Zionist Campaign Funds

Introduction

Obama's blatant and overt pandering to Israel before the representatives of 193 independent nations at the UN General Assembly on September 21, 2011, which followed the standing ovation for Abbas' call for Palestinian recognition, highlights one of the greatest US diplomatic defeats since the founding of the UN over 60 years ago.. This is the common opinion of foreign policy experts: Obama has led the US to an ignominious diplomatic defeat, deepening US isolation in the international system.

The White House's blatant parroting of Israel's position to continue bilateral negotiations, while Tel Aviv continued to colonize Palestinian land and forcibly evict its residents, alienated the 1.5 billion Muslims throughout the world. Obama's refusal to even mention the return to the 1967 borders as a basis for a "peace settlement" totally undermined any pretext that the US could act as an "honest broker" in Mid-East peace negotiations, even in the eyes of its most slavish supporters in the PLO. His one-sided reference to Israel's minimal casualties in maintaining the Occupation, while omitting any mention of the 12,000 Palestinian political prisoners, thousands of assassinations, everyday humiliation, routine torture of suspects and frequent defacement of Palestinian religious centers (mosques and churches, cemeteries and shrines), undermined any US effort to win favor among the millions of people involved in the pro-democracy social movements sweeping the Arab world from Tunisia and Egypt to the Gulf states.

Washington's insistence that its NATO allies line up with it in supporting continued "bilateral" negotiations has led to the German government's public humiliation when it followed Obama's line of pressuring Abbas back to 'negotiations', only to have Israeli Prime Minister Netanyahu announce the construction of 1,100 illegal Jews-only housing units in occupied Palestinian East Jerusalem

But was Obama's groveling before Israeli Prime Minister Binyamin Netanyahu really a 'failure' *in the eyes of the White House?* Or was his speech really a carefully crafted appeal to a domestic audience in order to raise hundreds of millions of dollars from pro-Israel billionaires to finance his re-election campaign?

There is a wealth of documentary evidence showing that Obama deliberately and forcefully sacrificed US international standing in order to satisfy the major American Jewish organizations who were demanding nothing less than his total and unconditional backing for Netanyahu's phony position of "peace negotiations" and colonization.

From the angle of satisfying the US Zionist power configuration (ZPC) and securing a massive flow of re-election financing, Obama's UN speech was a smashing success.

Obama's Rejection of World Opinion and the Zionist Payoff

Obama's re-election campaign from April to the end of September has received tens of millions of dollars from wealthy pro-Israeli Jewish fundraisers and contributors, as well as endorsements from rightwing US Jewish and Israeli politicians.

In the run-up to Obama's UN speech, Zionist lobbyists adopted "good cop/bad cop" tactics. Liberal Zionist Democratic Party advisers emphasized that he was "losing the Jewish vote and funding", highlighting the recent resignation of a disgraced Democratic Congressman from a district of Orthodox Jews because of his internet porno-exhibitionism as a sign of Obama's growing unpopularity among Jews. Some campaign strategists emphasized the "crucial Jewish vote in swing states" like Ohio and Pennsylvania (where *non-Jews*, who represent well over 80% of the voters, are not "crucial" in the eyes of these election experts!).

The 52 Presidents of the Major American Jewish Organizations took turns accusing Obama of "slandering Israel", for disobeying Netanyahu and "backing the Arabs", for protesting Israeli land grabs, even as Obama raised US government aid to Israel to an unparalleled $3 billion per annum, in the midst of a US economic recession with 18% of American workers unemployed or underemployed. Obama's pro-Israel critics overlooked his $205 million gift to Tel Aviv to build the *Iron Dome* rocket defense system together with the US military's latest fighter jets. The Zionist power configuration demanded total surrender even as they extracted more political and economic concessions. They ignored the enormous military imbalances in the Middle East in Israel's favor and the degradation of US standing in the region.

Hardball threats to end Jewish financial support by the rightwing Zionists was "complemented" by fundraising by liberal Zionists and promises of more to come if Obama ended his "public feuding" with Israel and vetoed Palestinian admission to the UN. Obama performed his well-rehearsed routine of the "absolute defender", now and forever, of every Israeli violation of Palestinian human rights.

Obama's Rush for the Gold

On June 20, 2011, months prior to Obama's speech opposing Palestinian admission to the UN, a pro-Israel Washington fundraising event for his re-election campaign raised over $1.5 million, assuring Obama that "Jewish donors" were not wavering as long as he followed Israeli Prime Minister Netanyahu's line of peace negotiations and land grabs.[73] During the fund raiser Obama reiterated his unconditional support for Israel's policies, including the settlements in the Palestinian West Bank. Following the dinner he met behind closed doors to elaborate on how far he was willing to go in opposing the Palestinian initiative at the UN.[74] A month earlier on May 22, 2011, Obama had spoken at the annual meeting of the American Israel Public Affairs Committee (AIPAC), directly appealing for funds in exchange for the United States' total submission to the AIPAC agenda.

Obama's dependence on Zionist funding was evident between April-June 2011: of the $68 million raised for his campaign, $37 million was raised by 244 "big cash bundlers"—individuals who round up multi-millionaire contributors. According to one count of the 244 bundlers, approximately 120 were identified as pro-Israel Jews. Among the Zionist "bundlers" are Penny Pritzker bagging contributions between $100,000-$200,000, Jeffrey Katzenberg putting the touch on contributors for $500,000 plus; Mark Gilbert, $500,000 plus; and Mark Stanley, $100,000 to $200,000.

Obama's fund raising and organizational success among Israeli right wingers and US Zionists multiplied following his UN speech opposing the recognition of Palestine. As *The New York Times* noted: ". . . Democratic officials maintain that they do not think that Mr. Obama is in danger of losing the Jewish vote—particularly given the President's muscular defense of Israel at the United Nations General Assembly last week".[75]

Following his UN speech Obama raised several million from wealthy Zionists in Manhattan and Hollywood at dinners ranging up to $35,800 a plate. The extremist right wing Israeli Foreign Minister, Avigdor Lieberman (influential among billionaire US Zionists), signaled his enthusiastic support for Obama, as did Abe Foxman, the notorious Israeli Firster and head of the Anti-Defamation League, and former-New York City Mayor Ed Koch, another fanatical-Zionist. Thanks to pro-Israel bundlers and hustlers, Obama had out-fundraised the leading Republican candidate, former Massachusetts Governor Mitt Romney, by more than a 4 to 1 margin by September 2011.[76]

The Consequences of Obama's Embrace of Netanyahu and Rejection of World Opinion

Immediately following Obama's UN speech, Netanyahu announced that Israel would build 1,100 new 'Jews-only' housing units in occupied Arab East Jerusalem with additional plans to displace tens of thousands of Bedouins from their villages to make way for new Jewish settlements. With firm assurances that American Zionist Jews have the American Presidency and Congress in their pocket, Netanyahu feels free to advance his long-stated policy of ethnic cleansing. Violent extremist Jewish colonial settlers, funded by millionaire US donors to Obama, feel free to continue their practice of defacing and burning mosques and subjecting Palestinians to daily humiliations. The US Congress and AIPAC wrote legislation eliminating S200 million dollars in funding to the Palestinian Authority because of its 'crime' of seeking admission for the Palestinian people to the United Nations. Obama's "muscular" knee bends for Israel at the UN have opened the door to more intense and brutal Israeli aggression against the Palestinians, new military threats toward Iran and increased pressure on Egypt's military rulers.

The White House's goal is to raise a billion dollars for the re-election campaign. This involves keeping the spigot open for big bucks from Zionist millionaires in Hollywood and Silicon Valley, as well as from smaller contributors among lawyers, dentists, doctors, professors and local business people in Florida, Pennsylvania, Ohio and elsewhere. Obama's strategy at the UN is designed to maximize Zionist loyalty and fundraising for his re-election. The White House has organized a campaign to *delay* any Security Council decision, removing the Palestinian issue from the limelight and putting it behind closed doors via procedural haggling. At the same time, Washington is pressuring Security Council members, especially Bosnia and Colombia, to block a three-fifths majority vote, which would then force the US to use its veto. If the White House does not secure the votes, Obama has promised Zionist fundraisers he will use the US veto to exclude Palestine from admission to the UN.

Obama will focus on his power to use the UN veto in order to increase fundraising among wealthy Zionists and to activate the Presidents of the 52 Major American Jewish Organizations to "get out the vote" among the electorate at large. The re-election campaign will remind Zionist mass media pundits (*CNN, FOX, CBS, NBC*) of how Obama "courageously stood up to" world public opinion—including that of leaders representing 90% of the world's population—in order to "defend Israel".

If foreign policy is an extension of domestic policy, as is clearly illustrated by Obama's truckling to Zionist fundraisers by acting on behalf of Israel in the United Nations, so too is domestic policy an extension of foreign policy. US overseas businesses cannot expect any "favored treatment" in

Muslim countries. Increased political hostility to the US and Israel will result in greater military spending leading to more fiscal deficits and more painful cuts in domestic social programs for the American people. This will increase domestic social and political polarization. In the short-run, Obama's sell-out to the Zionist power configuration has succeeded in filling the coffers of his re-election campaign. But in the near future it has raised insurmountable difficulties in dealing with overseas political conflicts and domestic economic crises.

Above all, Obama's game of mutual manipulation with the Zionist Lobby has further degraded US democratic political institutions and our international standing as a free and independent country.

The Freeing of Jonathan Pollard and Obama's Re-election: The Dirtiest Quid Pro Quo

In his gross servility to Israel and the American Zionist Lobby, President Barak Obama has surpassed all four of his predecessors with regard to the most egregious episode in Israel's many violations of US security. According to recent news reports, Vice-President Joe Biden announced that "President Obama was considering clemency for Jonathan Pollard".[77] While Biden originally claimed to have initially opposed this move, a week later, under intense pressure from Obama, he agreed to meet and discuss Pollard's release with American Jewish leaders, including the executive vice chairman of the Presidents of the Major American Jewish Organizations, Malcolm Hoenlein.[78]

Reagan, Bush-Senior and Junior and Clinton, all refused to reopen the Pollard case because the confessed American spy for Israel (who was awarded Israeli citizenship and a high military rank while in US Federal prison) did more damage to US national security than any spy in our history. At his trial, the FBI and Naval Intelligence revealed that Pollard, then a High Security Naval Intelligence analyst, had turned over tens of thousands of classified documents to his Israeli handler. Many were 'sold' to the Soviet Union. For his 'service to the Jewish State of Israel', a building, illegally built in occupied Arab East Jerusalem, is named Beit Yonatan.

All Israeli leaders, from Rabin to Netanyahu, have pressed US presidents to free their spy. But threats of mass protests and resignation from the US intelligence community prevented any serious discussion of releasing the traitor. Now, the entire spectrum of Zionist opinion from 'left to right'—from 'liberal' Congressman Barney Frank to extremist Israel Firster, Alan Dershowitz of Harvard, and including hundreds of rabbis—are pressuring Obama to free their 'hero'. Only a few prominent American Jews, like former US Navy Admiral Shapiro, are outraged and chagrined by the "Jewish Community's defense of a traitor".

ISRAELI BOMBERS:
AL QAEDA'S AIR FORCE

Introduction

Israel has committed repeated acts of war against countries that opposed its Zionist policies of colonization and annexation of Palestinian territory in East Jerusalem and the West Bank. Israeli leaders have secured arms and diplomatic support for their attacks through their Zionist proxies in the United States Congress and the Executive Branch.

The current series of Israeli bombing raids and missile strikes against Syria[79] are designed to strengthen the armed Syrian opposition and Islamist mercenaries seeking to destroy the government in Damascus. Israel intends to sabotage the upcoming round of peace negotiations. The Zionist state does not want a peaceful resolution to the current regional conflict. Its foreign policy depends on perpetual regional wars and political instability. Toward this end, Tel Aviv has the unconditional support of the 52 Presidents of the Major American Jewish Organization and all other Zionist organizations in the US.

Armed Conflict and Intervention in Syria

Since March 2011, Syria has increasingly been transformed into a battleground and humanitarian disaster. At first, there were domestic Syrian political and social organizations staging protests against the Ba'athist government. The early protestors included secular liberals, Muslims, democrats and socialists. They had engaged in mostly peaceful protest against the authoritarian, but multi-cultural, secular regime of Bashar al-Assad. The government clamped down heavily and arrested many protestors. This heavy-handed response helped to split the Syrian opposition. Peaceful civil society protestors remained in the country, although diminished in numbers, while many others went underground or fled to bordering countries and formed the early core of the armed opposition. They received military and financial support from NATO countries and Turkey, as well as from the corrupt Gulf Monarchies, especially Saudi Arabia. A cross-border war was launched in which

US and European special military forces played a leading role in organizing, training and directing a makeshift collection of armed Syrian groups. Turkey provided arms, training camps and logistical support. The funding came from the rich kingdoms of Saudi Arabia and the Gulf Monarchies, which have spent hundreds of millions of dollars. The Saudis recruited radical Islamist and Al Qaeda mercenaries and Wahhabi terrorists to fight the Damascus regime— targeting secular Syrians, Shiites, Alawites, Syrian Christians and Kurds.

In just a few years, the conflict underwent a radical change in character and in intensity from internal broad-based civil strife to an armed foreign-backed invasion with vicious sectarian overtones. Hundreds of thousands of Syrians fled from their home when thousands of mostly foreign, Islamist fighters attacked and occupied their cities, towns and villages, conducting campaigns of ethnic cleansing against non-Sunni and non-Arab Syrians. The government in Damascus responded by mobilizing ground troops and its air force to recover its vital highways and cities, and drive out this increasingly foreign occupation. This became especially critical toward the end of 2012, when Al Qaeda-linked extremists funded by the Saudi and Gulf monarchies gained ascendancy at a number of key fronts. These violent extremists overran and displaced the Western-backed 'internal' armed opposition who made up the so-called 'moderates'. The Saudi proxies attacked Kurdish militias in the semi-autonomous Syrian northeast in order to secure cross border supply routes to Iraq, thus regionalizing the war. This heralded a tremendous increase in terrorism and bombing against the Shiite government in Baghdad and majority Shia population.

As the Western-backed opposition retreated, the mercenaries linked to Al Qaeda fully expected their sponsors among the despotic Saudi oil billionaires to call on NATO and the US to launch missile strikes against the Syrian government. Without US and NATO air support, the jihadis would never take Damascus.

Meanwhile, the Islamist Turkish government had been playing a duplicitous role by allowing its border area to be used for terrorist camps, supply routes and a launch site for cross-border attacks against its neighbor. This has been very unpopular with the Turkish public. When it became evident that the Saudi-backed Al Qaeda terrorists were gaining the upper hand over Ankara's more 'moderate' Islamist Syrian clients, the Turks may have developed concerns that their border would become a regional center for Al Qaeda, with thousands of well-armed, battle-tested Islamist mercenaries. This may explain Ankara's recent approach to Teheran hoping to undercut the jihadi clients of the Gulf Monarchies.

With the Syrian opposition badly split and the US domestic opposition to a new war increasing, the US-NATO regimes withdrew their commitment to the Saudis to act as 'Al Qaeda's Air Force'. Faced with Congressional resistance due to public outrage at the prospect of further military engagement, US President Obama eagerly accepted Russian President Putin's offer to jointly oversee the dismantlement of Syria's chemical weapons stockpile rather than to make a missile strike on Syria in putative reprisal for its alleged use of chemical weapons, and to set up a peace conference between Syrian opposition factions not linked to Al Qaeda and the Syrian government.

Chemical Weapons, Disarmament and Peace: Who's in and Who's Out?

The Putin-Obama agreement was a significant advance for the US and Russia. President Obama did not have to face massive domestic and Congressional opposition to a new war with Syria and he was 'credited' with accepting a diplomatic solution. Russian President Vladimir Putin assumed the role of a world statesman in initiating the process, ensuring Syrian compliance and moving the parties toward a peace conference in Geneva to be held in late November. The European Union and the NATO powers were able to temporarily disentangle from their military commitments to the Syrian 'rebels' and their Saudi backers, and express their own indignation over US cyber-spying of their citizens and leaders. Furthermore, this gave the Obama Administration the opportunity to make a breakthrough in nuclear negotiations with Iran. Turkey, which had been flooded by desperate Syrian refugees, was facing rising nationalist pressures against its own military role in the Syrian 'civil war'. The Russian initiative allowed the Turks to further explore re-opening relations with Syria's ally, Iran.

This advance toward peace and disarmament weakened the military ambitions of the despotic Saudi regime and threatened the hegemonic position of the Israeli junta. The Saudi-Gulf States strategy had been to destroy the secular Syrian state via a mercenary Al Qaeda ground war supported by massive NATO-US air strikes against Damascus. The Saudis envisioned a replay of the Libyan invasion that saw the overthrow of the secular Gaddafi. A bloody jihadist victory in Damascus would strike a blow at Iran, the Saudis' (and the Israelis') ultimate target.

The US-Russian rapprochement and Obama's withdrawal of his threat to bomb Damascus had deprived the Saudi's Al Qaeda mercenaries of their long-awaited Western missile support. Across the Atlantic, in a fit of pique and high-pitched hysteria at NATO's refusal to serve as 'Al Qaeda's air force' for their pet mercenaries, the Saudis refused to sit take their appointed seat 'with the infidels' on the UN Security Council!

However, Israel was quick to step in with its own bombs and missiles to bolster the Islamist terrorists in Syria!

Israel viewed itself as a casualty of the Obama-Putin agreement; it had been clamoring for more overt Western involvement in the war against

Syria. Israel's strategy was to encourage the armed conflict, decimate the Syrian government, society and economy, and create a new client configuration composed of 'Egypt-Jordan-Syria' under joint Saudi-Israeli- US auspices (and financing).

The Israelis had expected US President Obama to unleash a massive NATO air strike against Syrian military installations, arms depots and vital civilian infrastructure. This would tip the military balance in favor of the armed Syrian opposition and foreign jihadist mercenaries, and precipitate the collapse of Damascus. Indeed the entire US Jewish-Zionist power structure, including the pro-Israel media troika (*The New York Times, Washington Post* and *Wall Street Journal*), called for the US to bomb Syria despite the fact that the majority of America citizens were increasingly vocal in their opposition to US involvement!

When Obama finally took note of US public opinion and embraced Vladimir Putin's proposal for Syrian peace and the dismantling of its chemical weapons arsenal, the media troika and the ZPC unleashed hysterical attacks, accusing President Obama of vacillation (for disobeying Netanyahu?), sacrificing Syrian lives (what about the Syrian victims of Israel's occupation of the Golan Heights?) and of betraying the 'rebels' (also known as Al Qaeda terrorists).

Israel and Saudi Arabia make logical 'allies': Both are sworn enemies of secular Arab nationalism and anti-colonialism; both have sponsored overseas terrorist groups against their opponents; both seek to destroy Iran and both are completely dependent on Western arms relying on imperialist wars to achieve their own regional aims. At the moment their plans for 're-drawing the map' of the Middle East has met a speed-bump in the form of Obama's reluctance to launch US missiles and bombs against Damascus.

The Israeli Air Force at the Service of Al Qaeda

In recent years Israel has committed numerous acts of war throughout the Middle East, including crimes against humanity in Gaza, the West Bank and Lebanon. It is no surprise that Israel, a colonial state and would-be regional hegemon, would bomb Syrian military bases and weapon depots on six occasions in 2013, despite the fact that Damascus was struggling for its survival against thousands of Saudi-financed Al Qaeda-linked mercenaries.

Israel's deliberate and unprovoked attacks against the beleaguered Syrian state are motivated by dangerous, sinister and cynical considerations on the part of Tel Aviv.

First, while Israel may dream of a client Saudi regime in Syria to counter the secular Ba'athists as well as their Shiite allies in Lebanon and Iran, they are willing to settle for the destruction of an adversary, despite the risks posed by having a strong Wahhabi/Al-Qaeda presence in the region. Their attacks against the Syrian military show their desire for the terrorists to continue ravaging Syrian cities and towns. This is essentially a tactical alliance between extremist Zionist-Jews and radical Sunni Muslims.

Second, Israel is calculating that its missile attacks against Syrian bases will provoke an armed response from Damascus which Tel Aviv could use as a pretext to declare war and unite the 'hawk and dove' Zionists in Israel, and especially in the US, to mobilize against another 'existential threat' to the 'Jewish State'. In other words, Israel intends to prod the US Congress and White House to launch an 'allied' bombing campaign against Damascus.

Thirdly, Tel Aviv views its missile strikes and bombing raids against Syria as a 'dress rehearsal' for its planned attack on Iran. In the context of Iranian President Rouhani's recent peace overtures toward the US, bombing Syria and provoking Damascus would scuttle any peaceful accord between the Washington and Teheran.

Israeli pilots are using Syria as a laboratory to test radar and communications, flight patterns, its bombing accuracy, interception technology and assets to further their readiness for a pre-emptive attack on Iran. The purpose for attacking the Syrian government and destroying defensive weapons destined for its Lebanese Shiite ally, Hezbollah, is to destroy any Lebanese capacity to resist Israeli aggression in a regional conflagration.

However, Israel's military-driven 'diplomacy' has failed. And yet the Jewish state refuses to reverse its brutal, colonial policies in the West Bank, re-think its working alliance with Al Qaeda in the Levant or formulate a realistic political settlement with Syria and Iran. Instead, the characteristic failure and mediocrity of Israeli policymakers have condemned them to rely exclusively on their first, last and only resort—greater brutality and aggression.

Netanyahu showed his disappointment with Obama by announcing the construction of 1500 new 'Jews-only' apartments in Occupied Palestinian East Jerusalem. Meanwhile, the Israeli Foreign Office denounced the Obama Administration for having revealed that Israeli planes and missiles had struck the major Syrian port of Latakia[80]—implying that Washington's revelation of Israel's attempted sabotage of the peace talks amounted to a 'betrayal' or 'crime' against the Jewish state!

The entire Zionist power configuration in Washington has lined up to support the Jewish state. When Israel commits an act of war against its neighbor, no matter how unjust and brutal the act, Zionists from the most religious to the most secular, the 'peaceniks' and neo-cons, all form a united chorus in praise of the righteous and moral 'Jewish Bombs' even as they fall on the besieged people of Syria today and Iran tomorrow. While the pro-Israel media troika in the US doesn't hesitate to denounce civilian suffering from Pentagon and CIA drones strikes in Pakistan, when Israeli missiles rain on Syria ... acts of pre-emptive war by the heirs of the Holocaust ... they are described as necessary for the defense of a peace-loving nation ... because Bibi Netanyahu said so!

Rank cant and mendacious special pleadings aside, the Saudis and their Israeli allies intend to finance, arm and serve as Al Qaeda's air force against the Assad regime in Syria. They mean to undermine any Syrian or Iranian peace process, that is, unless the US and Russia prevent them from provoking a major regional conflagration, threatening the welfare of hundreds of millions of people.

Conclusion

The Middle East has always been a mosaic of complex and changing alliances, marking shifts in the balance of imperial power. During the past decade, the US, Israel, Saudi Arabia and their satraps in Jordan, Egypt and Lebanon have ruled the roosts. Iraq, as an independent modern secular nation and multicultural society, was shattered and under the US military boot; the Taliban were in retreat ... Iran was isolated ... Syria was surrounded by invading foreign armed and trained terrorists and mercenaries.

Time passed and again circumstances have changed. The US has been forced to retreat from the horrific sectarian conflict it created in Iraq, while Iran gained political influence and stature in the region. Turkey captured lucrative regional markets. In Afghanistan, the Taliban have recovered, advanced and are preparing to take power as soon as the US withdraws support from its lackey in Kabul. The White House temporarily lost a dictator Mubarak in Egypt, only to gain a new dictatorial client in General El-Sisi, but the junta in Cairo faces an uncertain future with massive popular unrest. The King of Jordan may still be on the CIA/Mossad payroll but that country is a backward satrapy forced to rely on police state tactics. The corrupt Gulf Monarchies repress their dissident majorities at home while using their countries' incredible oil wealth to subsidize jihadi terrorists abroad. Their legitimacy and support is fragile: petro-billions, bombs and US military bases do not constitute a state!

Tactical relations are in flux. The Saudi monarch rejects the UN, repudiates the US for its rapprochement with Iran and embraces—its own hot air. Surely the Saudis understand that siding with Israel's air force against an Arab nation is a dangerous and desperate ploy that could backfire.

The Syrian and Iranian governments will continue with their peace agendas, democratic openings and calls for social co-existence, such as Hezbollah has successfully secured in Lebanon. The Russians support their overtures. If they are successful, even the US and Europe would reap immense economic benefits from a demilitarized and sanctions-free Middle East and Persian Gulf. The world economy would see lower energy prices and greater security, while the flow of rentier capital to the speculators in the City of London and Wall Street would reverse and benefit their own countries. We stand at the crossroads between turning toward peace or reverting to regional war, crisis and chaos.

THE BLOODY ROAD TO DAMASCUS: THE TRIPLE ALLIANCE'S WAR ON A SOVEREIGN STATE

Introduction

There is clear and overwhelming evidence that the uprising to overthrow President Assad of Syria is a violent, power grab led by foreign-supported fighters who have killed and wounded thousands of Syrian soldiers, police and civilians, partisans of the government and its peaceful opposition. The support has been so extensively documented that there is a Wikipedia page, titled "Foreign Involvement in the Syrian War", addressing the details and sources.[81]

The outrage expressed by politicians in the West and Gulf State and in the mass media, about the *'killing of peaceful Syrian citizens protesting injustice'* is cynically designed to cover up the documented reports of violent seizure of neighborhoods, villages and towns by armed bands brandishing machine guns and planting road-side bombs.

The assault on Syria is backed by foreign funds, arms and training. Due to a lack of domestic support, however, to be successful, direct foreign military intervention will be necessary. For this reason a huge propaganda and diplomatic campaign has been mounted to demonize the legitimate Syrian government. The goal is to impose a puppet regime and strengthen Western imperial control in the Middle East. In the short run, this will further isolate Iran in preparation for a military attack by Israel and the US and, in the long run, it eliminates another independent secular regime friendly to China and Russia.

In order to mobilize world support behind this Western, Israeli and Gulf State-funded power grab, several propaganda ploys have been used to justify another blatant violation of a country's sovereignty after their successful destruction of the secular governments of Iraq and Libya.

The Larger Context: Serial Aggression

The current Western campaign against the independent Assad regime in Syria is part of a series of attacks against pro-democracy movements and independent regimes from North Africa to the Persian Gulf. The imperial-militarist response to the Egyptian democracy movement that overthrew the Mubarak dictatorship was to back the *military junta's* seizure of power in 2013 and its murderous campaign to jail, torture and assassinate over 5,000 Muslim Brotherhood followers whose ranks were subsequently swelled by pro-democracy protestors. Notably, the Muslim Brotherhood has maintained a policy of peaceful resistance, despite the imprisoning of its democratically elected leadership and the early slaughter and ongoing killing of its followers.[82]

Faced with similar mass democratic movements in the Arab world, the Western-backed Gulf autocratic dictators crushed their respective uprisings in Bahrain, Yemen and Saudi Arabia. The assaults extended to the secular government in Libya where NATO powers launched a massive air and sea bombardment in support of armed bands of mercenaries thereby destroying Libya's economy and civil society. The unleashing of armed gangster-mercenaries led to the savaging of urban life in Libya and devastation in the countryside. The NATO powers eliminated the secular regime of Colonel Gaddafi, along with having him murdered and mutilated by its mercenaries. NATO oversaw the wounding, imprisonment, torture and elimination of tens of thousands of civilian Gaddafi supporters and government workers. NATO backed the puppet regime as it embarked on a bloody pogrom against Libyan citizens of sub-Saharan African ancestry as well sub-Sahara African immigrant workers—groups who had benefited from Gaddafi's generous social programs. The imperial policy of ruin and rule in Libya serves as "the model" for Syria: creating the conditions for a mass uprising led by Muslim fundamentalists, funded and trained by Western and Gulf State mercenaries.

The Bloody Road from Damascus to Teheran

According to the State Department '*The road to Teheran passes through Damascus*': The strategic goal of NATO is to destroy Iran's principal ally in the Middle East; for the Gulf absolutist monarchies the purpose is to replace a secular republic with a vassal theocratic dictatorship; for the Turkish government the purpose is to foster a regime amenable to the dictates of Ankara's version of Islamic capitalism; for Al Qaeda and allied Salafi and Wahabi fundamentalists a theocratic Sunni regime, cleansed of secular Syrians, Alawis and Christians, will serve as a trampoline for projecting power in the Islamic world; and for Israel a blood-drenched divided Syria will further ensure its regional hegemony. The armed anti-Syrian forces reflect a variety of conflicting political perspectives united only by their common hatred of the independent secular, nationalist regime which has governed the complex, multi-ethnic Syrian society for decades. It is worth bearing in mind that some of this hatred for the Assad dynasty may have been with good reason. In 1982, to quell a Muslim Brotherhood uprising in the town of Hama, the Syrian army under Assad, Sr. perpetrated a massacre, killing some 20,000 persons, according to Robert Fisk.[83] Known for torture, Syria has for years served as a rendition destination for CIA abductees, the most publicized being the kidnapping of Canadian citizen Maher Arar,[84] an indication of Assad, Sr.'s tacit alliance with the US at that time. But while the initial peaceful protest against the Assad regime may have had legitimate grounds, it was then hijacked by foreign forces, as the war against Syria became the principal launching pad for Gulf –state hegemonism and a further resurgence of Western militarism extending from North Africa to the Persian Gulf, buttressed by a systematic propaganda campaign proclaiming NATO's democratic, humanitarian and 'civilizing' mission on behalf of the Syrian people.

The Road to Damascus is Paved with Lies

An objective analysis of the political and social composition of the principal armed combatants in Syria refutes any claim that the uprising is in pursuit of democracy for the people of that country. Authoritarian fundamentalist fighters form the backbone of the uprising. The Gulf States financing these brutal thugs are themselves *absolutist monarchies*. The West, after having foisted a brutal gangster regime on the people of Libya, can make no further claim of *'humanitarian intervention'*—for the time being, at least, insofar as there is a Canadian Center for the responsibility to Protect, a Global Center for the Responsibility to Protect, and another in Australia, if not more elsewhere. [85] Western academics are invested in the notion.

The armed groups infiltrate towns and use population centers as shields from which they launch their attacks on government forces. In the process they force thousands of citizens from their homes, stores and offices which they use as military outposts. The destruction of the neighborhood of Baba Amr in Homs is a classic case of armed gangs using civilians as shields and as propaganda fodder in demonizing the government.

These armed mercenaries have no national credibility with the mass of Syrian people. One of their main propaganda mills is located in the heart of London, the so-called "Syrian Human Rights Observatory" where it coordinates closely with British intelligence turning out lurid atrocity stories to whip up sentiment in favor of a NATO intervention. The kings and emirs of the Gulf States bankroll these fighters. Turkey provides military bases and controls the cross-border flow of arms and the movement of the leaders of the so-called "Free Syrian Army". The US, France and England provide the arms, training and diplomatic cover. Foreign jihadist-fundamentalists, including Al Qaeda fighters from Libya, Iraq and Afghanistan, have entered the conflict. This is no "civil war". This is an *international conflict* pitting an *unholy triple alliance* of NATO imperialists, Gulf State despots and Muslim fundamentalists against an independent secular nationalist regime. The foreign origin of the weapons, propaganda machinery and mercenary fighters reveals the sinister imperial, 'multinational' character of the conflict. Ultimately the violent uprising against the Syrian state represents a systematic imperialist campaign to overthrow an ally of Iran, Russia and China, even at the cost of destroying Syria's economy and civil society, fragmenting the country and unleashing enduring sectarian wars of extermination against the Alawi and Christian minorities, as well as secular government supporters.

The killings and mass flight of refugees is not the result of gratuitous violence committed by a blood thirsty Syrian state. The Western backed militias have seized neighborhoods by force of arms, destroyed oil pipelines, sabotaged transportation and bombed government buildings. In the course of their attacks they have disrupted basic services critical to the Syrian people including education, access to medical care, security, water, electricity and transportation. As such, they bear most of the responsibility for this "humanitarian disaster" (which their imperial allies and UN officials blame on Syrian security and armed forces). The Syrian security forces are fighting to preserve the national independence of a secular state, while the armed opposition commits violence on behalf of their foreign paymasters—in Washington, Riyadh, Tel Aviv, Ankara and London.

Conclusion

The Assad regime's constitutional referendum held in February, 2012 drew millions of Syrian voters in defiance of Western imperialist threats and terrorist calls for a boycott. This clearly indicated that a majority of Syrians prefer a peaceful, negotiated settlement and reject mercenary violence. The Western-backed Syrian National Council and the Turkish and Gulf States-armed "Free Syrian Army" flatly rejected Russian and Chinese calls for an open dialogue and negotiations which the Assad regime has accepted. NATO and Gulf State dictatorships are pushing their proxies to pursue violent "regime change", a policy which already has caused the death of thousands of Syrians. US and European economic sanctions are designed to wreck the Syrian economy, in the expectation that acute deprivation will drive an impoverished population into the arms of their violent proxies. Echoing the Libya and Iraq scenarios, NATO proposes to "liberate" the Syrian people by destroying their economy, civil society and secular state.

A Western military victory in Syria will merely feed the rising frenzy of militarism. It will encourage the West, Riyadh and Israel to provoke a new civil war in Lebanon. After demolishing Syria, the Washington-EU-Riyadh-Tel

Aviv axes will move on to a far bloodier confrontation with Iran.

The horrific destruction of Iraq, followed by Libya's post-war collapse provides a terrifying template of what is in store for the people of Syria: A precipitous collapse of their living standards, the fragmentation of their country, ethnic cleansing, rule by sectarian and fundamentalist gangs, and total insecurity of life and property.

Just as the "left" and "progressives" declared the brutal savaging of Libya to be the *"revolutionary struggle of insurgent democrats"* and then walked away, washing their hands of the bloody aftermath of ethnic violence against black Libyans, they repeat the same calls for military intervention against Syria. The same liberals, progressives, socialists and Marxists who are calling on the West to intervene in Syria's *"humanitarian crisis"* from their cafes and offices in Manhattan and Paris, will lose all interest in the bloody orgy of their victorious mercenaries after Damascus, Aleppo and other Syrian cities have been bombed by NATO into submission.

Saudi Arabia: A Retrograde Rentier Dictatorship and Global Terrorism

Introduction

Saudi Arabia has all the vices and none of the virtues of an oil rich state like Venezuela. The country is governed by a family dictatorship which tolerates no opposition and severely punishes human rights advocates and political dissidents. Hundreds of billions in oil revenues are controlled by the royal despotism and fuel speculative investments the world over. The ruling elite relies on the purchase of Western arms and US military bases for protection. The wealth of productive nations is syphoned to enrich the conspicuous consumption of the Saudi ruling family. The ruling elite finances the most fanatical, retrograde, misogynist version of Islam, the "Wahhabi" sect of Sunni Islam.

Faced with internal dissent from repressed subjects and religious minorities, the Saudi dictatorship perceives threats and dangers from all sides: externally, secular nationalists and Shia ruling governments; internally, moderate Sunni nationalists, democrats and feminists; within the royalist cliques, traditionalists and modernizers. In response it has turned toward financing, training and arming an international network of Islamic terrorists who are directed toward attacking, invading and destroying regimes opposed to the Saudi clerical-dictatorial regime.

The mastermind of the Saudi terror network is Bandar bin Sultan, who has longstanding and deep ties to high level US political, military and intelligence officials. Bandar was trained and indoctrinated at Maxwell Air Force Base and Johns Hopkins University and served as Saudi Ambassador to the US for over two decades (1983-2005). Between 2005-2011 he was Secretary of the National Security Council, and in 2012 he was appointed as Director General of the Saudi Intelligence Agency. Early on Bandar became deeply immersed in clandestine terror operations, working in liaison with the CIA. Among his numerous "dirty operations" with the CIA during the 1980s, Bandar channeled $32 million dollars to the Nicaragua Contras engaged in a terror campaign to overthrow the revolutionary Sandinista government in Nicaragua. During his tenure as ambassador he was actively engaged in protecting Saudi royalty with ties to Osama bin Laden, accused of the 9/11 bombing of the Triple Towers and the Pentagon. Suspicion that Bandar and his allies in the Royal family had prior knowledge of the bombings by Saudi terrorists (11 of the 19) is suggested by the sudden flight of Saudi Royalty following the terrorist act. US intelligence documents regarding the Saudi-Bandar connection are under Congressional review.

With a wealth of experience and training in running clandestine terrorist operations, derived from his two decades of collaboration with the US intelligence agencies, Bandar was in a position to organize his own global terror network in defense of the isolated retrograde and vulnerable Saudi despotic monarchy.

Bandar's Terror Network

Bandar bin Sultan has transformed Saudi Arabia from an inward-looking, tribal based regime totally dependent on US military power for its survival to a major regional center of a vast terror network, as an active financial backer of rightwing military dictatorships (Egypt) and client regimes (Yemen) and military intervener in the Gulf region (Bahrain). Bandar has financed and armed a vast array of clandestine terror operations, utilizing Islamic affiliates of Al Qaeda, the Saudi controlled Wahhabi sect and numerous other Sunni armed groups. Bandar is a "pragmatic" terrorist operator: repressing Saudi Arabia's Al Qaeda adversaries in Saudi Arabia while financing Al Qaeda terrorists in Iraq, Syria, Afghanistan and elsewhere. While Bandar was a long-term asset of the US intelligence services, he has, more recently, taken an 'independent course' where the regional interests of the despotic state diverge from those of the US. In the same vein, while Saudi Arabia has a longstanding enmity toward Israel, Bandar has developed a "covert understanding" and working relation with the Netanyahu regime, around their common enmity toward Iran and, more specifically, in opposition to the interim agreement between the Obama-Rouhani regimes.

Bandar has intervened directly or via proxies in reshaping political alignments, destabilizing adversaries and bolstering and expanding the political reach of the Saudi dictatorship from North Africa to South Asia, from the Russian Caucuses to the Horn of Africa, sometimes in concert with Western imperialism, other times projecting Saudi hegemonic aspirations.

North Africa: Tunisia, Morocco, Libya and Egypt

Bandar has poured billions of dollars to bolster the rightwing pro-Islamic regimes in Tunisia and Morocco, ensuring that the mass pro-democracy movements would be repressed, marginalized and demobilized. Islamic extremists receiving Saudi financial support are encouraged to back the "moderate" Islamists in government by assassinating secular democratic leaders and socialist trade union leaders in opposition. Bandar's policies largely coincide with those of the US and France in Tunisia and Morocco, but not in Libya and Egypt.

Saudi financial backing for Islamist terrorists and Al Qaeda affiliates against Libyan President Gaddafi were in line with the NATO air war. However divergences emerged in the aftermath: the NATO backed client regime made up of neoliberal ex-pats faced off against Saudi backed Al Qaeda and Islamist terror gangs and assorted tribal gunmen and marauders. Bandar-funded Islamic extremists in Libya were bankrolled to extend their military operations to Syria, where the Saudi regime was organizing a vast military operation to overthrow the Assad regime. The internecine conflict between NATO and Saudi armed groups in Libya spilled over and led to the Islamist murder of the US Ambassador and CIA operatives in Benghazi. Having overthrown Gaddafi, Bandar virtually abandoned interest in the ensuing blood bath and chaos provoked by his armed assets. They in turn, became self-financing—robbing banks, pilfering oil and emptying local treasuries—relatively "independent" of Bandar's control.

In Egypt, Bandar developed, in coordination with Israel (but for different reasons), a strategy of undermining the relatively independent, democratically elected Muslim Brotherhood regime of Mohammed Morsi. Bandar and the Saudi dictatorship financially backed the military coup and dictatorship of General El-Sisi. The US strategy of a power-sharing agreement between the Muslim Brotherhood and the military regime, combining popular electoral legitimacy and the pro-Israel/pro NATO military, was sabotaged. With a $15 billion aid package and promises of more to come, Bandar provided the Egyptian military a financial lifeline and economic immunity from any international financial reprisals. None were taken of any consequences. The military crushed the Brotherhood, jailed and threatened to execute its elected leaders. It outlawed sectors of the liberal-left opposition which it had used as cannon fodder to justify its seizure of power. In backing the military coup, Bandar eliminated a rival, democratically elected Islamic regime which stood in contrast to the Saudi despotism. He secured a like-minded dictatorial regime in a key Arab country, even though the military rulers are more secular, pro-Western, pro-Israel and less anti-Assad than the Brotherhood regime. Bandar's success in greasing the wheels for the Egyptian coup secured a political ally but faces an uncertain future.

The revival of a new anti-dictatorial mass movement would also target the Saudi connection. Moreover Bandar undercut and weakened Gulf State unity: Qatar had financed the Morsi regime and was out $5 billion dollars it had extended to the previous regime.

Bandar's terror network is most evident in his long-term large scale financing, arming, training and transport of tens of thousands of Islamic terrorist "volunteers" from the US, Europe, the Middle East, the Caucasus, North Africa and elsewhere. Al Qaeda terrorists inside Saudi Arabia became "martyrs of Islam" inside Syria. Dozens of Islamic armed gangs in Syria competed for Saudi arms and funds. Training bases with US and European instructors and Saudi financing were established in Jordan, Pakistan and Turkey. Bandar financed the major 'rebel' Islamic terrorist armed group, the Islamic State of Iraq and the Levant, for cross border operations.

With Hezbollah supporting Assad, Bandar directed money and arms to the Abdullah Azzam Brigades in Lebanon to bomb Hezbollah-dominated South Beirut, the Iranian embassy and Tripoli. Bandar directed $3 billion to the Lebanese military with the idea of fomenting a new civil war between it and Hezbollah. In co-ordination with France and the US, but with far greater funding and greater latitude to recruit Islamic terrorists, Bandar assumed the leading role and became the principal director of a three front military and diplomatic offensive against Syria, Hezbollah and Iran. For Bandar, an Islamic takeover in Syria would lead to an Islamic Syrian invasion in support of Al Qaeda in Lebanon to defeat Hezbollah in hopes of isolating Iran. Teheran would then become the target of a Saudi-Israeli-US offensive. Bandar's strategy is more fantasy than reality.

Bandar Diverges from Washington: the Offensive in Iraq and Iran

Saudi Arabia has been an extremely useful but sometimes out of control client of Washington. This is especially the case since Bandar has taken over as Intelligence chief: a long-time asset of the CIA he has also, at times, taken the liberty to extract "favors" for his services, especially when those "favors" enhance his upward advance within the Saudi power structure. Hence, for example, his ability to secure AWACs despite AIPAC opposition earned him merit points. As did Bandar's ability to secure the departure of several hundred Saudi 'royalty' with ties to the 9/11 bombers, despite a high level national security lockdown in the aftermath of the bombing.

While there were episodic transgressions in the past, Bandar moved on to more serious divergences from US policy. He went ahead, building his own terror network, directed toward maximizing Saudi hegemony—even where it conflicted with US proxies, clients and clandestine operatives.

While the US is committed to backing the rightwing Maliki regime in Iraq, Bandar is providing political, military and financial backing to the Sunni terrorist "Islamic State of Iraq and Syria". When the US negotiated the "interim agreement" with Iran, Bandar voiced his opposition and "bought" support. Saudi Arabia signed off on a billion dollar arms agreement during

French President Hollande's visit in exchange for French Foreign Minister Laurent Faubius' attempt to forestall completion of nuclear negotiations with Iran by walking out. Bandar also expressed support for Israel's use of the Zionist power configuration to influence the Congress to sabotage US negotiations with Iran.

Bandar has moved beyond his original submission to US intelligence handlers. His close ties with past and present US and EU presidents and political influentials have encouraged him to engage in "Big Power adventures". He met with Russian President Putin to convince him to drop his support for Syria, offering a carrot or a stick: a multi-billion dollar arms sale for compliance and a threat to unleash Chechen terrorists to undermine the Sochi Olympics, if not. He has turned Erdogan from a NATO ally supporting 'moderate' armed opponents to Bashar al-Assad, into embracing the Saudi backed al Qaeda affiliate, the Islamic State of Iraq and Syria. Bandar has "overlooked" Erdogan's "opportunist" efforts to sign off on oil deals with Iran and Iraq, his continuing military arrangements with NATO and his past backing of the defunct Morsi regime in Egypt, in order to secure Erdogan's support for the easy transit of large numbers of Saudi trained terrorists to Syria and probably Lebanon.

Bandar has strengthened ties with the armed Taliban in Afghanistan and Pakistan, arming and financing their armed resistance against the US, as well as offering the US a site for a 'negotiated departure'.

Bandar is probably supporting and arming Uighur Muslim terrorists in western China, and Chechens and Caucasian Islamic terrorists in Russia, *even as* the Saudis expand their oil agreements with China and cooperate with Russia's Gazprom.

The only region where the Saudis have exercised direct military intervention is in the Gulf min-state of Bahrain, where Saudi troops crushed the pro-democracy movement challenging the local despot.

Bandar: Global Terror on Dubious Domestic Foundations

Bandar has embarked on an extraordinary transformation of Saudi foreign policy and enhanced its global influence. All for the worse. Like Israel, when a reactionary ruler comes to power and overturns the democratic order, Saudi arrives on the scene with bags of dollars to buttress the regime. Whenever an Islamic terror network emerges to subvert a nationalist, secular or Shia regime, it can count on Saudi funds and arms. What some Western scribes euphemistically describe as "tenuous effort to liberalize and modernize" the retrograde Saudi regime, is really a military upgrade of its overseas terrorist activity. Bandar uses modern techniques of terror to impose the Saudi model of reactionary rule on neighboring and distant regimes with Muslim populations.

The problem is that Bandar's "adventurous" large scale overseas operations conflict with some of the ruling Royal family's "introspective" style of rulership. They want to be left alone to accrue hundreds of billions collecting petrol rents, to invest in high-end properties around the world, and to quietly patronize high end call girls in Washington, London and Beirut—while posing as pious guardians of Medina, Mecca and the Holy sites. So far Bandar has not been challenged, because he has been careful to pay his respects to the ruling monarch and his inner circle. He has bought and brought Western and Eastern prime ministers, presidents and other respectable notables to Riyadh to sign deals and pay compliments to the delight of the reigning despot.

Yet his solicitous behavior to overseas Al Qaeda operations, his encouraging Saudi extremists to go overseas and engage in terrorist wars, disturbs monarchical circles. They worry that Saudis trained, armed and knowledgeable terrorists—dubbed as "holy warriors"—may return from Syria, Russia and Iraq to bomb the King's palaces and establish a very different kind of Islam than the formalist Wahhabism presently enforced by the Saudi monarchy. Moreover, oversea regimes targeted by Bandar's terror network may retaliate: Russia or Iran, Syrians, Egyptians, Pakistanis, Iraqis may just sponsor their own instruments of retaliation. Despite the hundreds of billions spent on arms purchases, the Saudi regime is very vulnerable on all levels. Apart from tribal legions, the billionaire elite have little popular support and even less legitimacy. It depends on overseas migrant labor, foreign "experts" and US military forces. The Saudi elite is also despised by the most religious of the Wahhabi clergy for allowing "infidels" on sacred terrain. While Bandar extends Saudi power abroad, the domestic foundations of rule are narrowing. While he defies US policymakers in Syria, Iran and Afghanistan, the regime depends on the US Air Force and Seventh Fleet to protect it from a growing array of adversarial regimes.

Bandar, with his inflated ego, may believe that he is building a new Islamic empire, but in reality, by waving one finger his patron monarch can lead to his rapid dismissal. One too many provocative civilian bombings by his Islamic terrorist beneficiaries can provoke an international crisis leading to Saudi Arabia becoming the target of world opprobrium.

In reality, Bandar bin Sultan is the protégé and successor of Bin Laden; he has deepened and systematized global terrorism. Bandar's terror network has murdered far more innocent victims than Bin Laden. That, of course, is to be expected; after all he has billions of dollars from the Saudi treasury, training from the CIA and the handshake of Netanyahu!

Iran-US Interim Agreement: Historic Breakthrough or Historic Sellout?

Introduction

The recent interim accord between the six world powers and Iran has been hailed as an "historic breakthrough", a "significant accomplishment" by most leading politicians, editorialists and columnists,[86] the exceptions being notably Israeli leaders and the Zionist power brokers in North America and Western Europe.[87]

What constitutes this "historic breakthrough"? Who got what? Did the agreement provide for symmetrical concessions? Does the interim agreement strengthen or weaken the prospects for peace and prosperity in the Gulf and the Middle East? To address these and other questions, one also has to include the powerful influence wielded by Israel on US and European policymakers.[88] Equally important, the current 'interim' agreement is just that—it is a first, limited agreement, which does not in any way spell out the strategic objectives of the major imperial powers. Any realistic appreciation of the significance of the interim agreement requires putting it into historical perspective.

The Historical Record: Past Precedents

For over a decade the major US intelligence agencies have published detailed accounts of Iran's nuclear program (see especially the National Intelligence Estimate 2007 (NIE)). The common consensus has been that Iran did not have any program for developing nuclear weapons (National Intelligence Estimate 2004, 2007). As a consequence of this 'absence of evidence', the entire Western offensive against Iran had to focus on Iran's "potential capacity" to shift sometime in the future towards a weapons program. The current agreement is directed toward undermining Iran's potential 'capacity' to have a nuclear weapons program: there are no weapons to destroy, no weapon plans exist, no war plans exist and there are no strategic offensive military operations on the Iranian 'drawing board'. We know this, because repeated US intelligence reports have told us that no weapons programs exist! So the entire current negotiations are really over weakening Iran's ongoing peaceful, legal nuclear program and undermining any future advance in nuclear technology that might protect Iran from an Israeli or US attack, when they decide to activate their "military option", similar to the pattern that marked the war to destroy Iraq.

Secondly, Iran's flexible and accommodating concessions are not new or a reflection of a newly elected President. As Gareth Porter has pointed out: nearly ten years ago, on November 15, 2004, Iran agreed "on a voluntary basis to continue and extend an existing suspension of enrichment to include all enrichment related and reprocessing activities".[89] According to Porter, Iran was ending "all manufacturing, assembly, installation and testing of centrifuges or their components". Despite these generous concessions, on March 2005, the Europeans and the US refused to negotiate on an Iranian proposal for a comprehensive settlement that would guarantee against enrichment toward weapons grade. Iran ended its voluntary suspension of all enrichment activity. The US, led by Zionists embedded in Treasury, (Stuart Levey) then escalated sanctions. Europe and the UN Security Council followed in kind. The practice of the US and Europe first securing major concessions from Iran and then refusing to reciprocate by pursuing a comprehensive settlement is a well established diplomatic practice. Iran's flexibility and concessions were apparently interpreted as "signs of weakness" to be exploited in their push toward 'regime change'.[90] Sanctions are seen as "effective" politico-diplomatic weapons designed to further weaken the regime. Policymakers continue to believe that sanctions should be maintained as a tool to divide the Iranian elite, disarm and dismantle the country's defensive capacity, and prepare for "regime change" or a military confrontation without fear of serious resistance from the Iranians.

The entire charade of Iran's 'nuclear weapons as a threat' has been orchestrated by the Israeli regime and its army of 'Israel Firsters' embedded in the US Executive, Congress and mass media. The 'Big Lie', promoted by Israel's propaganda machine and network of agents, has been repeatedly and thoroughly refuted by the sixteen major US Intelligence Estimates or NIE's, especially in 2004 and 2007. These consensus documents were based on extensive research, inside sources (spies) and highly sophisticated surveillance. The NIEs categorically state that Iran suspended all efforts toward a nuclear weapons program in 2003 and has not made any decision or move to restart that program. However, Israel has actively spread propaganda, based on fabricated intelligence reports, claiming the contrary in order to trick and push the US into a disastrous military confrontation with Israel's regional rival.

And the President of the United States ignores his own intelligence sources in order to repeat Israel's 'Big Lie'!

Given the fact that Iran is not a 'nuclear threat', now or in the past, and given that the US, European and Israeli leaders know this, why do they continue and even increase the sanctions against Iran? Why do they threaten to destroy Iran with pre-emptive attacks? Why the current demands for even more concessions from Teheran? The current negotiations and 'agreement' tell us a great deal about the 'ultimate' or final strategic aims of the White House and its European allies.

The 'Interim Agreement': A Most Asymmetrical Compromise

Iran's negotiators conceded to all the' 5 plus 1' major demands while they received the most minimum of concessions.[91]

Iran agreed to (1) stop all enrichment to 20 percent, (2) reduce the existing 20 percent enriched stockpile to zero, (3) convert all low enriched uranium to a form that cannot be enriched to a higher level, (4) halt progress on its enrichment capacity, (5) leave inoperable half of its centrifuges at Natanz and three-quarters of those at Fordow, and (6) freeze all activities at Arak heavy water facility which when built could produce plutonium. Iran also agreed to end any plans to construct a facility capable of reprocessing plutonium from spent fuel. The Iranian negotiators agreed to the most pervasive and intensive "inspections" of its most important strategic defense facilities by the International Atomic Energy Agency, which has been closely allied with the US and its EU counterparts. These "inspections" and data collection will take place on a daily basis and include access to Natanz and Fordow. The strategic military value of these inspections is inestimable because it could provide data, heretofore unavailable, for any future missile strike from the US or Israel when they decide to shift from negotiations to the 'military option'. In addition, the IAEA inspectors will be allowed to access other strategic facilities, including sites for developing centrifuges, uranium mines and mills. Future "negotiations" may open highly sensitive military defense sites such as Parchin, where conventional missiles and warheads are stored.

Obviously, there will not be any reciprocal inspections of the US missile sites, warships and military bases in the Persian Gulf, which store weapons of mass destruction aimed at Iran! Nor will the IAEA inspect Israel's nuclear weapons facilities in Dimona – despite Israeli threats to attack Iran. No comparable diminution of "military capacity" or nuclear weapons, aimed at Iran by some members of the '5 plus 1 and Israel' is included in this "historic breakthrough".

The '5 plus 1' conceded meager concessions: Unfreezing of 7% of Iranian-owned assets sequestered in Western banks ($7 billion of $100 billion) and 'allowing' Iran to enrich uranium to 5 percent—and even that "concession" is conditioned by the proviso that it does not exceed current stockpiles of 5% enriched uranium. While the Iranian negotiators claim they secured (*sic*) 'the right' to enrich uranium, the US refused to even formally acknowledge it!

In effect, Iran has conceded the maximum concessions regarding its strategic national defenses, nuclear facilities and uranium enrichment in what is supposedly the 'initial' round of negotiations, while 'receiving' the minimum of reciprocal concessions. This highly unfavorable, asymmetrical framework will lead the US to see Iran as 'ripe for regime change' and demand even more decisive concessions designed to further weaken Iran's defensive capacity. Future concessions will increase Iran's vulnerability to intelligence gathering and undermine its role as a regional power and strategic ally of the Lebanese Hezbollah, the current beleaguered governments in Syria and Iraq and the Palestinians under Israeli occupation.

The 'Final Settlement': Decline and Fall of the Islamic Nationalist Republic?

The real goals of the US sanctions policy and the recent decision to enter into negotiations with Iran have to do with several imperial objectives. The first objective is to facilitate the rise of a neoliberal regime in Iran, which would be committed to privatizing major oil and gas fields and attracting foreign capital even at the cost of strategic national defense.

President Rouhani is seen in Washington as the Islamic version of the former Russian President Mikhail Gorbachev. Rouhani, like his 'model' Gorbachev, 'gave away the store' while expecting Iran's imperial adversaries to reciprocate.

The '5 plus 1', mostly veterans of the 'imperial shakedown', will take all of Rouhani's concessions and demand even more! They will "allow" Iran to recover its own frozen assets in slow droplets, which the neoliberals in Teheran will celebrate as 'victories' even while the country stagnates under continued sanctions and the people suffer. The US Administration will retain sanctions in order to accommodate their Israeli-Zionist patrons and to provoke even deeper fissures in the regime. Washington's logic is that the more concessions Teheran surrenders, the more difficult it will be to reverse the process under public pressure from the Iranian people. This 'rift' between the conciliatory government of Rouhani and the Iranian people, according to CIA strategists, will lead to greater internal discontent in Iran and will further weaken the regime. A regime under siege will need to rely even more on their Western interlocutors. President Rouhani 'relying on the 5-plus-1' will be like the condemned leaning into the hangman's noose.

Rouhani and the Neoliberal Collaborators

The ascendancy of Rouhani to the Presidency brings in its wake an entire new politico-economic leadership intent on facilitating large-scale, long-term penetration by Western and Chinese oil and gas companies in the most lucrative sites. Iran's new oil minister, Bijan Namdar Zangeneh, has made overtures to all the oil majors, and offers to revise and liberalize the terms for investment and provide concessions designed to greatly enhance multinational profits in the most lucrative fields.[92] Zangeneh has kicked out the nationalists and replaced them with a cohort of liberal economists. He is preparing to eventually lay-off tens of thousands of public sector oil employees as an incentive to attract foreign corporate partners. He is prepared to lower fuel subsidies for the Iranian people and raise energy prices for domestic consumers. The liberals in power have the backing of millionaires, speculators and political power brokers, like Akbar Hashemi Rafsanjani, head of the key Expediency Council, which drafts policy. Many of Rafsanjani's followers have been appointed to key positions in President Rouhani's administration.[93]

Central to the 'Troika's (Rouhani-Rafsanjani-Zangeneh) strategy is securing the collaboration of multinational energy corporations. However that requires lifting the US-imposed sanctions against Iran in the shortest time possible. This explains the hasty, unseemly and one-sided Iranian concessions to the '5-plus-1'. In other words, the driving force behind Iran's giveaways is not the "success of sanctions" but the ascendancy to power of the Iranian comprador class and its neoliberal ideology which informs their economic strategy.

Several major obstacles confront the 'Troika'. The major concessions, initially granted, leave few others to concede, short of dismantling the entire nuclear energy infrastructure and lobotomizing its entire scientific and technical manpower, which would destroy the legitimacy of the regime. Secondly, having easily secured major concessions without lifting the sanctions, the '5-plus-1' are free to escalate their demands for further concessions, which in effect will deepen Iran's vulnerability to Western espionage, terrorism (the assassination of Iranian scientists and engineers) and preemptive attack. As the negotiations proceed it will become crystal clear that the US intends to force the 'Troika' to open the gates to more overtly pro-western elites in order to eventually polarize Iranian society.

The endgame is a weakened, divided, liberalized regime, vulnerable to internal and external threats and willing to cut off support to nationalist regimes in the Middle East, including Palestine, Iraq, Syria and Lebanon. The US recognized and seized upon the rise of the new neoliberal Rouhani regime and secured major unilateral concessions as a down payment to move step-by-step toward bloody regime change. Washington's "endgame" is the conversion of Iran to a client petrol-state allied with the Saudi-Israeli axis.

As far-fetched as that appears today, the logic of negotiations is moving in that direction.

The Israeli-US Differences: A Question of Tactics and Timing

Israeli leaders and their Zionist agents embedded in the US government howl, pull out their hair and bluster against the '5-plus-1' transitional agreement with Iran. They downplay the enormous one-sided concessions. They rant and rave about "hidden agenda", "deceit and deception". They fabricate conspiracies and repeat lies about secret "nuclear weapons programs" beyond the reach (and imagination) of any non-Zionist inspector. But the reality is that the "historic breakthrough" includes the dismantling of a major part of Iran's nuclear infrastructure, while retaining sanctions—a huge victory for the Zionists! The '5-plus-1' negotiated a deal which has secured deeper and more extensive changes in Iran while strengthening Western power in the Persian Gulf than all of Netanyahu's decade-long campaign of issuing 'military threats'.

Netanyahu and his brainwashed Zionist-Jewish defenders in the US insist on new, even harsher sanctions because they want immediate war and regime-change (to a puppet regime). Echoing his Israeli boss Netanyahu, New York Senator Chuck "the schmuck" Schumer, commenting on the interim agreement, brayed, "The disproportionality of this agreement makes it more likely that Democrats and Republicans will pass additional sanctions".[94] This is the same stupid policy that the embedded Zionists in Washington pursued with Iraq. Under the Bush Presidency, top neo-con Zionists like Wolfowitz, Ross, Indyk, Feith, Abrams and Libby, implemented Ariel Sharon's war dictates against Iraq: effectively, they 1) murdered Saddam Hussein (regime change); 2) destroyed Iraq's economy, society and modern infrastructure; and 3) provoked ethnic fragmentation and religious war—at a cost to the US of over 2 trillion dollars spent on the war, thousands of US lives (millions of Iraqi lives), and hundreds of billions in high oil prices to US consumers, further shattering the US domestic economy.

Among the few moderately intelligent and influential Zionist journalists who realizes the strategic value of the step-by-step approach of the Obama regime, Gideon Rachman has called for the White House "to take on the Israel lobby over Iran".[95] Rachman knows that if Israel's howling stooges in the US Congress drag the country into war, the American people will turn against the Israeli lobby, its fellow travelers and, most likely, Israel. Rachman and a few others with a grain of political sophistication know that the Rouhani regime in Tehran has just handed over key levers of power to the US. They know that the negotiations are moving toward greater integration of Iran into the US orbit. They know, in the final instance, that Obama's step-by-step diplomatic approach will be less costly and more effective than Netanyahu's military 'final solution'. And they know that, ultimately, Obama's and Israel's goal is the same: a weak neo-liberalized Iran, which cannot challenge Israel's military dominance, nuclear weapons monopoly, annexation of Palestine and aggression against Lebanon and Syria.

Conclusion

Having secured a "freeze" on Iran's consequential nuclear research and having on site intelligence on all Iran's major national defense and security facilities, the US can compile a data base for an offensive military strategy whenever it likes. Iran, on the other hand, receives no information or reports on US, European or Israeli military movement, weapons facilities or offensive regional capabilities. This is despite the fact that the '5-plus-1' countries and Israel have recently launched numerous devastating offensive military operations and wars in the region (Iraq, Afghanistan, Lebanon, Libya and Syria). Having set the agenda for negotiations as one of further unilateral concessions from Iran, the US can at any point, threaten to end negotiations – and follow up with its 'military option'.

The next step in the unilateral disarmament of Iran will be the US demand to close the strategic Arak heavy water plant. The US will demand that Iran produce a basic minimum amount of uranium and retain a stock pile to cover a few days or weeks for energy, research or medical isotopes. Washington will strip Iran of its capacity to enrich by imposing quantitative and qualitative limits on the centrifuges that Iran can possess and operate. During the next round of negotiations, the US will preclude Iran from undertaking the reprocessing of uranium at Arak or any other site. The US will tell 'the Troika' that the "right" (sic) to enrich does not extend to the right to reprocess. The US will demand stringent "transparency" for Iran, while maintaining its own high level secrecy, evasion and ambiguity with regard to its military, diplomatic and economic sanctions policy.

In a word, the US will demand that Iran surrender its sovereignty and subject itself to the colonial oversight of an imperial power, which has yet to make a single move in even reducing economic sanctions. The loss of sovereignty, the continued sanctions and the drive by the US to curtail Iran's regional influence will certainly lead to popular discontent in Iran – and a response from the nationalist and populist military (Revolutionary Guards) and the working poor. The crisis resulting from the Troika's adoption of the "Gorbachev Model" will lead to an inevitable confrontation. Overtime the US will seek out an Islamist strongman, an Iranian version of Yeltsin who can savage the nationalists and popular movements and turn over the keys to the state, treasury and oil fields to a "moderate and responsible" pro-Western client regime.

The entire US strategy of degrading Iran's military defenses and securing major neo-liberal "reforms" depends on President Rouhani remaining in power, which can only result from the Obama regime's compliance in lifting some of the oil and banking sanctions (FT 12/1/13, p. 6). Paradoxically, the greatest obstacle to achieving Washington's strategic roll-back goal is Netanyahu's power to block sanction relief – and impose even, harsher sanctions. The result of such an Israel Firster victory in the US would be the end of negotiations, the strengthening of Iran's nuclear program, the demise of the oil privatization program and added support to regional nationalist movements and governments. President Rouhani desperately needs western imperial reassurance of the benefits (sanction relief) of his initial giveaways. Otherwise his credibility at home would be irreparably damaged.

The imperial prize of a militarily weakened and neoliberalized Iran, collaborating in maintaining the status quo in the Middle East, is enormous but it still clashes with the Zionist Power Configuration, which insists on all power to the Jewish state from the Suez to the Persian Gulf!

THE ASSASSINATION
OF ANWAR AL-AWLAKI
BY FIAT

The killing of Anwar al-Awlaki a U.S citizen in Yemen by a CIA drone missile on September 30, 2011 was publicized by the mass media, President Obama and the usual experts on al-Qaeda as "a major blow to the jihadist network founded by Osama bin Laden" US officials called Awlaki "the most dangerous figure in Al-Qaeda".[96]

There is ample evidence to suggest that the publicity surrounding the killing of al-Awlaki greatly exaggerated his political importance and was an attempt to cover up the declining influence of the US in the Islamic world. The State Department's declaration of a major victory served to exaggerate US military capacity to defeat its adversaries. The assassination served to justify Obama's arbitrary use of death squads to execute overseas US critics and adversaries by executive fiat, denying the accused elementary judicial protections, contrary to international law. This instance was notable insofar as it concerned an American citizen. Shortly thereafter, al-Awlaki's 16 year old son, too, was killed by drone strike.

Myths About al-Awlaki

Al-Awlaki was an Islamist blogger in a small, poor Islamic country (Yemen). But before moving to Yemen, he had enjoyed frequent contact as a major media source (*National Geographic*, *The New York Times*) in relation to Islam, having condemned the 9/11 attacks, stating that "There is no way that the people who did this could be Muslim, and if they claim to be Muslim, then they have perverted their religion." *The New York Times* at that time claimed that al-Awlaki was "held up as a new generation of Muslim leaders capable of merging East and West."[97] In 2002, al-Awlaki was the first imam to conduct a prayer service for the Congressional Muslim Staffer Association at the US Capitol. While the 2002 PBC documentary, *Legacy of a Prophet*, includes a brief appearance of al-Awlaki, he left the US in that year, due to his perception of "a climate of fear and intimidation".[98]

In Yemen, Al-Awlaki was confined to propagandizing against Western countries, attempting to influence Islamic believers to resist Western military and cultural intervention. Within Yemen, his organizational affiliations were with a minority sector of the mass popular opposition to US backed dictator Ali Abdullah Saleh. His fundamentalist group was largely influential in a few small towns in southern Yemen. He was *not a military* or *political leader* in his organization, dubbed by the West as "Al-Qaeda in the Arabian Peninsula" (AQAP). Like most of what the CIA calls "Al-Qaeda", AQAP was a local autonomous organization, meaning that it was organized and controlled by local leaders even as it expressed agreement with many other loosely associated fundamentalist groups. Awlaki had a very limited role in the Yemeni groups' military and political operations and virtually no influence in the mass movement engaged in ousting Saleh. There is *no evidence*, documented or observable, that he was "a very effective propagandist" as ex-CIA and now Brookings Institution member Bruce Riedal claims. In Yemen and among the mass popular movements in Tunisia, Egypt, Bahrain or elsewhere his followers were few and far between. One "expert" cites such intangibles as his "spiritual leadership", which is as good a way as any to avoid the test of empirical evidence: apparently a crystal ball or a tarot read will do.

Given the paucity of evidence demonstrating Awlaki's political and ideological influence among the mass movements in North Africa, the Middle East or Asia, the US intelligence agencies claim his "real influence was among English-speaking jihadi, some of whom he groomed personally to carry out attacks on the US."

In other words Washington's casting Awlaki as an "important threat" revolves around his speeches and *writings*, since he had no *operational* role in organizing suicide bomb attacks—or at least no concrete evidence has been presented up to now.

The intelligence agencies "suspect" he was involved in the plot that dispatched bombs in cargo aircraft from Yemen to Chicago in October 2010. US intelligence claims he provided a "theological justification" via e-mail for US army Major Nidal Malik's killing of 13 people at Fort Hood. In other words, like many US philosophical writers and legal experts like Princeton's Michael Walzer and Harvard's Alan Dershowitz, Awlaki discussed "just wars" and the "right" of violent action. If political writings and speeches of publicists are cited by an assassin as the basis for their action, should the White House execute leading US Islamophobes like Marilyn Geller and Daniel Pipes, cited as inspiration by Norwegian mass murderer Anders Behring Brevik? Or does their Zionist affiliation provide them immunity from Navy Seal assaults and drone missiles?

Even assuming that the unsubstantiated "suspicions" of the CIA, MI6 and the Al Qaeda "experts" are correct and Awlaki had a direct or indirect hand in "terrorist action" against the US, these activities were absurdly amateurish and abject failures, certainly not a serious threat to US security. The "underwear bomber" Umar Farouk Abdul Mutallab's effort to ignite bomb materials on a flight to Detroit, December 25, 2009, led to his roasting his testicles! Likewise the bombs dispatched in cargo aircraft from Yemen to Chicago in October 2010 were another bungled job.

If anything the Yemenite AQAP's hopeless, hapless operational planning served to highlight its technical incompetence. In fact according to Mutallab's own admission, published on NBC news at the time, Awlaki played no role in the planning or execution of the bomb attack. He merely served to refer Mutallab to the Al Qaeda organization.

Clearly, Awlaki was a minor figure in Yemen's political struggles. He was a propagandist of little influence in the mass movements during the "Arab Spring". He was an inept recruiter of English-speaking would be bombers. The claims that he planned and "hatched" two bomb plots[99] are refuted by the confession of one bomber and the absence of any corroboratory evidence regarding the failed cargo bombs.

The mass media inflate the importance of Awlaki to the stature of a major al-Qaeda leader and subsequently, his killing as a "major psychological blow" to world-wide jihadists. This imagery has *no substance*. But the puff pieces do have a very *important propaganda purpose*. Worse still, the killing of Awlaki *provides a justification* for *extra-judicial state serial assassinations of ideological critics of Anglo-American leaders engaged in bloody colonial wars*.

Propaganda to Bolster Flagging Military Morale

Recent events strongly suggest that the US and its NATO allies are losing the war in Afghanistan to the Taliban: top collaborator officials are knocked off at the drop of a Taliban turban. After years of occupation, Iraq is moving closer to Iran rather than the US. Libya in the post-Gaddafi period is under warring mercenary forces squaring off for a fight for the billion dollar booty. Al Qaeda prepares to battle against neoliberal expats and Gaddafi renegades.

Washington and NATO's attempt to regain the initiative via puppet rulers in Egypt, Tunisia, Bahrain and Yemen is being countered by a "second wave" of mass pro-democracy movements. The "Arab Spring" is being followed by a "hot autumn". Positive news and favorable outcomes for Obama are few and far between. He has run out of any pseudo-populist initiative to enchant the Arab-Islamic masses. His rhetoric rings hollow in the face of his UN speech, denying recognition of an independent Palestinian state. His groveling before

Israel is clearly seen as an effort to bolster his re-election campaign financing by wealthy Zionists.

Diplomatically isolated and domestically in trouble over failed economic policies, Obama pulled the trigger and shot an itinerant Muslim preacher in Yemen to send a "message" to the Arab world. In a word he says, "If you, the Arabs, the Islamic world, won't join us we can and will execute those of you who can be labeled 'spiritual mentors' or are suspected of harboring terrorists."

Obama's defense of systematic killing of ideological critics, denying US constitutional norms of judicial due process to a U.S citizen and in blatant rejection of international law defines a homicidal executive.

Let us be absolutely clear what the larger implications are of political murder by executive fiat. If the President can order the murder of a dual American-Yemeni citizen abroad on the basis of his ideological-theological beliefs, what is to stop him from ordering the same in the US? If he uses arbitrary violence to compensate for diplomatic failure abroad what is to stop him from declaring a "heightened internal security threat" in order to suspend our remaining freedoms at home and to round up critics?

We seriously understate our "Obama problem" if we think of this ordered killing merely as an isolated murder of a "jihadist" in strife torn Yemen ... Obama's murder of Awlaki has profound, long term significance because it puts political assassinations at the center of US *foreign and domestic policy*. As Secretary of Defense Panetta states, "eliminating home grown terrorists" is at the core of our "internal security".

OLIGARCHS, DEMAGOGUES AND MASS REVOLTS . . . AGAINST DEMOCRACY

Introduction

In ancient Rome, especially during the late Republic, oligarchs resorted to mob violence to block, intimidate, assassinate or drive from power the dominant faction in the Senate.

While neither the ruling or opposing factions represented the interests of the plebeians, wage workers, small farmers or slaves, the use of the 'mob' against the elected Senate, the principle of representative government and the republican form of government laid the groundwork for the rise of authoritarian "Caesars" (military rulers) and the transformation of the Roman republic into an imperial state.

Demagogues in the pay of aspiring emperors aroused the passions of a motley array of disaffected slum dwellers, loafers and petty thieves (ladrones) with promises, pay-offs and positions in a New Order. Professional mob organizers cultivated their ties with the oligarchs 'above' and with professional demonstrators 'below'. They voiced 'popular grievances' and articulated demands questioning the legitimacy of the incumbent rulers, while laying the groundwork for the rule by the few. Usually, when the paymaster oligarchs came to power on a wave of demagogue-led mob violence, they quickly suppressed the demonstrations, paid off the demagogues with patronage jobs in the new regime or resorted to a discrete assassination of 'street leaders' unwilling to recognize the new order. The new rulers purged the old Senators into exile via expulsion and dispossession, rigged new elections and proclaimed themselves 'saviors of the republic'. They proceeded to drive peasants from their land, renounce social obligations and stop food subsidies for poor urban families and funds for public works.

The use of mob violence and "mass revolts" to serve the interests of oligarchical and imperial powers against democratically-elected governments has been a common strategy in recent times as well.

The choreographed "mass revolt" played many roles: it served to 1) destabilize an electoral regime; 2) provide a platform for its oligarch funders to depose an incumbent regime; 3) disguise the fact that the oligarchic opposition had lost democratic elections; 4) provide a political minority with a 'fig-leaf of legitimacy' when it was otherwise incapable of acting within a constitutional framework; and 5) allow for the illegitimate seizure of power in the name of a pseudo 'majority', namely the "crowds in the central plaza".

Some leftist commentators have argued two contradictory positions: One the one hand, some simply reduce the oligarchy's power grab to an 'inter-elite struggle' which has nothing to do with the 'interests of the working class', while others maintain the 'masses' in the street are protesting against an "elitist regime". A few even argue that with popular, democratic demands, these revolts are progressive, should be supported as "terrain for class struggle". In other words, the 'left' should join the uprising and contest the oligarchs for leadership of the stage-managed revolts!

What progressives are unwilling to recognize is that the oligarchs orchestrating the mass revolt are authoritarians who completely reject democratic procedures and electoral processes. Their aim is to establish a 'junta', which will eliminate all democratic political and social institutions and freedoms, and impose harsher, more repressive and regressive policies and institutions than those they replace. Some leftists support the 'masses in revolt' simply because of their 'militancy', their numbers and street courage, without examining the underlying leadership, and their interests and links to the elite beneficiaries of a 'regime change'.

All the color-coded "mass revolts" in Eastern Europe and the ex-USSR featured popular leaders who exhorted the masses in the name of 'independence and democracy' were pro-NATO, pro-(Western) imperialists and linked to neoliberal elites. Upon the fall of communism, the new oligarchs privatized and sold off the most lucrative sectors of the economy, throwing millions out of work. They dismantled the welfare state and handed over their military bases to NATO for the stationing of foreign troops and the placement of missiles aimed at Russia.

The entire 'anti-Stalinist' left in the US and Western Europe, with a few notable exceptions, celebrated these oligarch-controlled revolts in Eastern Europe, and some even participated as minor accomplices in the post-revolt neoliberal regimes. One clear reason for the demise of "Western Marxism" was its inability to distinguish a genuine popular democratic revolt from a mass uprising funded and stage-managed by rival oligarchs!

One of the clearest recent example of a manipulated 'people's power' revolution in the streets to replace an elected representative of one sector of the elite with an even more brutal, authoritarian 'president' occurred in early 2001 in the Philippines. The more popular and independent (but notoriously corrupt) President Joseph Estrada, who had challenged sectors of the Philippine elite and current US foreign policy (infuriating Washington by embracing Venezuela's Hugo Chavez), was replaced through street demonstrations of middle-class matrons with soldiers in civvies led by Gloria Makapagal-Arroyo. Mrs. Makapagal-Arroyo, who had close links to the US and the Philippine military, unleashed a horrific wave of brutality dubbed the 'death-squad democracy'. The overthrow of Estrada was actively supported by the left, including sectors of the revolutionary left, who quickly found themselves the target of an unprecedented campaign of assassinations, disappearances, torture and imprisonment by their newly empowered 'Madame President'.

Past and Present Mass Revolts Against Democracy: Guatemala, Iran and Chile

The use of mobs and mass uprisings by oligarchs and empire builders has a long and notorious history. Three of the bloodiest cases, which scarred their societies for decades, took place in Guatemala in 1954, Iran in 1953 and Chile in 1973.

Democratically-elected Jacobo Árbenz was the first Guatemalan President to initiate agrarian reform and legalize trade unions, especially among landless farm workers. Árbenz's reforms included the expropriation of unused, fallow land owned by the United Fruit Company, a giant US agro-business conglomerate. The CIA used its ties to local oligarchs and right-wing generals and colonels to instigate and finance mass protests against a phony 'communist-takeover' of Guatemala under President Arbenz. The military used the manipulated mob violence and the 'threat' of Guatemala becoming a "Soviet satellite" to stage a bloody coup. The coup leaders received air support from the CIA, slaughtered thousands of Arbenz supporters, and turned the countryside into 'killing fields'. Over the next 50 years political parties, trade unions and peasant organizations were banned, an estimated 200,000 Guatemalans were murdered, and millions were displaced.

In 1952 Mohammed Mossadegh was elected president of Iran on a moderate nationalist platform, after the overthrow of the brutal monarch. Mossadegh announced the nationalization of the petroleum industry. The CIA, with the collaboration of the local oligarchs, monarchists and demagogues, organized 'anti-communist' street mobs to stage violent demonstrations providing the pretext for a monarchist-military coup. The CIA-controlled Iranian generals brought Shah Reza Pahlavi back from Switzerland, and for the next 26 years Iran was a monarchist-military dictatorship, whose population was terrorized by the Savak, the murderous secret police. The US oil companies received the richest oil concessions; the Shah joined Israel and the US in an unholy alliance against progressive nationalist dissidents and worked hand-in-hand to undermine independent Arab states. Tens of thousands of Iranians were killed, tortured and driven into exile. In 1979, a mass popular uprising led by Islamic movements, nationalist and socialist parties and trade unions drove out the Shah-Savak dictatorship. The Islamists installed a radical nationalist clerical regime, which retains power to this day despite decades of a US-CIA-funded destabilization campaign which has funded both terrorist groups and dissident liberal movements.

Chile is the best-known case of CIA-financed mob violence leading to a military coup. In 1970, the democratic socialist, Dr. Salvador Allende, was elected president of Chile. Despite CIA efforts to buy votes to block Congressional approval of the electoral results and its manipulation of violent demonstrations and an assassination campaign to precipitate a military coup, Allende took office.

During Allende's tenure as president the CIA financed a variety of "direct actions", from paying the corrupt leaders of a copper workers union to stage strikes and the truck owners associations to refuse to transport goods to the cities, to manipulating right-wing terrorist groups like the Patria y Libertad (Fatherland and Liberty) in their assassination campaigns. The CIA's destabilization program was specifically designed to provoke economic instability through artificial shortages and rationing, in order to incite middle class discontent. The situation became notorious due to the street demonstrations of pot-banging housewives. The CIA sought to incite a military coup through economic chaos. Thousands of truck owners were paid not to drive their trucks leading to shortages in the cities, while right-wing terrorists blew up power stations, plunging neighborhoods into darkness, while shop owners who refused to join the 'strike' against Allende were vandalized.

On September 11, 1973, to the chants of 'Jakarta' (in celebration of a 1964 CIA coup in Indonesia), a junta of US-backed Chilean generals grabbed power from an elected government. Tens of thousands of activists and government supporters were arrested, killed, tortured and forced into exile. The dictatorship denationalized and privatized Chile's mining, banking and manufacturing sectors, following the free market dictates of Milton Friedman-trained economists (the so-call "Chicago Boys"). The dictatorship overturned 40 years of welfare, labor and land-reform legislation which had made Chile the most socially advanced country in Latin America. With the generals in power, Chile became the 'neo-liberal model' for Latin America. Mob violence and the so-called "middle class revolt", led to the consolidation of oligarchic and imperial rule and a 17 year reign of terror under General Augusto Pinochet dictatorship. The whole society was brutalized, and with the return of electoral politics, even former 'leftist' parties retained the dictatorship's neoliberal economic policies, its authoritarian constitution and the military high command. The 'revolt of the middle class' in Chile resulted in the greatest concentration of wealth in the hands of the oligarchs in Latin America to this day!

The Contemporary Use and Abuse of "Mass Revolts":
Egypt, Ukraine, Venezuela, Thailand and Argentina

In recent years "mass revolt" has become the instrument of choice when oligarchs, generals and other empire builders seek 'regime change'. By enlisting an assortment of chauvinist demagogues and imperial-funded NGO 'leaders', they set the conditions for the overthrow of democratically elected governments and stage-managed the installment of their own "free market" regimes with dubious "democratic" credentials.

Not all the elected regimes under siege are progressive. Many 'democracies', like that in the Ukraine, are already ruled by one set of oligarchs. In Ukraine, the elite supporting President Viktor Yanukovich decided that entering into a deep client-state relationship with the European Union was not in their interest, and sought to diversify their international trade partners while maintaining lucrative ties with Russia. Their opponents, who are currently behind the street demonstrations in Kiev, advocate a client relationship with the EU, stationing of NATO troops, and cutting ties with Russia. In Thailand, the democratically-elected Prime Minister, Yingluck Shinawatra, represents a section of the economic elite with ties and support in the rural areas, especially the North-East, as well as deep trade relations with China. The opponents are urban-based, closer to the military-monarchists and favor a straight neoliberal agenda linked to the US against the rural patronage-populist agenda of Ms. Shinawatra.

Egypt's democratically-elected Mohamed Morsi government pursued a moderate Islamist policy with some constraints on the military and a loosening of ties with Israel in support of the Palestinians in Gaza. In terms of the IMF, Morsi sought compromise. The Morsi regime was in flux when it was overthrown: not Islamist nor secular, not pro-worker but also not pro-military. Despite all of its different pressure groups and contradictions, the Morsi regime permitted labor strikes, demonstrations, opposition parties, freedom of the press and assembly. All of these democratic freedoms have disappeared after waves of 'mass street revolts', choreographed by the military, set the conditions for the generals to take power and establish their brutal dictatorship –jailing and torturing tens of thousands and outlawing all opposition parties. Elected to a four year term, Morsi wasn't given so much as a year to show what he could do: from the get-go, as Roger Annis noted, "the political and economic elite in Egypt set out to overthrow him by creating economic and social chaos—supplies of food, gasoline and other essentials were disrupted, police refused to perform their duties, causing crime rates to rise, and so on. The U.S. and the European countries used the threat of reducing aid as a pressure tactic to weaken the Morsi government and strengthen the opposition to it among the military and economic elite."[100] Once the military coup took place, Saudi aid poured in and overnight the shortages vanished. Morsi and other Muslim Brotherhood leaders were imprisoned, and the MB itself termed a terrorist organization, with a view to criminalizing their activities, their financing, and their membership. Anyone charged with supporting the MB "verbally or in writing" faces five years imprisonment.

Mass demonstrations and demagogue-led direct actions also actively target democratically elected progressive governments, like Venezuela and Argentina, in addition to the actions against conservative democracies cited above. Venezuela, under Presidents Hugo Chavez and Vicente Maduro, advances an anti-imperialist, pro-socialist program. 'Mob revolts' are combined with waves of assassinations, sabotage of public utilities, artificial shortages of essential commodities, vicious media slander and opposition election campaigns funded from the outside. In 2002, Washington teamed up with its collaborator politicians, Miami and Caracas-based oligarchs and local armed gangs, to mount a "protest movement" as the pretext for a planned business-military coup. The generals and members of the elite seized power and deposed and arrested the democratically-elected President Chavez. All avenues of democratic expression and representation were closed and the constitution annulled.

In response to the kidnapping of 'their president', over a million Venezuelans spontaneously mobilized and marched upon the Presidential palace to demand the restoration of democracy and Hugo Chavez to the presidency. Backed by the large pro-democracy and pro-constitution sectors of the Venezuelan armed forces, the mass protests led to the coup's defeat and the return of Chavez and democracy. All democratic governments facing manipulated imperial-oligarchic financed mob revolts should study the example of Venezuela's defeat of the US-oligarch-generals' coup. The best defense for democracy is found in the organization, mobilization and political education of the electoral majority. It is not enough to participate in free elections; an educated and politicized majority must also know how to defend their democracy in the streets as well as at the ballot box.

The lessons of the 2002 coup-debacle were very slowly absorbed by the Venezuelan oligarchy and their US patrons who continued to destabilize the economy in an attempt to undermine democracy and seize power. Between December 2002 and February 2003, corrupt senior oil executives of the nominally 'public' oil company PDVSA (Petróleos de Venezuela) organized a 'bosses' lockout stopping production, export and local distribution of oil and refined petroleum products. Corrupt trade union officials, linked to the US National Endowment for Democracy, mobilized oil workers and other employees to support the lockout in their attempt to paralyze the economy. The government responded by mobilizing the other half of the oil workers who, together with a significant minority of middle management, engineers and technologists, called on the entire Venezuelan working class to take the oil fields and installations from the 'bosses'. To counter the acute shortage of gasoline, President Chavez secured supplies from neighboring countries and overseas allies. The lockout was defeated. Several thousand supporters of the executive power grab were fired and replaced by pro-democracy managers and workers.

Having failed to overthrow the democratic government via "mass revolts", the oligarchs turned toward a plebiscite on Chavez rule and later called for a nationwide electoral boycott, both of which were defeated. These defeats served to strengthen Venezuela's democratic institutions and decreased the presence of opposition legislators in the Congress. The repeated failures of the elite to grab power led to a new multi-pronged strategy using: (1) US-funded NGOs to exploit local grievances and mobilize residents around community issues; (2) clandestine thugs to sabotage utilities, especially power, assassinate peasant recipients of land reform titles, as well as prominent officials and activists; (3) mass electoral campaign marches and (4) economic destabilization via financial speculation, illegal foreign exchange trading, price gouging and hoarding of basic consumer commodities. The purpose of these measures is to incite mass discontent, using their control of the mass media to provoke another 'mass revolt' to set the stage for another US-backed 'power grab'. Violent street protests by middle class students from the elite Central University were organized by oligarch-financed demagogues. 'Demonstrations' included sectors of the middle class and urban poor angered by the artificial shortages and power outages. The sources of popular discontent were rapidly and effectively addressed at the top by energetic government measures: Business owners engaged in hoarding and price gouging were jailed; prices of essential staples were reduced; hoarded goods were seized from warehouses and distributed to the poor; the import of essential goods were increased and saboteurs were pursued. The Government's effective intervention resonated with the mass of the working class, the lower-middle class and the rural and urban poor and restored their support. Government supporters took to the streets and lined up at the ballot box to defeat the campaign of destabilization. The government won a resounding electoral mandate allowing it to move decisively against the oligarchs and their backers in Washington.

The Venezuelan experience shows how energetic government counter-measures can restore support and deepen progressive social changes for the majority. This is because forceful progressive government intervention against anti-democratic oligarchs, combined with the organization, political education and mobilization of the majority of voters can decisively defeat these stage-managed mass revolts.

Argentina is an example of a weakened democratic regime trying to straddle the fence between the oligarchs and the workers, between the combined force of the agro-business and mining elites and working and middle class constituencies dependent on social policies. The elected-Kirchner-Fernandez government has faced "mass revolts" in a series of street demonstrations whipped up by conservative agricultural exporters over taxes; by the Buenos Aires upper-middle class, angered at 'crime, disorder and insecurity'; as ell as a nationwide strike over 'salaries' by police officials who 'looked the other way' while gangs of 'lumpen' street thugs pillaged and destroyed stores. Taken altogether, these waves of mob action in Argentina appear to be part of a politically-directed destabilization campaign by the authoritarian Right who have instigated or at least exploited these events. Apart from calling on the military to restore order and conceding to the 'salary' demands of the striking police, the Fernandez government has been unable or unwilling to mobilize the democratic electorate in defense of democracy. The democratic regime remains in power but it is under siege and vulnerable to attack by domestic and imperial opponents.

Conclusion

Mass revolts are two-edged swords: They can be a positive force when they occur against military dictatorships like Pinochet or Mubarak, against authoritarian absolutist monarchies like Saudi Arabia, a colonial-racist state like Israel, and imperial occupations like against the US in Afghanistan. But they have to be directed and controlled by popular local leaders seeking to restore democratic majority rule.

History, from ancient times to the present, teaches us that not all 'mass revolts' achieve, or are even motivated by, democratic objectives. Many have served oligarchs seeking to overthrow democratic governments, totalitarian leaders seeking to install fascist and pro-imperial regimes, demagogues and authoritarians seeking to weaken shaky democratic regimes and militarists seeking to start wars for imperial ambitions.

Today, "mass revolts" against democracy have become standard operational procedure for Western European and US rulers who seek to circumvent democratic procedures and install pro-imperial clients. The institutional practice of democracy is denigrated while the mob is extolled in the imperial Western media. This is why armed Islamist terrorists and mercenaries are called "rebels" in Syria and the mobs in the streets of Kiev (Ukraine) attempting to forcibly depose a democratically-elected government are labeled "pro-Western democrats".

The ideology informing the "mass revolts" varies from "anti-communist" and "anti-authoritarian" in democratic Venezuela, to "pro-democracy" in Libya (even as tribal bands and mercenaries slaughter whole communities), Egypt and the Ukraine.

Imperial strategists have systematized, codified and made operational "mass revolts" in favor of oligarchic rule. International experts, consultants, demagogues and NGO officials have carved out lucrative careers as they travel to 'hot spots' and organize 'mass revolts' dragging the target countries into deeper 'colonization' via European or US-centered 'integration'. Most local leaders and demagogues accept the double agenda: 'protest today and submit to new masters tomorrow'. The masses in the street are fooled and then sacrificed. They believe in a 'New Dawn' of Western consumerism, higher paid jobs and greater personal freedom . . . only to be disillusioned when their new rulers fill the jails with opponents and many former protestors, raise prices, cut salaries, privatize state companies, sell off the most lucrative firms to foreigners and double the unemployment rate.

When the oligarchs 'stage-manage' mass revolts and take over the regime, the big losers include the democratic electorate and most of the protestors. Leftists and progressives, in the West or in exile, who had mindlessly supported the 'mass revolts' will publish their scholarly essays on "the revolution (sic) betrayed" without admitting to their own betrayal of democratic principles.

If and when the Ukraine enters into the European Union, the exuberant street demonstrators will join the millions of jobless workers in Greece, Portugal and Spain, as well as millions of pensioners brutalized by "austerity programs" imposed by their new rulers, the 'Troika' in Brussels. If these former demonstrators take to the streets once more, in disillusionment at their leaders' "betrayal", they can enjoy their 'victory' under the batons of "NATO and European Union-trained police" while the Western mass media will have moved elsewhere in support of 'democracy'.

CONCLUSION

This book is not a treatise about imperialism in the abstract—it is written to update, refine and take account of the changes in the structure and operations of empire building in the second decade of the 21st century. The study focuses in particular on the Middle East because it has been the *centerpiece* of imperial policymakers: the region where the United States has expended greater arms, military personnel and financial resources, and suffered the greatest losses.

The major 'findings' derived from out study highlight several key propositions about the politics of US empire building in the 21st century.

At the most general level imperial policy is *not* a set of rigid formulas deduced by the 'laws of capital accumulation'. Our study illustrates the importance of the *outcome* of political struggle—wins and losses—in shaping the scope and intensity of imperial interventions and imperial retreats. A series of imperial victories in the 1990s led to the escalation of imperial wars; prolonged, costly wars and defeats led to retreat and significant changes in operations, theaters of engagement and tactics.

Ideology is as much a material force influencing imperial policy as 'material interests': despite heavy losses to major corporate investors, especially in the petroleum industry, US policymakers engaged in warfare and economic sanctions which devastated lucrative markets in Iraq, Libya, Syria and Iran . Military metaphysics, the idea that political conflicts can only be resolved through the use of imperial force trumped the market logic of economic actors.

The decline of the US empire is not a zero-sum-game—the steady fall of empire has not been accompanied by the rise of an alternative global power or alternative socialist system.

Empire-builders have harnessed up-to-date information technology to political assassinations via drones, to spying on allies and adversaries, to gain political and economic advantages. Imperial needs increasingly dictate some of the most advanced research in IT innovations to sustain the most retrograde interests.

Empire building especially under electoral systems ("formal

democracies") requires citizen submission, sacrifice and obedience. Imperial policymakers depend on stable domestic foundations to pursue wars of conquest. Lacking consent and in the face of rising opposition, imperial policymakers increasingly resort to police state measures: absent the carrot of imperial plunder to buy off the domestic public, the stick becomes the principal instrument for buttressing the domestic foundations of empire.

Empire building in the US has one unique idiosyncrasy which differentiates it from all previous empires: a powerful domestic power configuration (Zionist) embedded in state policymaking circles acting on behalf of a foreign power (Israel). In the specific region of this study—the Middle East—the Zionist power configuration has played a major role in harnessing the US Empire to serving the regional power projections of Israel. This fact underlines the importance of the *domestic political power relations* in shaping US imperial policy; the importance of military ideology over economic interests; and the role of "dual citizens" with foreign allegiances in subverting a potentially democratic foreign policy.

In summary understanding imperial politics requires 1) analyzing its changing structure and operational code; 2) identifying its ideology and technological innovations; 3) analyzing the *domestic* foundations of empire and the interplay between overseas expansion and internal decay; and 4) locating idiosyncratic domestic *political configurations* which influence and direct the particular policies and strategies of empire builders.

ENDNOTES

1   Carried by RSN as Nick Turse, TomDispatch, "America's Secret Wars in 134 Countries," 1/16/14 <http://readersupportednews.org/opinion2/266-32/21537-americas-secret-war-in-134-countries>
2   *Financial Times*, 12/8/13, p. 4.
3   Ibid.
4   *Financial Times*, 12/ 13/13.
5   *Financial Times*, 12/10/13, p. 2.
6   See inter alia, James Petras, *The Power of Israel in the United States*, Clarity Press, 2006; *Zionism, Militarism and the Decline of US Power*, Clarity Press, 2008.
7   "What was the Israeli Involvement in Collecting U.S. Communications Intel for the NSA?", *Haaretz*, June 8, 2013.
8   BBC News, 8/16/13; Al Jazeera 9/16/13.
9   *La Jornada* (Mexico City) 8/16/13, p. 22; *Financial Times*, 8/10-11/13. "T he exact threat to US missions has yet to be made public."
10 *Financial Times*, 8/8/13, p. 2 and *Financial Times* 8/10-11 2013 p 2; 'McClatchy Washington Bureau' 8/5/13.
11 *Financial Times*, 8/8/13, p. 2.
12 Ibid.
13 *Financial Times*, 8/12/13, p.2.
14 Morris Morley: *Washington, Somoza and the Sandinistas: State and Regime in US-Nicaraguan Relations 1969-1981*, Cambridge 1994.
15 Clinton joined forces with right-wing Republicans in 1999 to facilitate banks engaging in broad speculation with their clients' money.
16 James Henry, *The Price of Offshore Revisied*, <http://www.taxjustice.net/cms/upload/pdf/The_Price_of_Offshore_Revisited_Presser_120722.pdf>
17 See a multiple tally of JPMorgan Chase wrongdoings at Eyder Peralta, "JPMorgan to pay $1.7 billion to Madoff Victims," The Two-Way, NPR, 01/07/14 <http://www.npr.org/blogs/thetwo-way/2014/01/07/260442151/jpmorgan-chase-to-pay-1-7-billion-to-madoff-victims>
18 Here is a timeline of BDS successes: <http://www.bdsmovement.net/timeline> The *Financial Times* on 2/3/2014 noted: "Norway's $810 billion government pension fund Global has been barred from investing in two Israeli companies due to their 'serious violations of individual rights'. See also <http://www.haaretz.com/news/diplomacy-defense/1.571849>
19 See <http://www.irmep.org/ten.htm>
20 Ibid.
21 Daniel Larson, "Jundallah and Israel's False Flag Operation in Iran", The American Conservative, 01/13/12 <http://www.theamericanconservative.com/larison/jundallah-and-israels-false-flag-operation-in-iran/>
22 Janet McMahon, "More Secretive Than Stealth PACS: Super PACS and 501©(4)s Financing 2012 Presidential Race", Washington Report on Middle East Affairs, October 2012 <http://www.wrmea.org/pdf/201210pac_charts.pdf>
23 *Daily Alert*, October 24, 2013.
24 *Financial Times*, 10/18/2013, p.6.
25 *Financial Times*, 10/29/2013, p.1.

26   Ynet.com, 9/6/13.
27   *Cleveland Jewish News*, 9/6/13.
28   For full coverage of the daily activities and the uncritical reportage of the major media see *The Daily Alert*, the official mouthpiece of 52 Presidents of the Major American Jewish Organizations, especially March 4-6, 2012.
29   See the AIPAC video reports and the list of speakers at <http://www.aipac.org>, 3/2/2012 and subsequent reports.
30   *White House press release* of Obama's declaration that US subordinate relation to Israel is "sacrosanct", 3/4/12. <http://www.whitehouse.gov/the-press-office/2012/03/04/remarks-president-aipac-policy-conference-0>
31   The reference is to Noam Chomsky whose laughable effort to downplay the influence of the Zionist power configuration is widely rejected and is once again refuted by the most superficial observation of the proceedings, pledges and prostrations of all top US policy makers at the AIPAC meeting.
32   Netanyahu's public pronouncements and AIPAC speech were duly recorded, amplified and supported by *The New York Times, Wall Street Journal*, and especially the *Washington Post* (2/6/2012). He explicitly called on the US to militarily attack Iran on behalf of Israel, on the basis of Teheran's 'capacity' to make a nuclear weapon. According to Netanyahu "we can't afford to wait much longer ..." *Prime Minister's Office* 3/5/12.
33   *The New York Times*, 3/5/12.
34   *Prime Minister's Office* as quoted in the *Daily Alert*, 3/6/12.
35   AIPAC video daily reports, 3/6/12.
36   For example, just one of the numerous Zionist billionaires, the casino czar, Sheldon Adelson, has already contributed "tens of millions of dollars" to influence the current presidential elections. *Haaretz*, 2/29/12. Haim Saban, another Israel-Firster billionaire, bought the principal Spanish language TV outlet in the US, UNIVISION, and then proceeded to promote sensationalist Israeli propaganda about an Iranian-Islamist "takeover" of Latin America.
37   AIPAC press releases, 3/7/12 – 3/10/12.
38   A survey of the *Daily Alert* from March 4 to March 9 reveals there is not one single article that discusses the alternative of a diplomatic settlement with Iran, while over a dozen articles feature calls for war.
39   For documentation and details on the decisive role of Zionist policy makers in launching the US war against Iraq, see my *The Power of Israel in the United States* (Atlanta: Clarity Press 2006).
40   For a list of these agencies, go to <http://www.businessinsider.com/17-agencies-of-the-us-intelligence-community-2013-5?op=1>
41   *The New York Times*, 3/1/12.
42   The 52 Presidents of the Major Jewish Organizations repeatedly endorsed Netanyahu's pretext for war. See *Daily Alert*, 3/6/2012.
43   Quoted in <http://Mondoweiss.net>, 3/2/12.
44   Ibid.
45   Key Zionist Congressional operatives include Representatives Berman, Cantor, Harman, Lieberman, Ros- Lehtinen, and Levin as well as their Christian side-kicks, like McConnell and Pelosi among others who appeared at the AIPAC war fest. *AIPAC promotional flyer* 3/2/12.
46   *Financial Times*, 3/6/12, p. 9
47   See "On Bended Knees: Zionist Power in American Politics" in James Petras, *War Crimes in Gaza and the Zionist Fifth Column* (Atlanta: Clarity Press 2010).
48   *The Power of Israel in the United States*, supra.
49   Though Ross has formally resigned, he is still a key Obama adviser on the Middle East. See *Haaretz*, 1/27/12.
50   One of the key Zionist operatives is Jeffrey Feltman, Assistant Secretary of State for Near Eastern Affairs. He played a crucial role in support of Israel's bombing of Lebanon in 2006, during his term as Ambassador, calling Hezbol-

lah a "terrorist organization". He dictated policy to the Lebanese US client ruler, Fouad Siniora. Feltman twice served in Israel. He was stationed in Gaza where he collaborated with the occupying Israeli Defense Forces. He worked with uber-Zionist, US Ambassador Martin Indyk, backing Israel's position in the phony "Peace Process" from 2000 to 2001. Other Zionists in key positions include Jack Lew, former Chief of Staff to President Obama and current Secretary of the T reasury; David Plouffe, senior adviser to President; Dan Shapiro, Ambassador to Israel, and Eric Lynn, Middle East policy advisor. See *Jewish Virtual Library,* a Division of the American-Israeli Enterprise: <http://www.jewishvirtuallibrary.org/jsource/US-Israel/obamajews.html>

51   Prominent Zionists, who formerly served in strategic positions in the foreign policy realm of the Obama regime included Rahm Emanuel, Chief of Staff to the President; David Axelrod, Senior Advisor; James Steinberg, Deputy Secretary of State; Steven Simon, former Head of Middle East/North Africa Desk at the National Security Council; and Richard Holbrooke, Special Envoy to Pakistan/Afghanistan (deceased).

52   Several studies estimate that Jews make up about 25% of the Forbes 400 richest Americans; over half are contributors to Israel or Zionist organizations or causes. J.J. Goldberg in his book on Jewish power estimates that 45% of Democratic fundraising comes from pro-Israel Jews. *Jewish Power: Inside the Jewish Establishment,* (Reading: Addison-Wesley, 1996).

53   See *The Power of Israel in the United States,* supra

54   Steve Rosen, a top policy director of AIPAC, along with his colleague, Keith Weissman, admitted to handing over confidential documents to the Israeli embassy. Rosen later filed suit against AIPAC for firing him and Weissman, and refusing to pay their legal fees; he claimed that the Lobby frequently condoned its employees' receipt and illegal transfer of classified US government information citing numerous AIPAC documents to back-up his case. *The Jewish Daily Forward,* 12/15/2010.

55   The owner and publisher of the *Atlanta Jewish Times,* Andrew Adler, urged Netanyahu to order the Israeli secret spy service, the *Mossad,* to assassinate President Obama, *Haaretz,* 1/21/12. Rabbi Michael Lerner, a moderate Zionist critic of Israel, has been subject to four attacks on his home in the past two years, while accused of being a '*self-hating Jew*' by Zionist fanatics. Mainstream Zionist organizations dissociate themselves from physical violence, while slanderously labeling opponents and critics of Israel as "anti-semites", which has created precisely the political climate that encourages the less balanced among their audience to violent activity. Leading Zionist ideologues have been extremely active in inducing colleges and universities to fire critics of Israel, as was the case in the failure of DePaul University to renew the contract of a widely published scholar like Norman Finkelstein. Professors Walt and Mearsheimer, authors of an erudite study, *The Israel Lobby,* were subject to vitriolic attacks by American Zionist leaders, including A. Foxman of the Anti (*sic*) Defamation League as well as a superficial critique by left-Zionist Noam Chomsky. The racist rantings of uber-Zionists like David Horowitz and Pamela Geller helped to detonate the Islamophobic and Zionophilic mass murderer, Anders Breivik, in Norway.

56   See the *Atlantic Jewish Times* editorial, 1/20/12.

57   The editor of the *Atlantic Jewish Times* who called for Obama's assassination was not charged with any federal security offense. The confessed Zionist spy, Colonel Ben-Ami Kadish, who stole secret US nuclear weapon plans for Israel, did not spend a single day in jail although he paid a $50,000 fine for handing over scores of documents to Israel. (See Grant Smith *Foreign Agents* (Washington, DC: Institute for Research Middle East Policy (IRMEP), 2008). On AIPAC spying see IRMEP 2/6/12. <http://www.irmep.org/>

58   Not to be ignored, the rarified atmosphere in high level scientific research

journals has been politicized—most outrageous is the censorship of a genetic-immunologic study (by a leading international team of scientists) showing the close genetic relationship, if not identity between Levantine Jews and Palestinians. University libraries around the world were advised to 'tear-out' (eyes closed) the offending study from the pages of the journal, *Human Immunology*, lest such data might undermine the racist 'raison d'être' for an exclusively Jewish state. (see "Journal axes gene research on Jews and Palestinians", Robin McKie, *Guardian-Sunday Observer* (London), 11/25/01 and *Hum. Immunol.* 62 (9): 889–900.)

59   A review of news reports and editorials of *The New York Times, Washington Post* and *Wall Street Journal*, published by the *Daily Alert* during the AIPAC conference reveals a close alignment with the extremist militarist position of the Israeli regime and AIPAC leaders. See Steve Lendman, "*New York Times* Promotes War on Syria and Iran", 3/3/12. <http://www.opednews.com/articles/New-York-Times-Promotes-War-by-Stephen-Lendman-120322-87.html>

60   During the month of February 2012, the Israeli Army and armed paramilitary Jewish settlers carried out 145 attacks on Palestinians, killing and wounding dozens, demolishing homes, seizing thousands of acres of land and uprooting scores of families: The Wall and Settlements Information Center, Palestinian Authority 3/1/12. Neither *The New York Times* or the *Wall Street Journal* or the *Washington Post* reported on these Israeli crimes against Palestinian civilians.

61   See Jewish Virtual Library, which contends that the percentage is 2.2%. <http://www.jewishvirtuallibrary.org/jsource/US-Israel/usjewpop.html>

62   Among Chertoff's current clients are the manufacturers of the intrusive and nationally detested 'body scanners' used at US airports. He was also instrumental in the release and repatriation of a dozen Israeli Mossad agents arrested in New York and New Jersey within 24 hours of the 9/11 terrorist attack. Three of the nine justices, Ginsberg, Breyer and Kagan, are Zionists unwilling to challenge the Executive usurpation of war powers and promotion of torture and rendition. The others are all affiliated with the Roman Catholic Church. Not a single Protestant-affiliated Justice (numerically the majority religion in the US) has been appointed to the Supreme Court since the 1990 appointment of respected constitutional scholar, David Souter (by George Bush the First), because of their 'unreliability' (codeword for upholding the Bill of Rights and Constitution). The recent appointment of Justice Elena Kagan, whose lackluster academic career did not deter uber-Zionist Laurence Summers from appointing her Dean of the Harvard Law School, underscores the mediocre criteria used in the high judiciary. The most recent appointment of Sonya Sotomayor to replace the brilliant (and *Zionistically* 'unreliable') J.P. Stevens, was promoted heavily for the Supreme Court on the basis of her strong ties to Israel, starting with her first (of many) 'leadership' tours to Israel (see Ron Kampeas, "Life story Israel trips tie Sotomayor to Jews", *The Jewish Chronicle*, 5/ 26/09, <http://thejewishchronicle.net/view/full_story/2637245/article-Life-story--Israel-trips-tie-Sotomayor-to-Jews-#ixzz1pCoJROGS>).

63   *Financial Times,* 3/6/12, p. 9.

64   Howard Kohr, AIPAC executive director, during his vitriolic war mongering speech at the conference, exceeded even Netanyahu's explicit call for an immediate military attack on Iran. See *AIPAC daily report*, 3/16/12.

65   Most experts agree that the oil price increase has stymied 'economic recovery' and if it continues to rise will plunge the world back into deep recession.

66   Obama's speech to the AIPAC meeting pointedly called on the Israeli leaders to tone down on their military rhetoric, clearly linking rising oil prices to Israeli warmongering.

67   See Grant Smith, "AIPAC Directors Use of Classified Missile Data, Harmed National Security–US State Department," *Business Wire*, 2/6/12.

68   *Financial Times,* 3/1/12, p. 17.

69   Jane Eisner, "Salary Survey 2013: Who Earns What at America's Biggest Jewish Non-Profits Salary Survey Shows Who Is in Charge and What They Take Home", The Jewish Daily Forward (undated). The article provides an extensive list of executives and organizations, beyond those names provided here. See <http://forward.com/articles/189219/who-earns-what-at-americas-biggest-jewish-non-prof/#ixzz2qh6doRIV>

70   "Poll: Israelis Dissatisfied with Cease Fire", *USA Today*, N11/23/12 <http://www.usatoday.com/story/news/world/2012/11/23/poll-israelis-dissatisfied-cease-fire/1722005/>

71   Gilad Sharon, "A decisive action is necessary", *Jerusalem Post*, 11/18/12.

72   Brett Wilkins, "Israli Lawmaker: There are no innocents in Gaza: Mow them down," *The Digital Journal*, November 19, 2012. <http://digitaljournal.com/article/337203> Notably, the *Jerusalem Post* version is not available.

73   *The Jewish Daily Forward*, 6/29/11.

74   Ibid.

75   Helene Cooper, "Obama Turns to Biden to Reassure Jewish Voters and Get Them to Contribute, too," *The New York Times*, 9/30/12. <http://www.nytimes.com/2011/10/01/us/politics/obama-turns-to-biden-to-reassure-the-jews-and-get-them-to-contribute-too.html?_r=0>

76   Alister Bull, "Obama's West Coast Swing Shows Fundraising Strength, *Reuters*, 9/27/11 < http://www.reuters.com/article/2011/09/27/us-usa-campaign-obama-idUSTRE78O0GH20110927>

77   *The New York Times*, 9/30/11; *Jerusalem Post*, 10/02/11.

78   Natasha Mozgovaya, "Jonathan Pollard won't survive another year in U.S. Jail, wife says," *Haaretz*, 11/2/11 <http://www.haaretz.com/news/diplomacy-defense/jonathan-pollard-won-t-survive-another-year-of-u-s-jail-wife-says-1.396869>

79   "Israel has been accused several other times this year of launching airstrikes inside Syria, including once in January. In the January incident, a U.S. official said Israeli fighter jets bombed a Syrian convoy suspected of moving weapons to Hezbollah." Barbara Starr, "Israeli Planes Strike Syrian Military Base, US Official Says," CNN, 10/21/13 <http://www.cnn.com/2013/10/31/world/meast/syria-civil-war/>

80   Ibid.

81   See <https://en.wikipedia.org/wiki/Foreign_involvement_in_the_Syrian_Civil_War>

82   Adam Morrow, Inter Press Service, 12/29/13 <http://www.parapolitics.info/parapolitical/2013/12/29/122913-adam-morrow/>

83   Robert Fisk, "Freedom, democracy and human rights in Syria", *The Independent*, 09/16/10. <http://www.independent.co.uk/voices/commentators/fisk/robert-fisk-freedom-democracy-and-human-rights-in-syria-2080463.html>

84   "Maher Arar: My Rendition & Torture in Syrian Prison Highlights U.S. Reliance on Syria as an Ally," DemocracyNow, 06/13/11 <http://www.democracynow.org/2011/6/13/maher_arar_my_rendition_torture_in>

85   See Canadian Centre for the Responsibility to Protect, <http://ccr2p.org/>; Global Centre for the Responsibility to Protect, New York <http://www.globalr2p.org/about_us#staff>; and University of Queensland's Asia Pacific Centre for the Responsibility to Protect <http://www.r2pasiapacific.org/>

86   *Financial Times*, 11/26/13, p. 2

87   *Financial Times*, 11/26/13, p. 3

88   Stephen Lendman, lendmanstephen @gmail.com <http://sjlendman.blogspot.ca/> 11/26/13; 11/27/13.

89   Gareth Porter, Inter Press Service, 11/26/13.

90   "An Unusual Success for Sanctions Policy", *Financial Times*, 11/27/13, p. 10.

91   *Financial Times*, 1/25/13, p. 2.

92   *Financial Times*, 11/27/13, p. 2.

93   *Financial Times*, 11/26/13, p. 3.

94   *Barrons*, 12/2/13 p. 14.

95   *Financial Times*, 11/26/13, p. 10

96   *Financial Times,* Oct. 1 and 2, 2011.

97   Laurie Goodstein, "A Nation Challenges: The American Muslims: Influential American Muslims Temper Their Tone," The New York Times, 10/19/01 < http://www.nytimes.com/2001/10/19/us/nation-challenged-american-muslims-influential-american-muslims-temper-their.html>

98   For greater detail, see <https://en.wikipedia.org/wiki/Anwar_al-Awlaki#cite_ note-85>

99   *Financial Times*, 10/01/11; 10/02, p. 2

100   Roger Annis, "Silence is Complacency: Against the Coup in Egypt," rabble. ca, 10/10/13. <http://rabble.ca/news/2013/08/silence-complacency-against-coup-egypt>

INDEX